An Introduction to
English Runes

An Introduction to English Runes

R. I. PAGE

Emeritus Professor of Anglo-Saxon, University of Cambridge, and
Fellow of Corpus Christi College, Cambridge

Second Edition

THE BOYDELL PRESS

First published 1973

Second edition 1999
The Boydell Press, Woodbridge

ISBN 0 85115 768 8

The Boydell Press is an imprint of Boydell & Brewer Ltd
PO Box 9, Woodbridge, Suffolk IP12 3DF, UK
and of Boydell & Brewer Inc.
PO Box 41026, Rochester, NY 14604–4126, USA
website: http://www.boydell.co.uk

A catalogue record for this book is available
from the British Library

Library of Congress Cataloging-in-Publication Data
Page, R. I. (Raymond Ian)
    An introduction to English runes / R.I. Page. – 2nd ed.
    p.   cm.
    Originally published: London : Methuen, 1973.
    Includes bibliographical references and indexes.
    ISBN 0–85115–768–8
    1. Runes.   2. Inscriptions, Runic.   3. Inscription,
    English (Old)   I. Title.
    PD2003.P3 1999
    430 21 – dc21

This publication is printed on acid-free paper

Printed in Great Britain by
St Edmundsbury Press Ltd, Bury St Edmunds, Suffolk

Contents

Figures

Abbreviations

Most of the abbreviations I have used are self-evident. Readers who are not linguists may like to have the explanation of the following:

Gmc	Germanic
MLat	Mediaeval Latin
OE	Old English
OHG	Old High German
ON	Old Norse
PrOE	Primitive Old English
PrON	Primitive Old Norse
WGmc	West Germanic
WS	West Saxon

Acknowledgments

© For permission to reproduce certain of the photographs in this book the author and publisher would like to thank the following:

The British Library for figs 1, 13; the British Museum for figs 28, 46, 55, 61 (Dept of Medieval and Later Antiquities) and 68 (Dept of Coins and Medals); the Master and Fellows of Corpus Christi College, Cambridge, for figs 18, 69 and 75; the President and Fellows of St John's College, Oxford, for fig. 16; the Museum of Antiquities, Newcastle-upon-Tyne, for fig. 12; the National Museum, Copenhagen, for fig. 27; Sunderland Museum and Art Gallery ('lyne and Wear Museums) for fig. 44.

Preface

The first edition of this book, commonly known as *The Little Red Rune Book*, came out in 1973. It has long been out of print, and there have been many requests for a second impression. In the twenty-five years since that work was written English runic studies have developed a good deal, so a straightforward reissue would serve no useful purpose. Some radical revision was needed, and this I have attempted.

Though much of the original remains, I have re-examined, rewritten, and restructured parts, and added new material, including a complete chapter, no.14. I have excised passages as fresh evidence made them otiose or inaccurate. I hope what remains reads coherently. What I have tried to do overall is adjust to changed patterns of knowledge and opinion on the Anglo-Saxon runic material. But what, it may be asked, has happened in this field over a quarter of a century to make changes necessary? I cite four points:

First, a significant number of new inscriptions has appeared. The index of the first edition listed sixty-two undoubted Anglo-Saxon runic texts, excluding coin legends. The present edition supplies over twenty more – exact numbers cannot be quoted because of the uncertainty of some identifications. To these must be added the multitude of recently discovered runic coins, some of them variants of known issues, others completely new in type and legend. New inscriptions continue to surface: two more since this presentation was completed.

Second, newly-found inscriptions do not simply expand the Anglo-Saxon runic corpus: they require us to modify our appraisal of it. To the thirty-six rune-stones and fragments of 1973, only one, Whithorn II, is to be added. In 1973 there were seventeen inscriptions on metal; now we have a dozen more. To 1973's five texts on the fugitive material bone we can add a further five. A completely new inscription type has come to light in travellers' runic graffiti spotted in Italy. There is a modification of known distribution patterns, chronological, topographical and perhaps educational. Now we have relatively more inscriptions from the south and east of England and from the early (pre-650) period. This is supported by newly-found coin material, which also strengthens the evidence from these regions in early and middle Anglo-Saxon times. An added problem is that both the multiplicity and the scatter of these new finds encourage the detecting public to identify runes on a variety of objects – often chunks of metal or bone –where in fact we have only casual marks, usually accidental, on a surface. New discoveries bring new pseudo-discoveries in their train as a glance through auction catalogues and detecting magazines will demonstrate. And of course, new discoveries of runic texts are not confined to England. Many new Continental and Scandinavian runes have emerged, and these have required me to revise statements about the script's early distribution and significance, and England's runic links to other countries.

This leads to a third point, the need to refine and extend the theoretical basis of English runic study. We must revise conclusions about the early stages of the script's employment in this and neighbouring countries, the expansion of the *futhark* among the Anglo-Saxons and its subsequent development, the relationship between epigraphical and manuscript runes, the connection between sound-change and runic convention. Younger, and therefore cleverer, scholars have appeared in recent years, eager to challenge long-standing theories and to apply new thought patterns to the examination of inscribed texts; for example, to define runic literacy and its relevance to contemporary social structures. Defying the wreckful siege of battering days, I have introduced some of these novelties into my text, though I fear there will remain theories that need revision, perhaps replacement. All runologists carry with them a *bagage intellectuel* that needs to be unpacked from time to time and its contents sorted out, though we do not always remember to do it.

My fourth point is less a matter for revision, more one for stressing. It is more trivial but not therefore to be neglected; the growth of an uninformed enthusiasm for runes in recent decades. Part of this is innocent enough, if imperceptive – the popularity in literature and applied art of what have come to be thought of as runes. Fantasy literature often includes runes in mediaeval or fictional settings. We see runic script forms used to decorate jewellery and clothing. With the growth of the 'heritage' industry has come exploitation of various aspects of 'heritage', and in parts of the United Kingdom this has brought with it an awareness of runic forms, but too often an uninformed, limited awareness, a failure to realise how the script differed from date to date, region to region, people to people. Graphs from different traditions are mingled together, in meaningless combination. Sometimes this lack of understanding leads to absurdity. For example, a popular if not learned book on runes was recently advertised in a respected Book Club. The blurb explained that the runic script was one used in Viking times for a variety of purposes ranging from the legal to the epigraphical, but despite that it 'never evolved as a spoken language': a stunning inability to distinguish language from writing system.

This, though amusing enough, is relatively harmless. More insidious is the way runes are now touched by the flight from reason so characteristic of our pragmatic, scientific and down-to-earth times; the attempt, often in most vulgar terms, to promote some link between runes and the supernatural. There is nothing new about this (as certain chapters in my book demonstrate), but modern assertions about 'reading the runes', linking the script to other fashionable ways of foreseeing the future or of discovering a true self, go beyond a reasoned discussion of the evidence and are likely to lead the study of runes into contempt among the thoughtful. I hope this book will help to redress the balance.

Because the book derives from an earlier work it is likely to contain inconsistencies in presentation. I hope I have kept these to a minimum. However, one or two are new introductions, and I admit them in this preface in the hope of drawing the teeth of keen-eyed critics who value consistency above clarity, precision or common sense. The most evident is in my method (or rather methods) of transliterating runes. It is common practice, in recording Continental and Scandinavian inscriptions, to use **bold** for the runic transliteration. I do this when presenting non-Anglo-Saxon inscriptions. For the latter I use the system I adumbrated in 1984 of transliterating into s p a c e d roman between single inverted commas. There are, however, some inscriptions whose affinities are hard, indeed impossible, to define – an obvious example is the legend of the **skanomodu** solidus which may be English or may be Frisian. I therefore give it in bold. There are other cases which are likely or certain to be English, but of so early a date that we cannot know how far the diagnostic sound-changes have developed; whether, for instance, ᚨ, ᚩ should be transcribed 'æ', 'œ', or if they still represent their earlier sounds, the back vowels /a/, /a:/, and /o/, /o:/ preceding *i*-mutation, and so are better transliterated **a**, **o**. Examples are the Undley bracteate and the Watchfield fitting. There is no difficulty here for those who recognise the purpose of transliteration – to indicate graph rather than sound. But to inexperienced rune-readers, transcribing Watchfield's first word as 'h æ r i b œ c i' rather than **hariboki** may be forbidding. Of course, this is not the only inconsistency in my practice. I transliterate with different degrees of precision in different circumstances or for different purposes, as I confess in chapter 4. The stern critic must be aware of this and at least note my intentions.

Some will find fault with my reluctance to use phonetic and phonemic notation, thinking my way of presenting earlier forms often imprecise or outdated. Here I believe imprecision may be a virtue, for we know so little about how Old English was pronounced in its various regions and at varying dates that it is unwise to be dogmatic. Similarly, I doubt if we know enough about the linguistic awareness of Anglo-Saxon rune-carvers to make specific phonemical claims on their presentation of words. My imprecision is an admission of ignorance. It is also a clue to the purpose of this book, which should certainly serve linguists, but also archaeologists and historians who might find technical vocabulary and conventions off-putting.

In this edition I have made changes too because the world has changed. Geography has not remained fixed. Place-names confidently ascribed in 1973 to the USSR must be revised to fit new regions of authority. I hope I have got them right. In the United Kingdom successive kindly governments have decided they know better how counties should be bounded and named than their inhabitants. I have tried to keep up with fashion here, and give both traditional and modern county name where there is a distinction. For little known or ambiguous place-names I have added (in brackets) county names at the first mention, and sometimes later where geographical distribution is significant. Here I hope I am consistent in my inconstancy. I have also given the present location of most of the runic monuments I discuss. Sometimes this is not possible – there may be no established location, or it may be unknown to me (as when an object is 'in private hands'), or indeed an object may have been moved in recent years. A few pieces are not known to survive and indeed may not survive.

In the matter of footnotes my first edition was limited by publisher's requirements. I did not object to this, holding an unfashionable belief that most pages of a book should contain text rather than references or added discussion. This revised edition supplies notes slightly more freely in view of the many new inscriptions and studies that have appeared in twenty-five years. Details of them need to be available to beginners in rune-reading. In particular I draw attention to the excellent Norwegian annual *Nytt om Runer* whose issues contain many of the earliest find-reports. I hope in all this to have avoided the pedantry that scholarly supervision encourages nowadays.

Two final apologiæ, one on structure, one on style. There is a certain amount of repetition in this book. When a small body of material must be looked at from various viewpoints, geographical, chronological, typological, linguistic and so on, it is inevitable that individual bits of evidence serve multiple purposes. Reservations about their use, limitations on their reliability, have to be repeated. I have tried to cut this down to a minimum but I doubt if I have succeeded to the satisfaction of all readers. On style, a helpful colleague suggests I should have a note on 'irony'. This is a quality found in much English prose: we do not always say in simplicity what we mean. It certainly enters my own style – here and there. However, there are people into whose souls the irony has not entered, and I should perhaps warn them of the dangers inherent in my way of writing, and hope they will read delicately.

This book could not have been written, or rewritten, without the help of colleagues, so numerous that it is impossible to name them all here. Indeed, over the years runologists from many countries have shared their knowledge with me and challenged my opinions. No runologist can work without the co-operation of museum curators and librarians and of incumbents and vergers of the churches that preserve so many of our runic relics. I thank these men of learning and of God for their hospitality and friendliness. A modern runic scholar needs the help of archaeologists, art historians, numismatists, historians and historical linguists, and here too I have been fortunate in my colleagues. I thank four in particular, for they valiantly worked through an earlier draft of this work and made invaluable suggestions for improvement: Michael Barnes of University College, London, Kathryn Lowe of the University of Glasgow, Leslie Webster of the Department of Medieval and Later Antiquities, British Museum, and Sir David Wilson, former Director of the British Museum.

1

Runes and Runesters

As their entries in the *Oxford English Dictionary* show, the words 'rune' and 'runic' can mean a number of different things. The primary meaning of the noun is given there as 'A letter or character of the earliest Teutonic alphabet, which was most extensively used (in various forms) by the Scandinavians and Anglo-Saxons.' There is also an extended sense of 'a similar character or mark having mysterious or magical powers attributed to it', an obsolete or rare sense 'incantation or charm denoted by magic signs', and a technical sense, 'A Finnish poem, or division of a poem, *esp.* one of the separate songs of the Kalevala', whence derives the general, 'Any song, poem, or verse'. The adjective 'runic' is characterised as 'Consisting of runes', 'Carved or written in runes; expressed by means of runes', 'Inscribed with runes', 'Of or pertaining to runes', four meanings which are not always easy to distinguish when the word is in use. But there is also: 'Of poetry, etc.; Such as might be written in runes . . . *esp.* ancient Scandinavian or Icelandic.' The word can or could be applied 'to ancient Scandinavia or the ancient North', and can be used 'Of ornament: Of the interlacing type (originally Celtic) which is characteristic of rune-bearing monuments, metal-work, etc.' And the dictionary continues with four uses of 'runic' as a noun, one of which is 'The ancient Scandinavian tongue'.

In this book I take the two related words in their primary meanings. I use 'rune' for a letter of the characteristic alphabet that recorded early Germanic texts, North, East and West, though I concentrate on the distinctive branch of the script the Anglo-Saxons developed, commonly for their inscriptions and – so surviving evidence suggests – minimally for their writings; and by 'runic' I mean consisting of runes, carved or written in runes, inscribed with runes, or concerned with runes. The extended meanings of both words are unimportant to my purpose, but it is worth using a little space to explore some of them, for they trace the course of runic studies in this country and help to account for some misconceptions that survive still.

Though there is an Old English word *run*, the modern 'rune' and 'runic' are words of the seventeenth century, deriving from late Latin *runa* and *runicus*, probably reinforced by their Scandinavian equivalents.[1] Their appearance in the English language reflects the enthusiasm for the Dark Ages, their history and antiquities, which became such a feature of European scholarship in that century. It was perhaps the Dane, Ole Worm, whose work provided the most vigorous stimulus to runic studies in this country. His books, *Runer, seu Danica Literatura Antiquissima*, published in Copenhagen and Amsterdam in 1636, *Danicorum Monumentorum Libri Sex* (Copenhagen 1643) and *Specimen Lexici Runici* (Copenhagen 1650), English scholars read eagerly and quoted often. Worm illustrated his *Monumenta* with woodcuts of rune-inscribed stones and other objects in Norway, Sweden and Denmark. His *Specimen* is an Old Norse-Latin dictionary, with the headwords printed in both runic and roman types. Consequently, seventeenth-century writers came to use the word 'runic' both of the epigraphical script of these monuments, which is its proper signification, and of the mediaeval Scandinavian language of Worm's lexicon and the literature that was written in it. The great predominance of Scandinavian runic remains over those in other countries and other tongues has led to the word 'runic' being intimately associated with Scandinavia down to the present day, while confusion between script and language was to remain at any rate into the nineteenth century.

But as early as 1700 some Englishmen had realised that runes were not exclusively Scandinavian. George Hickes, compiler of the encyclopaedic *Thesaurus*,[2] Humfrey Wanley, our first great authority on Anglo-Saxon manuscripts and palaeography, and such amateurs as William Nicolson, archdeacon and then bishop of Carlisle, had become aware of the runic remains of this country. In his catalogue of Old English manuscripts Wanley asserted that the Anglo-Saxons used the script and were responsible for bringing it to England with their invasions; and Nicolson kept a sharp eye open for their monuments while on his pastoral visitations through the north-west of England.

A century or more earlier runes had already been remarked and tentatively examined by English scholars. Robert Talbot, the Tudor antiquary, found them in manuscripts and copied them into his commonplace book.[3] Reginald

[1]   C.E.Fell has examined these uses in 'Runes and Semantics' in Bammesberger, *Old English Runes*, 195–229.
[2]   *Linguarum Vett.Septentrionalium Thesaurus. . . .* 2 vols (Oxford 1705).
[3]   Now Corpus Christi College, Cambridge, MS 379, with a list of runes taken from St John's College, Oxford, MS 17; R.I.Page, 'A Sixteenth-Century Runic Manuscript', *Studies in Honour of René Derolez*, ed. A.M.Simon-Vandenberger (Gent 1987), 384–90, reprinted with some corrections in Page, *Runes and Runic Inscriptions*, 289–94.

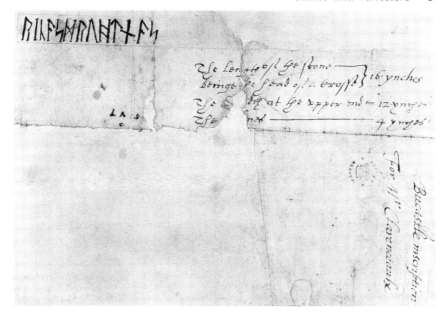

Fig.1. The runes of the lost Bewcastle cross head as recorded in a letter
to William Camden (British Library MS Cotton Julius F.vi).

Bainbrigg, schoolmaster of Appleby, recorded for the historian William
Camden the inscription on the font at Bridekirk (Cumberland/Cumbria) and
part of the great text on the cross at Ruthwell (Dumfries and Galloway)
though only the first of these achieved print, in the 1607 edition of Camden's
Britannia.[4] The characters baffled Bainbrigg. The Bridekirk runes he supposed were 'either the Arabians', or the Syrians' letters before Esdras for they
resemble them very much', and he thought the Ruthwell cross to be inscribed
peregrinis literis, 'with foreign letters'. In 1615 the broken head of the high
cross at Bewcastle (Cumberland/Cumbria) was 'found', acquired by Lord
William Howard of Naworth, a well-known collector of sculptured stones,
and shown by him to Sir Henry Spelman and Camden (fig.1). Thereafter Sir
Robert Cotton saw it, and members of his circle copied the inscription and
transliterated it fairly accurately into roman characters, showing they recognised the runes for what they were.[5]

4   Bainbrigg's sketches are now British Library MS Cotton Julius F.vi, fos. 305, 352.
    The Ruthwell cross drawing achieved publication belatedly in R.I.Page, 'An Early
    Drawing of the Ruthwell Cross', *Medieval Archaeology* 3 (1959), 285–8.
5   R.I.Page, 'The Bewcastle Cross', *Nottingham Medieval Studies* 4 (1960), 54–6.
    See also the postscript in *Runes and Runic Inscriptions*, 70.

Fig.2. The Manchester ring, from Hickes's *Thesaurus*.

Again, however, it was the scholars of the late seventeenth and early eighteenth centuries who put English runic studies on a sound basis. Hickes distinguished clearly between character and language, realising that Old English was occasionally recorded in runes though he thought the Anglo-Saxons learnt them from the Vikings. His *Thesaurus* contained a large amount of runic material, most of it published for the first time. For much of it Wanley was responsible, and it is to his skill as transcriber and care as proof-reader that the eighteenth century owed much of its runic knowledge. We are still in his debt, since for some monuments, like the Anglo-Saxon *Runic Poem* whose manuscript went up in the Cotton library fire of 1731, the *Thesaurus is* our only source. Hickes was the first to publish the partly runic Manchester/ Lancashire ring, then in Sir Hans Sloane's collection (fig.2), and the pseudorunic Sutton, Isle of Ely, brooch, which disappeared shortly after Hickes produced his engraving of it and did not come to light again until 1951. In the third section of the *Thesaurus*, called *Grammaticæ Islandicæ Rudimenta*, he printed a group of runic alphabets in part from Anglo-Saxon manuscripts, and copied the inscriptions of the Bridekirk font and the Ruthwell cross from Archdeacon Nicolson's drawings. He reproduced some runic passages in literary manuscripts – a few of the Exeter Book riddles and Cynewulf's signatures in his poems *Christ* and *Juliana*. In another of his plates he tried, anticipating later runologists, to trace the relationship between runic, Greek and roman characters. Book 2 of the *Thesaurus* is Wanley's catalogue of manuscripts containing Anglo-Saxon. In his introduction to it Wanley suggested that the Anglo-Saxons knew runes before they learnt the roman letters that were to supersede them, and he noted that they continued to include two runes, *thorn/þorn* and *wynn*, in their later bookhand. Wanley's list of manuscripts shows he was on the look-out for runes in them, for he noted several cases, as the runic *pater noster* in the Corpus Christi College, Cambridge, MS 422 text of the *First Poetical Dialogue of Solomon and Saturn*, runic scribbles added to MSS 41 and 326 in the same collection, and the drawing of the Bewcastle head runes in British Library MS Cotton Domitian xviii.

In the century or so that followed the publication of Hickes's *Thesaurus* the study of English runes proceeded slowly and desultorily. Individual discoveries were made and recorded – the amulet ring found near Bramham Moor (West Yorkshire) and published in Francis Drake's *Eboracum* in 1736 (fig.3), the piece of an inscribed cross taken from the ruined church at

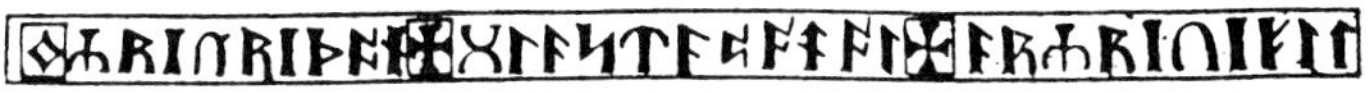

ᛒᚱᛁᚲᚱᛁᚦᛖᛗᚷᛚᚡᛡᛏᚠᛖᚠᛒᚠᛁᛟᛖᚱᚱᛟᚱᛁᚲᛁᛡᛁ

Fig.3. The Bramham Moor ring, from Drake's *Eboracum*.

Alnmouth (Northumberland) in 1789, and the fragmentary standing cross dug up in Lancaster churchyard in 1807 and quickly purloined by a collector of curiosities and put into a Kendal museum. But there was no general interest in runic, or indeed in Anglo-Saxon studies. Antiquaries sometimes failed to recognise runes when they saw them – in his cabinet Ralph Thoresby of Leeds (1658–1725) had two of the Anglo-Saxon runic coins known as *sceattas* (now often called 'pennies' by numismatists) without recognising the script of their legends, even though he was pursuing the subject of runic coins.[6]

Scandinavian scholars, on the other hand, remained active, so it is not surprising that in the later eighteenth century, with the rise in interest in Norse culture of which Bishop Percy's translation of Paul-Henri Mallet's *Northern Antiquities* (London 1770) is a symbol, 'runic' retained the implication 'Scandinavian'. Percy's *Five Pieces of Runic Poetry translated from the Islandic Language* (London 1763) has a title-page partly in Norse runes though the poems themselves have nothing strictly runic about them, being free translations of Eddic and skaldic verse. Percy excused his title with the comment, 'The word Runic was at first applied to the letters only; tho' later writers have extended it to the verses written in them.' Thomas James Mathias had even less reason for his *Runic Odes. Imitated from the Norse Tongue* (London 1781) for he made no attempt to link his poems, three adaptations from Old Norse, one imitation of it, and two whose inspiration is Celtic, to the script. 'Runic' was rapidly becoming one of the Gothick words, contrasting with the staid, formal and Classical 'Roman'. It had the connotations 'magical', 'mystic', 'eerie' as well as 'barbarous', 'Germanic', 'Northern', and only at some remove was it remembered as the name of a set of letters.

One result of this semantic imprecision was that when Englishmen did recognise the script of their runic monuments, they appealed to learned Scandinavians to tell them what the texts meant. And the Scandinavians, though they may have been erudite in their own character and language, made a mess of interpreting the English ones. An excellent example of this is the work of the Icelander, Finn Magnusen (Finnur Magnússon), in the early nineteenth

---

[6] R.I.Page, 'Ralph Thoresby's Runic Coins', *British Numismatic Jnl* 34 (1965), 28–31.

century. Magnusen was an industrious student of Danish runes, but his efforts on the English ones were ludicrous. After absurd but brief attempts on the Kingmoor (Cumberland/Cumbria) amulet ring and the Lancaster standing cross, Magnusen published an elaborate reading of the Ruthwell cross inscriptions, in what Kemble, rhetorically but innumerately, called '105 stupendous pages'. The Icelander got scarcely a word right, for he read the text as a mixture of Old Norse, Old Saxon, Old Frisian, Old English and Netherlandish, a blend that surprised even Magnusen.[7]

As a direct reaction came the work of the first great English runologist of modern times, John Mitchell Kemble (1807–57), whose article, 'On Anglo-Saxon Runes', published in *Archaeologia* 28 in 1840, is full of good sense and mordant wit. Kemble distinguished firmly between the runes of Anglo-Saxon England and those of Scandinavia. He recognised that the two versions of the script were related, but so distantly that Scandinavian scholars had no special qualifications for dealing with the English characters. So he sardonically rebuked the Northern scholars for being 'so obliging as to attempt to decypher them for us', and wrote his paper 'to save them this trouble in future'. This article of Kemble's set the foundations on which later English runologists built. It asserted the distinctive character of the English runic tradition, cognate with that of Northern Europe but separate from it. Henceforth there was no occasion to equate 'runic' with 'Scandinavian'. In so far as the confusion remains today, it is because of the huge numbers of runic monuments in Scandinavia and its colonies compared with the dearth of them elsewhere.

Kemble was a scholar of some distinction, intelligent, careful and, for his day, well-trained. Yet even he was not infallible where runes were in question as the sad case of the Chertsey bowl shows. This was a copper dish found in that town's monastic ruins. Kemble published it, identifying it as an alms dish and reading its text as a mixture of runes and uncials.[8] It was later found to be in modern Greek (fig.4). It is unfortunate, though entertaining, that the nineteenth-century runologists who succeeded Kemble followed him rather in this credulity than in the rigorous scholarship that was more typical of him.

By their nature runes attract the attention of two distinct groups of scholars. Historical linguists are interested in runes as records of language, and so tend, mistakenly, to forget about the object they are inscribed on and to think

---

[7] 'Om obelisken i Ruthwell og om de angelsaxiske runer', *Annaler f. nordisk Old-kyndighed* 1 (1836–7), 243–337.

[8] '. . . Observations on . . . a Runic Copper Dish found at Chertsey', *Archaeologia* 30 (1844), 39–46.

Fig.4. The Chertsey bowl 'runes', from Stephens's
Old-Northern Runic Monuments.

only of the text. Many have come to grief through studying an inscription, perhaps in transliterated form, without taking note of what it was inscribed upon, what were the physical constraints upon the carver. On the other hand, archaeologists and art historians are usually ill-trained in linguistic method, and will concentrate their interest on the object inscribed, its design, purpose, materials, and the circumstance of its discovery. All they want to know about the wording is 'What does it mean?', and it is sometimes impossible to give a succinct answer to that question. The perfect runologist would be learned in all these disciplines, but perfection is rare even among runologists and the best we can hope for is one who is primarily a competent historical linguist, but who is aware of and sympathetic to the results and methods of archaeology, art history and related subjects, and is prepared to seek expert and up-to-date advice on these matters.

Kemble was well grounded in the new linguistic learning of nineteenth-century Germany but his successors in the main were not. Most were antiquaries, and their work, often idiosyncratic and fantastical, lurks in the journals of the newly founded local archaeological societies. There are people like the 'prince of English runesters' Daniel Henry Haigh (1819–77), Anglican devout and Catholic convert, whose imagination worked full-time both when he saw and when he interpreted inscriptions, who wrote extensively on the runes found on Anglo-Saxon coins and on the monuments of Kent and Yorkshire, and who fought a bitter feud against John Maughan, rector of Bewcastle and guardian of its great cross; and George Forrest Browne (1833–1930), Disney Professor of Archaeology at Cambridge, and bishop of Stepney and then of Bristol, whose knowledge of many things was extensive but of Old English was slight, and who lectured learnedly, incessantly and inaccurately on runes before the University. But in runic matters all these men were dwarfed by the extravagant figure of George Stephens, for nearly forty years (1855–93) Professor of English at Copenhagen, and author of four astounding volumes, *The Old-Northern Runic Monuments of Scandinavia and England now first collected and deciphered* (London, Copenhagen, Lund 1866–1901, vol.4 published several years after Stephens's death). In the *Dictionary of National Biography* Henry Bradley summed Stephens up icily:

The conscientious labour which Stephens devoted to securing accurate copies of the inscriptions is deserving of the highest praise, and as a storehouse of materials for runic studies, his work is invaluable. On the other hand, his own contributions to the interpretation of the inscriptions are almost worthless, owing to his want of accurate philological knowledge. His method of translation consisted in identifying the words of the inscriptions with any words of similar appearance that he could discover in the dictionaries of the ancient or modern Scandinavian languages, and then forcing them into some plausible meaning without regard to grammar.

Bradley's criticism of Stephens's linguistic work is just, for this influential book has misled generations of runic ignoramuses. It abounds in absurdities like the elaborate runic reading of a stone from Brough which later turned out to be in ancient Greek – even George Forrest Browne spotted that. It is customary to scoff at Stephens, but rather we should stress the positive qualities which even Bradley admitted in him, the abounding vigour and enthusiasm that led him to become a collecting point for Anglo-Saxon runic studies through the second part of the nineteenth century. Until the publication in 1961 of Hertha Marquardt's English volume of the *Bibliographie der Runeninschriften nach Fundorten* (a bibliography of runic inscriptions arranged alphabetically according to find-spots), runologists looking for information turned naturally to Stephens in the first instance. He is the only man to have achieved anything like a full corpus of English runes, the first to publish a number of these important monuments, and is our primary authority for some provenances. Indeed, his extensive correspondence, much of it preserved in the Royal Library, Stockholm, and in Lund University Library, is rich in runic information not known from anywhere else. He alone preserved the report of the discovery of a coin at Wijk-bij-Duurstede (Netherlands) which is now known to be an issue of King Beonna of East Anglia.[9] Without Stephens's record of the Selsey (West Sussex) gold fragments scholars would never have persisted in searching the British Museum's stores where they had lurked, unknown and wrongly labelled, for decades. His correspondence preserves a detailed and vastly entertaining account of the appearance and adventures of the Coquet Island (Northumberland) ring, a piece which no longer survives but which is pictured in his book. In short, Stephens's *Old-Northern Runic*

[9]   H.E.Pagan, 'A New Type for Beonna', *British Numismatic Jnl* 37 (1968), 10–15; also M.M.Archibald, 'The Coinage of Beonna in the Light of the Middle Harling Hoard', *British Numismatic Jnl* 55 (1985), 35.

Monuments is a splendid reference work – provided you check every state-ment in it.

Stephens had no successor. Though several modern runologists rival him in the fertility of their imaginations, none has taken his place as the central figure in Anglo-Saxon runic studies, and none has produced such a remark-able collection of facts and fictions about English runes. Later scholars worked on a smaller scale and, at their best, with greater linguistic discipline, for it is in the careful publication of new finds and the painstaking analysis of earlier ones that the best of more recent runic scholarship shows itself. To give examples. A.S.Napier made an austere and intelligent examination of the Auzon/Franks casket texts which, though published at the beginning of the twentieth century, has never been bettered.[10] Bruce Dickins accompanied his 'A System of Transliteration for Old English Runic Inscriptions' with a mini-corpus of Anglo-Saxon texts; with typical retinence he gave the results of his study without detailing the course of his thought.[11] More recently R.Derolez and U.Schwab have written an elegant account of the important Anglo-Saxon runic graffiti at the church of St Michael, Monte Sant' Angelo, Gargano (Italy).[12] The numismatist Mark Blackburn has prepared an immensely perceptive and revealing survey of the English runic coins which runologists will ignore at their peril.[13] Individual rune-stones have been set in their historical contexts in the county volumes of the British Academy's *Corpus of Anglo-Saxon Stone Sculpture* (CASS 1984–   ).

I have begun with this short historical introduction partly because of the intrinsic interest of the tale itself, but principally because it serves to warn the student and to introduce some of the themes of this book. As a warning it shows how the words 'rune' and 'runic' developed a number of diverse mean-ings so that we must be careful about accepting them at their face value, certainly in writings from early modern times, and sometimes even in present-day accounts; it cautions against accepting too readily early descrip-tions, readings and interpretations, and in particular against trust in Ste-phens's remarkable corpus of texts; and it suggests that there may still exist

10 'The Franks Casket', *An English Miscellany presented to Dr Furnivall . . .* (Oxford 1901), 362–81.
11 *Leeds Studies in English* 1 (1932), 15–19.
12 'The Runic Inscriptions of Monte S.Angelo (Gargano)', *Academiae Analecta* 45 (1983), 95–130.
13 'A Survey of Anglo-Saxon and Frisian Coins with Runic Inscriptions' in Bammes-berger, *Old English Runes*, 137–89.

misconceptions about the nature of runes which derive from mistaken theories of earlier and speculative runologists.

On the positive side, it points to the necessary distinction between script and language, directing the reader's attention to the specifically Anglo-Saxon forms of the runic characters which are the subject of this book; it introduces the beginner to the variety of disciplines the runologist must call upon to help him in his work; and it suggests the uncertainty of much of our interpretation of the texts, and the range of different meanings the student may find given for any one inscription.

This last point needs further development. A witty, not to say mischievous, Viking archaeologist has defined the first law of runic studies as 'for every inscription there shall be as many interpretations as there are runologists studying it'. The work of runic scholars over the years has encouraged such sardonic comment. Some years ago I reviewed a book by the Danish linguist, Niels Åge Nielsen, which exemplifies the rule from Swedish sources. Examining a group of Viking Age rune-stone texts, Nielsen listed six diverse readings and interpretations of the Sparlösa, Västergötland, stone.[14] This monument presents quite a long text, fairly well preserved; so there should be enough for the runologist to get his teeth into. Interpretations of one baffling section of it range from the practical, 'May Eiríkr, son of Griótgarðr in Véby, acquire . . .' to the informative, 'I am guardian of the sanctuary. I cut these runes, may he read them who can. I make them binding . . .'; from the threatening, 'A holy thing must not be profaned. He who alters this inscription, let him be outlawed, a pervert, openly known to all the people' to the romantic, 'The priestess's mighty work. I slaughtered Alrik's horse in the gods' sanctuary, and Arngunn drove the chariot of the sun with the horse.' Despite the multiplicity and variety of existing suggestions Nielsen managed to add another. A case like this – and it is not unique – may lead the beginner to think that runology is nothing but inspired guesswork, or even simple guesswork.

It is perhaps true that no Anglo-Saxon runic inscription has so beguiling a range of interpretations, but one from Chessell Down (Isle of Wight) approaches it. This consists of seven letters, clearly divided into two distinct groups, scratched on the back of a decorated scabbard mount (fig.5). Archaeologists date this piece to the sixth century, firmly in the pagan period when Anglo-Saxons used no script other than runes. Scholars have usually taken the inscription to be the name of the sword belonging to the scabbard, though Sonia Chadwick Hawkes's observations that the rune-inscribed plate is an

14 *Runestudier* (Odense 1968), 25–8.

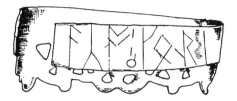

Fig.5. The Chessell Down scabbard mount runes. (1:1)

addition to the original mount, and that the runes were cut shortly before the sword was buried with its owner, make this less likely. Translations of the text include Stephens's absurd 'destruction to the armour (of the foe)', George Hempl's 'self defence', Hermann Harder's 'I strengthen the power of Swari', R.W.V.Elliott's 'increase to (or augmenter of) pain', Karl Schneider's 'Terrible one, wound!' and Bengt Odenstedt's 'to Thor, the charioteer'.[15] A more recent case is the Loveden Hill (Lincolnshire) cremation urn with its fifteen runes apparently divided into three groups. In 1980 Odenstedt interpreted them as a sentence, 'Siþæbæd gets bread'; in 1989 Elliott as a three-fold description of a cinerary urn: 'bed for the journey (of death)'; 'dwelling'; 'sepulchre'; in 1990 Eichner as 'Siþæbald consecrates you. Grave-mound'; in 1991 Bammesberger as 'Sȝþæbæd' ‖ 'female servant' ‖ 'tomb'.[16] These valiant attempts do not have a lot in common.

In fact, examples like these illustrate a primary epigraphical difficulty facing us when we deal with peoples who were otherwise illiterate. We have little idea of the sort of text – form, content and register – they would think

[15] S.C.Hawkes and R.I.Page, 'Swords and Runes in South-east England', *Antiquaries Jnl* 47 (1967), 11–18; Stephens, *Old-Northern Runic Monuments*, vol.3, 460; G.Hempl, 'The Runic Inscription on the Isle of Wight Sword', *PMLA* 18 (1903), 95–8; H.Harder, 'Die Runen der ags. Schwertinschrift im Britischen Museum', *Archiv f. d. Stud. d. neueren Sprachen* 161 (1932), 86–7; R.W.V.Elliott, *Runes, an Introduction* (Manchester 1959), 79–80, and 2.ed. (1989), 104–5; K.Schneider, 'Six OE Runic Inscriptions Reconsidered', *Nordica et Anglica: Studies in Honor of Stefán Einarsson*, ed. A.H.Orrick (The Hague 1968), 40–3; B.Odenstedt, 'The Chessell Down Runic Inscription', *Archaeology and Environment* 2 (1984), 113–26. Odenstedt has since retracted this interpretation.

[16] B.Odenstedt, 'The Loveden Hill Runic Inscription', *Ortnamnssällskapets i Uppsala Årsskrift* (1980), 24–37; Elliott, *Runes*, 2.ed., 50–2; H.Eichner, 'Die Ausprägung der linguistischen Physiognomie des Englischen anno 400 bis anno 600 n. Chr.' in Bammesberger and Wollmann, *Britain 400–600*, pp.324–5; A.Bammesberger, 'Three Old English Runic Inscriptions' in Bammesberger, *Old English Runes*, pp.125–8.

appropriate to cut on a stone, a piece of bone, a weapon or tool, brooch or ring, simply because they have left no other writings to tell us. We have no recorded context of thought to help us understand an inscription, and modern parallels may be misleading. There may be cases where we are in little doubt as to meaning, where an inscription is unambiguous in accidence, syntax and morphology, and contains only roots which are easily recognisable. Or where it is one of a group of texts which cast light upon each other. Or where the relationship between inscribed object and text looks so suggestive as to give a strong clue as to meaning. But unless such conditions apply, our examination is liable to end in speculation. For many of the earliest Anglo-Saxon inscriptions, and even for some of the later, we can only speculate: as, for example, with the roe-deer's astragalus (ankle-bone – such bones were used as playing-pieces in some sort of board game) from a cremation urn at Caistor-by-Norwich, the Loveden Hill urn, the two small bits of gold from the foreshore near Selsey, the Ash or Gilton/Guilton (Kent) sword-hilt, the Dover brooch, the cattle-bone dug up at *Hamwih* (Southampton), the bracteate from Welbeck Hill (Lincolnshire/South Humberside), the bronze pail from Chessell Down, the badly corroded tweezers from Heacham (Norfolk), the jet disc from Whitby (North Yorkshire) and the wooden spoon from York.

It follows that the runologist needs two contrasting qualities, imagination and scepticism. The first gives him insight into the possible meanings a letter group may express: the second restrains his fancy and holds his erudition in the bonds of common sense. In practice, of course, runologists tend to lean to one side or the other, to be primarily imaginative or primarily sceptical.

One runological problem that illuminates this division, indeed conflict, of qualities, is that of the original purpose of runes; what the early Germanic peoples, who were otherwise illiterate, needed them for. Imaginative runologists have often regarded the script as essentially magical, as giving access to supernatural powers, being linked to Germanic paganism and in some way an expression of it. They are influenced by an etymology of the Old English word *run* which implies a meaning 'mystery, secret'.[17] Faced with an obscure text people who think like this are tempted to explain it as magico-religious. An extreme example of this approach is the work of the German runologist Karl Schneider, whose immensely learned book *Die germanischen Runennamen: Versuch einer Gesamtdeutung* (Meisenheim am Glan 1956) tried to show how runes reflected aspects of pagan belief and practice, and whose interpretations of inscriptions leant towards the mystical, and sometimes fell flat into it. To give an example of his results: the Manchester gold ring has a

---

[17] On this Fell, 'Runes and Semantics', 205–16.

legend, partly runic and partly roman, which, reads, +æDRED MEC AH EAnRED MEC agROf, '+ Ædred owns me, Eanred inscribed me.' To the sceptical runologist this is no more than a record of owner and maker of the ring. Schneider, making great play with the names of the runes used in the legend, thought it 'an eminently pagan fertility and prosperity charm cunningly contrived and cleverly camouflaged', its purpose 'to grant its owner vitality and increase of property in the form of harvest and cattle for the ethical obligation of hospitality'.[18]

Few will follow Schneider thus far, but numbers of workers in the field accept a more moderate expression of the link between runes and magic and perhaps Germanic paganism; and many present-day dabblers in runes have found it profitable to adduce the mystical significance and indeed power of the script. Sceptical runologists, on the other hand, usually regard runes as just another script type, used in the same ways, for religious, magical or plain practical ends, as any other alphabet. The Danish scholars Anders Bæksted and Erik Moltke exemplified this attitude. In his monograph *Målruner og Troldruner* (Copenhagen 1952), Bæksted reassessed the evidence for rune-magic and tried to refute the conclusions some had drawn from it. Moltke wrote explicitly, 'Runes are perfectly ordinary letters used for exactly the same purposes as the Latin characters we employ today';[19] and in his last book, published shortly after his death, he remained characteristically dogmatic: 'All talk about the priesthood needing writing [i.e. runes] for secret, magical purposes is nonsense, partly . . . because application of writing to such ends is always secondary.'[20]

Schneider and Bæksted-Moltke take up extreme positions, and between them are a multitude of intermediate ones for the judicious runologist. R.W.V.Elliott's *Runes, an Introduction* (Manchester 1959) and some of his runic articles give the case for rune-magic in restrained form. (The second edition of his book (Manchester 1989) shows some modification of these views.) For myself, I look upon Schneider's work as so much misplaced erudition, while I think that Bæksted, in firmly rejecting magical values of runes, had sometimes to resort to special pleading. Consequently, I am prepared to accept that runes were sometimes used to enhance magical activities, and even to suspect that they may sometimes have been a magical script, or at least an esoteric one that could be used in magical practices, without wanting

---

[18] 'Six OE Runic Inscriptions', 51.
[19] *Skalk* 2 (1965), 16.
[20] *Runes and their origin: Denmark and elsewhere* (Copenhagen 1985), 69.

to think them essentially magical during the Anglo-Saxon era, or to interpret all difficult or obscure texts in magical terms.

Thus early in the book I introduce a subject of controversy since I want to make clear from the beginning what opportunity for dispute rests in Anglo-Saxon runic studies, how little certain information we can draw upon. This is partly because for many years there was too little competent and critical work done on the Anglo-Saxon runic corpus – we are now more fortunate in that a number of capable younger scholars have entered the field. But there is also the problem that the corpus is so very small. We have no idea how representative a sample it supplies, what percentage survives of the inscriptions that were once cut; though we can be fairly sure it is tiny. Inevitably it is hard to establish principles of studying the corpus. Old English runic texts are still scarce despite the new finds that are appearing annually. Apart from the coin legends, which do not fit easily into a statistical count, there are about ninety runic inscriptions known either from Anglo-Saxon England itself, or from Continental regions in contact with it, as well as a few others that contain rune-like signs that may not be runes proper.

Of this modest number about twenty are either so damaged or so fragmentary that they yield little information. Two more are lost, and we know them only through early drawings which may be inaccurate. Another, that on the metal plate attached to the base of the Brunswick/Gandersheim casket, is of doubted authenticity. The texts of four (or five if the Anglo-Saxon sundial dug from the walls of Orpington (Kent) church is included here) are mainly in roman characters, with only a few runes. Three more are magic gibberish.

Of the remainder there are twenty or so whose interpretations are uncertain, whose meanings are disputed or unknown. There remain perhaps forty significant texts, and several of these consist only of personal names in the nominative case. Otherwise, the longest are the Ruthwell cross inscriptions, with over 320 runes remaining or recorded, and the Auzon/Franks casket, with over 260, some of them cryptic. More typical of the longer Anglo-Saxon runic legends are those of the reliquary or casket at Mortain in Normandy (thirty-eight runes giving six words), the Thornhill (West Yorkshire) III memorial stone (fifty-four runes and ten words) and the bone plate traditionally ascribed to Derby (twenty-four runes and seven words).

A corpus of this size and nature presents a minimal body of material to base conclusions on. Moreover, it is spread over a wide period of time, the whole of the Anglo-Saxon period, and over a large geographical area, stretching from Kent as far north as Edinburgh; and runic usages may have varied from age to age and from region to region. As a consequence it is difficult to define runological principles from the Anglo-Saxon material alone. To take only a few examples of difficulty. We cannot know with any precision the full range of sounds that individual runes represented, nor can we distinguish with certainty some early rune types from some later ones. We know practically nothing of the audience the inscriptions appealed to, nor indeed whether it was the same sort or size of audience throughout the period. The runemaster's standing in the community and his training in his skill are unknown to us, and we cannot tell what spelling traditions he inherited. We cannot be sure if the sparsity of extant runes shows that the Anglo-Saxons carved few runic texts, or if they cut many on perishable materials which have duly perished. This leads to the related question; is our understanding of English runes distorted because we have lost most of the informal inscriptions, those on wood and perhaps on bone and non-precious metals? Might these have had a more 'demotic' content than the formal memorial inscriptions on stone that we are more accustomed to? We can only conjecture about the relationship between runic and roman scripts, the amount of prestige each had, and the reasons why one died out in the early Middle Ages while the other survives today. And there is room for a good deal of disagreement over whether later Anglo-Saxon scribes were equally conversant with the runic as with the roman alphabet, as I discuss in chapter 14.

On some of these points we can appeal to the evidence of Continental or Scandinavian monuments, but there will remain many unanswered and perhaps unanswerable questions, topics where certainty cannot be achieved and we have to be content with likelihood or even bare possibility. In recent years there have been important and creative re-examinations of some of the principles of runic study, as in Derolez's discussion of the relationship between epigraphical and manuscript runes in England,[21] but unfortunately they do not always bring us greater understanding. Sometimes they only lead into deeper darkness. New discoveries and new studies of older theories have turned some of the certainties I put into the first edition of this book into doubts; or have required more complex interpretations of the material; or have simply suggested a new range of evidence. The difficulty about writing a general introduction lies in these areas of uncertainty where, however hard he tries to be objective, the writer's opinion controls the way he presents the sparse data, and where the arguments for or against a point of view are too detailed and technical to put into such a book. All the writer can do is caution his readers to be on the watch for his prejudices. I do so now by admitting myself a sceptical runologist.

---

[21] R.Derolez, 'Epigraphical versus Manuscript English Runes: One or Two Worlds?', *Academiae Analecta* 45 (1983), 69–93; developed in D.Parsons, 'Anglo-Saxon Runes in Continental Manuscripts' in Düwel, *Runische Schriftkultur*, 176–94.

2

When and Where

Where, when and why runes were invented are matters for dispute, and are often disputed. Luckily these questions are not our concern. More important for this book is a related one; by what route or routes did runes come to England? We can plot the scatter of known early runic inscriptions, though we must always keep in mind that only a tiny fraction of what was cut is likely to have survived.[1] The second edition of Wolfgang Krause's *[Die] Runeninschriften im älteren Futhark* (Göttingen 1966), with that author's views informed by Herbert Jankuhn's archaeological expertise, gave a clear picture of the early distribution of the script as it was then understood. By the time of the Anglo-Saxon invasions, by the mid fifth century, runes were quite widespread in Norway, they occurred here and there in what is now Sweden – in Bohuslän, Skåne, Uppland, Östergötland and the island of Gotland – and they were fairly common in the Danish isles of Sjælland and Fyn, on the Jutland peninsula, and at its neck in Schleswig. Outside the north Krause's corpus gives the solitary northern German example of the Liebenau (Mittelweser) brooch, in Lower Saxony, and five pieces from eastern Europe, from Kovel (Ukraine), Dahmsdorf (Germany), Rozwadów (Poland), Pietroassa (Rumania) and Szabadbattyán (Hungary). Despite these curious early outliers in the east, the weight of this distribution is in Scandinavia, and this, together with the fact that the inventor(s) of runes certainly knew the roman alphabet, led Erik Moltke to suggest Denmark as the homeland of the script, a thesis that is both persuasive and unproven.[2] However that may be, from an Anglo-Saxon point of view it is a group at the south of the Jutland peninsula that attracts attention, for some of the Germanic tribes who settled England reputedly came from near there.

---

[1] R.Derolez, 'The Runic System and its Cultural Context', *Michigan Germanic Studies* 7 (1981), 20.

[2] 'Er Runeskriften opstået i Danmark?', *Fra Nationalmuseets Arbejdsmark* (1951), 47–58. More recently in his *Runes and their Origin*, 64–5.

More recent discoveries of runes have added to Krause's list but hardly modified its geographical thrust. In the east only one addition is to be made: an inscription from Leţcani (Rumania), From Denmark – Jutland and the islands, as well as Skåne which in early times formed part of Denmark – there is a mass of new material. In 1994 Marie Stoklund, Denmark's leading runologist, listed the pre-400 inscriptions in south-Scandinavian territory, including Schleswig: those from the great marsh-finds of Illerup, Vimose, Torsbjerg/Thorsberg and Nydam; individual finds of inscribed brooches, from Himlingøje, Vaerløse, Skovgårde, Nøvling, Næsbjerg, Gårdlösa and Møllegårdsmarken, and a wooden box from Stenmagle whose date is uncertain – altogether some twenty-seven runic objects.[3] So much for geographical scatter, but geography is not everything. All these inscriptions are on objects that are easy to carry, and their find-spots may be some distance from where their runes were cut. Indeed, archaeologists have suggested that marsh-finds like those of Vimose, Torsbjerg and Illerup were war-booty, taken from defeated enemies and sacrificed by victorious locals. These objects may have reached Jutland from afar, though in some, possibly most, cases inscriptions may have been added shortly before sacrifice. More radically, scholars have begun to question whether geographical distribution is of the first importance; to suggest we should rather attend to matters such as social standing, interrelationship of families of rank, and gift exchange, with runes identified as a script used by a minority, among certain aristocratic groups, across tribal borders.

To return to geography. The later distribution of runic monuments shows interesting developments. Scandinavia continues important, and again there are occasional examples from eastern Europe. But runes also appear in Frankish and Alemannic territories, in what are now southern and western Germany, and sporadically in modern Belgium, France and Switzerland, and there is an apparently significant though small group from the Frisian (Netherlands and Ostfriesland) coastal region. At first glance this last-named should be relevant to our purpose, since the Old English and early Frisian languages are intimately linked, and this link may be reflected in the runic systems of the two countries.

Though rigorous and prejudiced philologists will contest the terminology, it is helpful and sufficiently accurate to group together the inscriptions from Schleswig, Denmark, Norway and Sweden as North Germanic, and to call those of the Frankish-Alemannic-Frisian territories West Germanic. Between the two is a region in north-west Germany. Until recently no runes had

3 'Von Thorsberg nach Haithabu' in Düwel, *Runische Schriftkultur*, 96, 98–105.

emerged there save for those of Liebenau, which are marginal to the area. Thus it formed a convenient boundary zone between the two runic groups, which have similar alphabets apart from a few letter forms that appear to distinguish North from West Germanic types. The latest discoveries have compromised this convenient boundary.

In the first place runes have begun to appear in the hitherto almost rune-less territory. Known since the 1930s is a group of rune-inscribed animal bones from sites on the lower Weser River (Oldenburg, Lower Saxony). Some of the inscriptions have letter and word forms that look most suspect; until recently the whole group had been thought fakes. Now Peter Pieper has conducted detailed scientific tests to suggest that at least some of the Weser runes are genuine.[4] A possible date is early fifth-century. More important are very recent finds from Wremen, near Cuxhaven, where a major excavation uncovered a runic text of great importance cut on the footstool to a decorated wooden chair, set in a fifth-century high-status context.[5] Thus we can no longer regard northern Germany as rune-less, though it is still sparse in runes compared with Scandinavia, and even compared with Frisia.

A second point affects distinctions in rune form between North and West Germanic inscriptions. Chief among these is the **h**-rune. In the North Germanic area this has a single cross-stave Ͱ; in the West a double cross-stave Ħ. Perhaps the earliest runic inscription yet recognised in England is on a deer's astragalus (ankle-bone). This was taken with over thirty others, uninscribed, from a cremation urn in the large cemetery at Caistor-by-Norwich. It has six runes carefully scratched on it. Five of them are types common to North and West Germanic alphabets. The sixth, no. 4 in the letter sequence, is an **h**-rune of the North Germanic type, with single cross-stave (fig.6). Since the urn where the bone lay resembles pots from late fourth- and fifth-century Fyn and from Angeln (North Germany), it was at first assumed that the inscription was North Germanic in inspiration. This theory was convincing until there emerged, in England, several other inscriptions with single-barred **h**. An example is on one of the cremation urns from the south Lincolnshire cemetery of Loveden Hill, which has, cut crudely round it before it was fired, a runic text that seems to contain a single-barred **h**-rune, though the legend has not been interpreted with any certainty so we cannot be sure. The Loveden Hill runes were identified in the 1960s and since then there have appeared other early inscriptions from England with the single-barred **h**.

---

4   P.Pieper, 'The Bones with Runic Inscriptions from the Lower Weser River. New Results of Scientific Investigations Concerning the Problem: Original(s) or Fake(s)' in Bammesberger, *Old English Runes*, 343–58.
5   K.Düwel, 'Neue Runenfunde aus Deutschland', *Nytt om Runer* 9 (1994), 14–16.

Fig.6. The Caistor-by-Norwich astragalus runes. (2:1)

There is the baffling sequence **buhu** or possibly **buhui** cut on a brooch from Wakerley (Northamptonshire). More important is a sixth-century find from Watchfield (Oxfordshire), a copper-alloy fitting belonging to a leather case containing scales and weights, and with a text beginning **hariboki**, clearly having a first element *hari-*, 'army', perhaps as part of a personal name. In neither of these cases need we suggest North Germanic influence. Yet later Anglo-Saxon inscriptions, certainly from the end of the seventh century onwards, use only the West Germanic double-barred **h** ᚻ.

This form, with two cross-staves, also occurs on the Continent in several sixth-century inscriptions from Germany, on a brooch from Kirchheim (Württemberg), a wooden staff from Neudingen in the same region, a silver buckle from Pforzen (Bavaria) and a brooch and a buckle from Weimar (Thuringia). In Frisia the double-barred form occurs first on a coin or jewel from Harlingen, *c.*600, which records the personal name **hada**. We have to explain how the double-staved **h** came to be on the Continent; why early England evidences the single-staved form and later England only the double-staved version. Were there two distinct introductions of runes to this country, first from North and later from Continental West Germanic territory? Or was the double-barred **h** developed in England and exported to the Continent? Does the chronology of forms allow this possibility?

There is a second, much less decisive, formal test. The rune we transliterate as **k** began as ᚲ, and in the north eventually developed to ᚴ. In England the equivalent form is ᚳ, also found in a few Continental West Germanic inscriptions, most convincingly in the words **kabu**, **kobu**, two forms of the word 'comb', on bone combs from Oostum and Toornwerd, both in Frisia.[6]

The evidence I have presented so far is consistent with two alternative hypotheses: (i) runes came to England from south Scandinavia, developed a couple of individual forms here and were then exported to those lands on the Continent where the West Germanic inscriptions occur, or (ii) runes came to

6 K.Düwel and W.-D.Tempel, 'Knochenkämme mit Runeninschriften aus Friesland . . .', *Palaeohistoria* 14 (1970 for 1968), 363–7, 369–70.

England from south Scandinavia, but also travelled south from that region by some land route which left a large area of north-west Germany virtually free of them; on the Continent certain new forms developed and these too spread over the Channel to England where they eventually superseded the North Germanic types.

The weakness of (i) is that it hardly allows for the early appearance of runes in West Germanic territory, certainly by the first half of the sixth century.[7] There is a second difficulty too. England had closer runological links with Frisia than with the rest of the Continent. Only in these two areas are the new vowel runes ᚨ and ᚩ found. Since their creation seems linked in some way – though what way is a matter of fierce dispute – to developments in pronunciation common to English and Frisian, it is natural to assume they were invented at a time when English and Frisian formed part of a continuum within the group of West Germanic dialects that some learned philologists have named Ingvaeonic.[8] The weakness of hypothesis (ii) above is in part chronological. From what survives it seems likely that runes appeared rather earlier in England than in Frisia. Indeed, most Frisian inscriptions are so late as to suggest that runes were a comparatively tardy development there. The earliest of the Frisian runes to be dated with precision are those on the gold *solidi* from Harlingen and Schweindorf (Ostfriesland, Germany), both *c*.600 (unless one accepts a very early – fifth-century – date assigned to a bone comb-case from Kantens, with two runic or rune-like graphs on it).[9] Several English runic texts antedate the Frisian solidi. Moreover, again judging by what survives, the Anglo-Saxons used runes more purposefully than the Frisians. In England the tradition was more robust and practical, which implies there was more reason for the Anglo-Saxons to adopt the script than for the Frisians.

In all probability both hypotheses are too simplistic and stemmatic. To some extent they rely on modern political divisions that are misleading in early mediaeval terms. In, say, the fifth and sixth centuries there were likely to be influences in both directions across the North Sea, between the insular

---

7 Up-to-date details of dates of German inscriptions are in the catalogue to the exhibition, *Schmuck und Waffen mit Inschriften aus dem ersten Jahrtausend*, held in Göttingen, 7 August–6 September 1995.

8 Recent years have seen intensive examination of this subject by H.F.Nielsen and other scholars: summarised in his 'Ante-Old Frisian: a Review', *NOWELE* 24 (1994), 91–136.

9 There has been much published on the Frisian inscriptions recently. For a brief summary and references see my 'On the Baffling Nature of Frisian Runes', *Amsterdamer Beiträge zur älteren Germanistik* 45 (1996), 131–50, and other articles in the same volume.

Anglo-Saxons and the various North Germanic and Continental West Germanic speakers, as indeed archaeological evidence implies. Users of runes might have picked up new usages and forms and allowed older ones to fall into disuse. For all that it remains important for us to note regional differences that characterise surviving runic monuments.

In Anglo-Saxon England runes continued in epigraphical use for some six hundred years. The Caistor-by-Norwich runes are placed on archaeological grounds in the fourth or early fifth century. Among the latest of surviving Anglo-Saxon runic monuments proper, if we can trust art historians, is a late tenth- or early eleventh-century grave-stone, Whithorn I (Wigtownshire/ Dumfries and Galloway), with runes cut along one edge. Within this long period of time we can plot only imprecisely the incidence of surviving examples. Already I have implied some of the uncertainties of dating. The Caistor-by-Norwich burial is set within fairly wide limits, and even when we have dated the burial we have not necessarily dated all objects connected with it. Theoretically the rune-bearing astragalus could have been old when buried, and theoretically could have been brought to this country, already engraved, from southern Scandinavia (though that seems unlikely since the object is not of great intrinsic value). The Whithorn I stone is placed within half a century or so on stylistic grounds, but the inscription, cut curiously down the edge, may be a casual addition to a finished object.

There are few English runes that we can assign to a close date. Most important are runic coins from regal issues, pennies of Offa (757–96), Coenwulf (796–821) and Ceolwulf I (821–3) of Mercia, and *stycas* of Eanred (*c*.808–40), Æthelred II (840–9), Redwulf (844) and Osberht (849–67) of Northumbria, and Æthelberht of East Anglia (d.794). Less precisely dated is the quite rich coinage of Beorna/Beonna of East Anglia, a mid eighth-century king known only from post-Conquest sources, and there has recently been found a single coin of his approximate contemporary Alberht/Æthelberht. Only one other runic object has a precise date on historical grounds, the wooden coffin which the Lindisfarne monks gave to St Cuthbert's body at its elevation in 698.

However, historical evidence can be used more generally for dating runic monuments. To take a crude example, many of the rune-stones are explicitly Christian, as are also such miscellaneous objects as the Whitby (North Yorkshire) comb and the Derby bone plate with their references to God, the Auzon/Franks casket with its portrayal of the Magi, and the Mortain (Normandy) chrismal which may have been a reliquary or a box for the consecrated host. Evidently none of these could be earlier than the beginning of the seventh century. The name-stones of Lindisfarne (Northumberland), Hartlepool (Durham/Cleveland) and Monkwearmouth (Durham/Tyne and Wear) are so alike that they must surely be linked to the religious houses in those places, and this puts them between the seventh century when the monasteries were founded, and the ninth when the Vikings crushed them.

For closer dating we can only resort to typological studies by archaeologists, art historians, numismatists and linguists, and though these produce results, they also reveal problems. S.C.Hawkes's meticulous examination of the runic mount of the Chessell Down scabbard and the sword it held shows how complex the discussion may have to be.[10] She suggests that the hilt of the sword was a composite piece, made up of parts from different dates and provenances, from Scandinavia and England of the fifth and sixth centuries. The scabbard mount is probably English work of the early sixth, but the strip of silver carrying the runes looks like a repair to it, while the runes themselves, being very little worn, may well have been scratched only a short time before the burial, perhaps in the mid sixth century. In this case the archaeological provenance was clear, and Hawkes was able to study the inscribed object in such detail, aided by parallels both in this country and Scandinavia, that she could suggest a fairly close dating. But often – and particularly in these metal-detecting times – there is no precise archaeological context for an inscribed object, and the scholar can place it only generally within a century. For instance, Sir David Wilson, a leading authority on later Anglo-Saxon metalwork, could only date the Kingmoor amulet ring roughly to the ninth century on the evidence of its use of gold and niello.[11] As regards the rune-stones and runic crosses, which are included in the Corpus of Anglo-Saxon Stone Sculpture scholars are only now working out a detailed chronology – largely on the uncertain basis of typology – and there is still room for difference of opinion.

Dating on numismatic grounds, which is important when we consider coins that bear no king's name – or which bear the name of a king only imprecisely dated, – is similarly liable to vary and alter. In 1960 the numismatist S.E.Rigold published a study of the pale gold and silver coins struck in the name of the moneyer Pada. He thought the series began *c*.680. Some years later, in the light of new evidence, he re-examined the dating and pushed it back ten or fifteen years, accepting *c*.665–70. Another scholar, J.P.C.Kent, wished to go back as far as 655–60 (which was in fact a return on new grounds to an old dating long since discarded, which put these coins in the 650s because the Pada of their legends was identified with Peada, son of Penda of Mercia, who flourished in that decade). Recently, in a magisterial

10 Hawkes and Page, 'Swords and Runes in South-east England', 11–18.
11 *Anglo-Saxon Ornamental Metalwork 700–1100 in the British Museum* (London 1964), 23.

survey, Mark Blackburn has returned the Pada coins to the slightly later date, *c*.660–70.[12]

Dating on linguistic grounds is still more tentative. Its principle is simple enough. Throughout the Old English period the language was continually changing, in pronunciation, morphology, semantics and syntax, the first two being the most important for our purposes. If we could assign dates to the various linguistic changes, we could date inscriptions by reference to them. Simple though the principle is, its practice is perilous. It is worth listing a few of the difficulties. Some of the linguistic changes are hard, and some are impossible to date. Dating and localisation are interrelated, since sound-changes (with consequent changes in methods of representing sounds by graphs) occur at different dates in different places; so before a text can be dated we ought to know what local dialect it represents. As comparative material for dating purposes we use written texts, assuming that there is a correlation between manuscript and epigraphical English. This may not always be the case, but what alternative approach is there? The written texts we use as controls can themselves often be dated and localised only approximately. There are no Old English manuscripts before 650, and they are rare enough before 800, so we have no control texts corresponding to our earliest inscriptions, which are thus not susceptible to close linguistic dating. Surviving Old English manuscripts cover only part of the country, omitting large areas such as Lindsey, western Northumbria and East Anglia, so control texts are lacking for these areas too. Scribes may use a variety of styles of Old English, legal, poetical, learned, which are distant from those of rune-carvers. Inscriptions are generally short, and inevitably supply few localising or dating features. Memorial-stone texts may use old-fashioned forms of the language embedded in traditional formulae – as they sometimes do today. Professional letter carvers may have used in their work some sort of formal dialect which has no equivalent in the written tradition. They may have worked far from their homes and used a dialect not equivalent to that of the neighbourhood where their monuments were raised. We should be aware of physical restraints on the runic material we study – the space available to the carver or the need for tidy lay-out of his inscription. Such considerations may have affected the form of his text.[13] Clearly, linguistic dating can only be approxi-

---

[12] 'A Survey of Anglo-Saxon and Frisian Coins with Runic Inscriptions' in Bammesberger, *Old English Runes*, 137–89.

[13] I discuss these points in detail in 'Dating Old English Inscriptions: the Limits of Inference', *Papers from the 5th International Conference on English Historical Linguistics*, edd. S.Adamson *et al.* Current Issues in Linguistic Theory 65 (Amsterdam and Philadelphia 1990), 357–77.

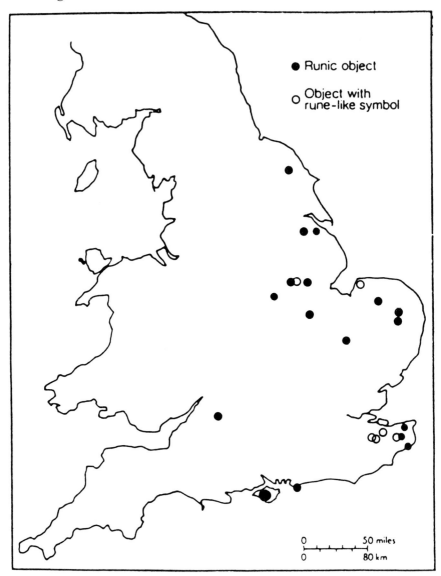

Fig.7. Pre-650 runic monuments.

mate; to give an example, all I feel safe to say of the quite lengthy Falstone (Northumberland) inscription is that its language points most readily to the eighth century, while the ninth is possible, but the seventh and tenth are unlikely. The Corpus of Anglo-Saxon Stone Sculpture is a little more precise, 'mid eighth to mid ninth century', but on what grounds is not too evident.

It is sometimes possible to combine several methods so as to produce a more precise dating for an object. A spectacular example is the Auzon casket, where the art historian, the linguist and runologist and the palaeographer combine to give *c*.700 as a likely date. But the combination of methods does not always produce such clarity. Some art historians have put the Lancaster standing cross in the tenth century, but to the historical linguist its text can hardly be later than the ninth and on the whole looks rather earlier. Sometimes inscriptions from different sites can be brought together to cast light upon one another. On historical grounds the name-stones from Hartlepool and Lindisfarne, and the tiny fragment of a similar stone from Monkwearmouth date between, say, 650 and 850. Designs of the various stones show marked similarities, and a body of opinion among art historians ascribed them to the seventh or eighth century. The Corpus is a little hesitant here: 'last quarter of seventh to first quarter of eighth century'/'eighth century' (Hartlepool and Monkwearmouth), 'mid seventh to mid eighth century'/'first half of eighth century'/'eighth century' (Lindisfarne). The linguistic evidence from Lindisfarne very tentatively suggests the eighth or ninth century. An eighth-century date fits the Hartlepool language. The common element is the eighth century, and as a group, therefore, these stones are most likely to belong then. The stronger evidence of Hartlepool and Lindisfarne can be used to support the meagre information from the Monkwearmouth fragment. In these and similar cases, however, one must be wary of the circular argument; where the art historian gives a date on the basis of a linguistic assessment, which is found, when probed, to depend on a dating suggested by an earlier art historian.

Clearly it would be useful if we could date and localise closely most of our runic monuments, and so draw a series of distribution maps, one for each century from the fifth to the eleventh, illustrating the spread and decline of epigraphical runes in Anglo-Saxon England. Equally clearly we cannot, since so much of our dating and our knowledge of provenances is tentative. Moreover, I must again stress that we have only a small and perhaps unrepresentative sample of runic material surviving. What I have tried to do is produce two maps with 650 as the dividing point, for we have a number of provenances for objects which are certainly (or almost certainly) pre-650, and a larger number for those which are certainly (or almost certainly) post-650. The dividing date, 650, I fixed on in 1973 and even with the runic finds made since then it seems to work adequately. It is arbitrary or rather pragmatic, a date that fits better than any other I have come upon, but that is all. Whether future finds will alter the distribution patterns radically or significantly nobody can tell. The two maps make only elementary and temporary statements of date and place, and no deeper conclusions should be drawn from them. I give them in figs. 7, 8. The difference between the two plots is sur-

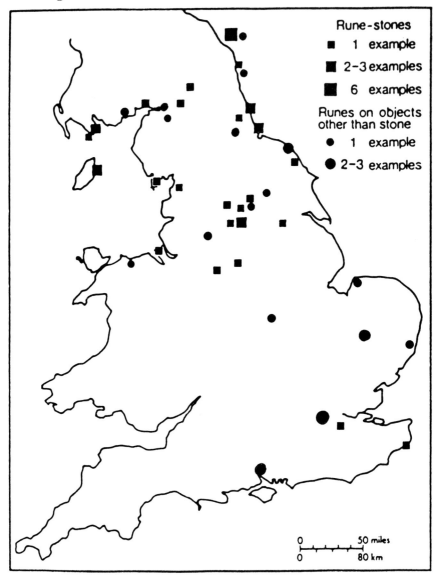

Fig.8. Post-650 runic monuments.

prising and revealing. Both show Wessex and the west Midlands virtually empty of runes, but in the first the weight of distribution is in the south-east, East Anglia and the east Midlands, whereas in the second it is in north Mercia and Northumbria.

Before I discuss these distribution patterns in detail, it is as well to know just what has been plotted. In every case but one the only direct indication of localisation that we have is the object's find-spot in modern times. The one exception shows how unreliable this sort of evidence is. It is the coffin of St Cuthbert, discovered in Durham cathedral in 1827. Bede recorded that the monks of Lindisfarne made it, and Symeon of Durham described how the members of St Cuthbert's community bore it from the harried island through Northumbria, resting for a time at Chester-le-Street, but finally going to Durham at the saint's firm command.[14] Some of the other runic objects I have plotted could be far away from their places of manufacture without our knowing it. Of course, there are degrees of probability involved. It would be easy enough to take around the country a sword or ring, a box, brooch or bracteate; a set of scales and weights (like those linked to the Watchfield inscription) were presumably designed for carrying about for use in commerce or accounting; valuables are likely to have passed from hand to hand in the course of trade, or by inheritance, gift exchange or plunder.

Something like this certainly happened to three inscribed boxes found abroad, whose runes make it clear they are Anglo-Saxon. They are the chrismal which has been one of the treasures of the collegiate church of S.Évroult, Mortain, Normandy, for as far back as our records of it go; the whale's bone casket which Sir Augustus Wollaston Franks gave to the British Museum, and which can be traced back to a family in Auzon, Haute-Loire (France) in the nineteenth century; and the elegantly decorated bone box in the Herzog Anton Ulrich-Museum at Brunswick, which may have come from the church treasury at Gandersheim in the same province.[15] On the other hand, the carvers who worked the huge stones which form the Bewcastle and Ruthwell crosses very likely lodged in those places, for the toil of transporting loads like these would have been harsh. We tend, therefore, to think the modern provenances of the rune-stones more secure evidence for their places of origin, and this despite the fact that some stones, the small ones from Lindisfarne and Hartlepool for example, are portable enough; and despite Symeon of Durham's account of how the fleeing monks of Lindisfarne took with them to Durham, as well as Cuthbert's body, the shattered high cross of bishop Ethelwald.[16]

Noteworthy about the first distribution map (pre-650) is that it includes no rune-stones. The only stone which might have qualified is that usually attributed to Sandwich, though in fact Richborough (Kent) is a closer provenance

---

[14] Bede, *Prose Life* (ed. B.Colgrave), xlii; Symeon, *Historia Dunelmensis Ecclesiae* (Rolls Series), ii.10–13, iii.l.

[15] I consider these three boxes and the problems of their provenances in 'English Runes Imported into the Continent' in Düwel, *Runische Schriftkultur*, 177–80.

[16] *Historia Dunelmensis Ecclesiae*, i.12.

for it. Stephens thought it heathen on quite inadequate grounds, for the inscription remains uninterpreted and almost unread, and the stone's shape is unparalleled and so undated.[17] Apart from the Caistor-by-Norwich astragalus, the Loveden Hill urn, the Undley (Suffolk) bracteate (a single-sided stamped metal disc used as a pendant) and probably the rune-stamped pots of Spong Hill (Norfolk), all objects plotted on this map are sixth- or seventh-century and of metal, and several are of precious metal with the runes roughly scratched in. They fall mainly in the rich Kentish kingdom and the Jutish region linked to it in the Isle of Wight and the mainland nearby, and in East Anglia and the East Midlands. Two are sword-pommels, from Sarre and Ash/Gilton (both Kent); one is a scabbard mount, from Chessell Down (Isle of Wight). Also from the Chessell Down cemetery is a bronze bowl of eastern Mediterranean manufacture with a cryptic and now damaged runic text scratched across it. From Dover comes a splendid gold, silver, garnet and shell brooch with two inscriptions on its back. To these items I have added (though with a distinguishing symbol) a small group of similar objects that fit into the same cultural context. They have on them marks which may be runic or may be rune-like patterns, so the identification of the script is uncertain. They are from Kent: sword-pommels from Faversham and Ash, an inlaid spear-head from Holborough, and a disc-brooch with 'graphs' cut on its back from Boarley. I also add, taking something of a liberty, the two bits of a zigzag piece of gold (?ring fragments) picked up on the foreshore near Selsey (West Sussex). These retain only fragmentary letter groups and cannot be dated, but the fact that they are of precious metal and with roughly scratched runes makes them so like others in this group that I think myself justified in adding them.

The East Anglian runic material has increased quite dramatically since my 1973 discussion. Then the only certain runes from that region, other than on coins, were those on the Caistor-by-Norwich astragalus. Noteworthy now are two other pre-sixth century finds: the Undley bracteate and a group of cremation urns from Spong Hill, Beetley, North Elmham, which use a common stamp with runic letters on it. A seventh-century disc brooch from Harford Farm, Caistor-by-Norwich, has an inscription added on its back recording its repair. There is also a swastika brooch from Hunstanton (Norfolk) with rune-like forms cut on its face. Further inland is a group of runic metal objects from the east Midlands: five runes cut on a sixth-century brooch from

---

17 Most recently studied by D.Parsons, 'Sandwich: the Oldest Scandinavian Rune-stone in England?', *Developments around the Baltic and the North Sea in the Viking Age*, edd. B.Ambrosiani and H.Clarke. Birka Studies 3 (Stockholm 1994), 310–20.

Wakerley (Northamptonshire), a solitary ᛗ scratched on a mid-sixth-century brooch from a Sleaford (Lincolnshire) cemetery, and the solitary ᚠ cut inside the base of a copper bowl from Willoughby-on-the-Wolds (Nottinghamshire). Further north are: a silver bracteate with a retrograde runic legend that looks very like some Scandinavian bracteate inscriptions, from a sixth-century grave at Welbeck Hill (Lincolnshire); and runes/rune-like scratches on a ?early seventh-century copper-alloy hanging bowl from Cleatham, Manton (Lincolnshire/Humberside); and going north again, from Heslerton (North Yorkshire) a sixth-century cruciform brooch with four runes scratched on its back. Quite out of a usual geographical context is the inscribed fitting from Watchfield (Oxfordshire), which is one of the very few bits of evidence of epigraphical runes in the west of the country.

The second map (post-650) should perhaps include all rune-stones: certainly it includes all those we can assign a date to. Almost all these are in the north and north Midlands, the only outliers being two in Kent, the Dover grave-slab and the Orpington sundial with its extensive roman texts and its few runes. Except for these two, the southern boundary of the rune-stones is marked by those from Overchurch in the Wirral (Cheshire/Merseyside), Leek (Staffordshire) and Crowle (Lincolnshire/Humberside). There is a group on the Northumbrian-Mercian border, of which dated examples are the Thorn-hill (three examples) and Collingham (West Yorkshire) stones. Firmly in Northumbria are rune-stones from a wide range of dates between the late seventh or early eighth centuries and the eleventh: Alnmouth, Bewcastle, Chester-le-Street (Durham), Falstone, Great Urswick (Lancashire north of the sands/Cumbria), Hackness (North Yorkshire), Hartlepool (two examples), Lancaster, Lindisfarne (six examples), Monkwearmouth (two examples), Ruthwell, and St Ninian's cave and Whithorn (two examples) in Wigtown-shire (Dumfries and Galloway). On the Isle of Man and presumably connected with the Northumbrian specimens are two name-stones from Maughold.

Among the portable objects from the later period is a small group in the south of England. The river Thames yielded two objects, perhaps Kentish, which archaeologists date to the late eighth and tenth centuries, a silver mount, perhaps the binding of a knife sheath, and an inlaid scramasax (a one-edged short sword). From excavations at the Royal Opera House, London, site comes a bone handle with a curious, retrograde, sequence of runes on it, as yet uninterpreted.[18] Also from the south is the inscribed bone from *Hamwih*, the early settlement site of Southampton, and on historical

---

[18] R.I.Page, 'Runes at the Royal Opera House, London', *Nytt om Runer* 12 (1997), 12–13.

Fig.9. The Bakewell rune-stone fragment.

grounds this is more likely to be after 650 than before it. It could relate to the Kentish-Isle of Wight sphere of influence, but *Hamwih* was a major port and the inscription could be the work of a traveller, perhaps even a Frisian, as is suggested faintly by one of its rune forms and perhaps more clearly by its wording. Probably among these should be included a fragment of a bone plaque with the remnant of a runic text, also from Southampton.

There is a small group of comparatively new finds in East Anglia. From Heacham (Norfolk) comes a pair of tweezers with two baffling inscriptions, much damaged by corrosion. Early this century Blythburgh (Suffolk) yielded an ?eighth-century bone writing tablet, but not until the 1980s were runes spotted incised on its rim and in the recess for the wax writing surface. From a middle-Saxon habitation and perhaps church site in Brandon (Suffolk) are three runic pieces: a metal fragment perhaps of a pair of tweezers, a disc-headed pin and a bone handle. From the east Midlands comes a copper-alloy artefact, perhaps part of the connecting plate from a set of linked pins, found by metal detectors at Wardley (Leicestershire/Rutland). Part of an engraved runic inscription, probably a woman's name, remains on it. It may be from the eighth century.

Most of the later portable runic monuments are in the north and north Midlands: a group of related amulet rings from the neighbourhood of Bramham Moor (West Yorkshire), Kingmoor and Linstock Castle (both

Fig.10. The Leeds runic fragment, from Stephens's *Old-Northern Runic Monuments*.

Cumberland/Cumbria); other rings from Wheatley Hill (Durham), Llysfaen (Caernarvonshire/Gwynedd); and one formerly attributed generally to Lancashire but now known to come from Manchester; St Cuthbert's coffin, from Lindisfarne; a wooden spoon from Viking Age York; a comb and jet disc (?spindle whorl) from Whitby, presumably linked to the monastery of *Streoneshalh*. The language of the Auzon casket shows it to be Northumbrian or north Mercian, and the Mortain casket may be from the west Mercian area, though its dialect is less convincing evidence. Arguing from probability and on the basis of the distribution maps, the lead Coquet Island ring, now distintegrated into powder, belongs to the later group.

In this last example I have introduced another dating method, admittedly a dangerous one, that of 'fit'. The Coquet Island ring fits into the later distribution map but not into the earlier, and so I have suggested the later date for it; and here I am supported by the fact that, if the ring comes from the Coquet Island monastery site as is usually supposed, it could hardly be pre-650. Using the same principle we can add several more find-spots to the maps. Presumably the inscribed bone from the Anglian phase of a habitation site at Mote of Mark (Kirkcudbrightshire/Dumfries and Galloway) belongs here, though the archaeological evidence is inconclusive. Here too we could place three more stone inscriptions. At Bakewell (Derbyshire) and Leeds were discovered two tiny bits of runic stones. The former survives in the Sheffield City Museum (fig.9); nobody has seen the latter since the nineteenth century but there is a drawing of it that looks authentic enough (fig.10). Neither fragment has any carving to help the art historian, and neither inscription is long or complete enough to provide facts for the historical linguist. Geographically speaking, the Bakewell stone fits in well with the Overchurch and Leek stones in the north Midlands, and the Leeds one into the West Yorkshire group of Collingham and Thornhill. To the latter too may belong a stone fragment at Kirkheaton (West Yorkshire), whose text has no clear dating features and whose decoration is too crude for subtle dating analysis. Perhaps we should add the Bingley (West Yorkshire) 'font', a hollowed-out trough-like stone which the nineteenth century recognised as an article of church furniture though previously the local grammar school boys had been in the habit of using it on 'certain natural and necessitous occasions'. This has Anglo-Saxon carving which art historians have tended to avoid examining, and the very weathered remains of an inscription that could well have been runic, though no letters remain certainly recognisable.

Acting as a link between the three runic areas of the south-east, East Anglia and the north, and over the important seventh-century period, are the runic coins. I discuss these in detail in chapter 9, but a short summary is fitting here. Coins cannot be fitted readily into my distribution maps for of necessity they were produced in quantity and travelled far from their mint towns, and it is the mints that are significant. Yet where the towns are not named, numismatists deduce the general areas of minting from the distribution of coin finds. On the find evidence the earliest Anglo-Saxon runic coins, of gold and very few indeed, belong to the south. They date from the first half of the seventh century. The runic *sceattas* (or silver 'pennies' as they are now called) are a non-regal coinage from the later seventh and the early eighth centuries. Mark Blackburn ascribes the earliest series to Kent (those in the name of Pada, which demonstrate the transition from pale gold to silver as the metal of currency); again from Kent (the early silver coins of Epa/Æpa) and East Anglia (the later coins of Epa and those of Wigræd, Til-berht and Æþiliræd). Mid eighth-century East Anglian coins (broad pennies) of the kings Beonna and Æthelberht use runes, though Beonna also has coins with roman and mixed runic-roman legends. The issues of a second East Anglian Æthelberht have roman letters for the king's name, runes for that of the moneyer Lul. Mercian pennies from the late eighth and early ninth centuries which use runes in the same degree are probably by East Anglian money-ers. On later coins from this kingdom there are only occasional runes within otherwise roman legends. Thereafter the only English coins to use the script are *stycas* (small and of base metal) of Northumbrian kings in the mid ninth century.

From the distribution patterns, sustained by the coin evidence, it seems clear that runes came into use first in the south and east of England, and there may have been independent imports of the script into Kent and its neighbour-ing counties and into East Anglia and the east Midlands. In the early stages runes were particularly favoured for cutting on metal, and this use persisted into the ninth century, alongside one on stone. Recent occasional finds of runes on bone (as at Blythburgh, Brandon and Southampton) may imply a wider use of the script on more transient materials which have survived only exceptionally to our day – wood is an obvious suggestion. In the seventh century the character spread north, enjoying a wide range of uses there until the end of Anglo-Saxon England. Indeed, it seems to have flourished and developed in the north, for it was the rune-masters of that region who, as we shall see, achieved the most sophisticated runic practices.

Before we accept this summary as valid, it is worth considering whether external factors may have affected distribution patterns. Though I do not think the rune maps are appreciably distorted, I have some reservations about them. The south-east is rich in splendid grave-goods. The interest they have attracted could have led scholars to examine them more carefully than the poorer material of the north, and to find more of the runes cut on them. I think this point has some force. A careful and ordered examination of the huge catalogue of base metal artefacts might reveal more runic inscriptions, more evenly spread over the country. In recent times the metal detector has brought to our attention a number of runic inscriptions on metal pieces (especially coins), and this may have distorted our picture of runic use. The north has plenty of stone suitable for carving, so the distribution of rune-stones could represent, not a pattern of usage, but a pattern of the availability of materials on which runes would survive until modern times. This is fairly unlikely since Anglo-Saxon stones with non-runic inscriptions exist in various areas of the country – East Anglia and Wessex for example – where there are no rune-stones. Since many rune-stones came to light when churches were rebuilt or restored, the later map may merely show that the industrial north and north Midlands were more liable to pull down or enlarge their old churches than the agricultural and pastoral south and east. Or the various distribution maps may in some degree plot the energy or activity of local antiquaries and archaeological societies. Considerations like these are hard to assess and discount, and they add a further element of uncertainty to our conclusions. Yet there is no strong evidence to suggest that the distribution maps are seriously at fault, and provisionally we must accept them as making statements about how Anglo-Saxon runes were used at various times. I say 'provisionally', and in that word is a warning. If readers compare the distribution maps of the present edition with those of 1973 they will note remarkable changes, most notably in the regions of East Anglia and the east Midlands. The corpus of Anglo-Saxon runic inscriptions identified is small, so conclusions drawn from it are bound to be provisional – even a modest increase in the numbers may lead us to amend our opinions, or even to change them dramatically.

The maps I have plotted are crude ones, primarily useful for showing how much the early and later runes differ. They are weak in that they must omit important inscriptions if they have no precise find-spots or no close dating. A serious case of this is the newly found inscribed potsherd from Worcester. If it is genuine – and the archaeological report seems good evidence for that – it represents an important new area of runic usage, the west country. But until the archaeological evidence is fully deployed, we cannot date the piece clearly enough to allow it to be included.[19]

Moreover each of the two maps is likely to confuse different traditions of runic usage. The early one, as I have suggested tentatively, may plot together runes of Scandinavian inspiration (the Caistor-by-Norwich astragalus, the Welbeck Hill bracteate, the Spong Hill urns) and those with apparent links to Frisia and the Continent south of Schleswig (the Undley bracteate, the Chessell Down scabbard mount). The Kentish monuments form a homogeneous group and quite a large one if we accept the Faversham, Ash and Holborough symbols as runes. The practice of scratching runes on metalware is quite common throughout the Continent in early times, and the sixth century, from which most English examples come, produces numbers of inscribed brooches from both West and North Germanic regions, and a few inscribed weapons. It looks as though the Kentish rune-masters followed the practices of their Continental precursors and were perhaps in touch with their Continental contemporaries. The use of runes by metalsmiths may explain why they occur on coin dies, and why they persist for moneyers' names on coins until quite late. In the south and in East Anglia the runes seem to have continued until the ninth century or later, though they were not particularly common towards the end. The traditional explanation for their decline is that they were overwhelmed by the roman alphabet, backed as it was by the might of the Christian church, but the new finds from Brandon and Blythburgh, which indicate quite late runes in learned or ecclesiastical contexts, cast doubt upon this.

In the north it is quite certain that the Christian church accepted runes, as their appearance on so formal an object as St Cuthbert's coffin shows. Most of the rune-stones are explicitly Christian, in their texts or their contexts. They occupy ancient sites in or close by churches as do the Bewcastle and Ruthwell crosses, or were found as fragments re-used in church buildings as the Leeds, Thornhill or Kirkheaton stones, or they come from Christian cemeteries or churchyards as those of Hartlepool and Lancaster. Far from letting runes fall into desuetude, the church in north England seems to have preserved them, extended their use, applied them to formal and public purposes. Educated people, literate also in other scripts, produced some of the northern runic monuments. This is clear from St Cuthbert's coffin where holy names may be in runic or roman, the Falstone stone, Monkwearmouth II and some

---

[19] R.I.Page, 'Epigraphical Runes in Worcester', *Nytt om Runer* 9 (1994), 17.

of the Lindisfarne name-stones where the scripts occur side by side; it is implied at Hartlepool where, of a group of name-stones, some had roman and some runic legends but the scripts were never mingled, and at Hackness where the rune-stone has other, discrete, inscriptions in roman capitals. The Chester-le-Street and Alnmouth stones use occasional runes in predominantly roman inscriptions, and so do two rings, Manchester and Llysfaen. Lancaster and Thornhill have yielded, as well as runic stones, others with Old English texts in roman scripts. The elegant runes of the Whitby comb are the work of a craftsman who knew enough Latin to spell out *dæus mæus*. The Auzon casket has a curious mixture of texts, both runic and non-runic, in a decorative scheme that has learned analogues. All these I examine in more detail in chapter 14.

On the other hand, not all northern texts had this background of education. The Whitby disc has three runes, unfortunately not interpreted; they look like owner's marks, and may have been made by a person of humbler attainments than those of the comb from the same site. The York spoon again seems to have runic owner's marks. There is nothing to be derived from the Coquet Island ring drawings which suggests that the rune-master was a man of learning. The church that thundered against charms would hardly have countenanced – at any rate officially – the magical inscriptions of the Bramham Moor, Kingmoor and Linstock Castle amulet rings, so their erudition is of a different type. Probably the northern runic texts represent quite a wide range of runic practices. The church is obviously important, and indeed the Anglo-Saxon rune-stone may be the church's invention, derived from the memorial cross with roman inscription. Certainly, Continental West Germania had no tradition of raising rune-stones, and the ones of the Viking Age north are very different from the English examples.

In this discussion of distribution in time and place I have managed to accommodate nearly all the known runic inscriptions from Anglo-Saxon England, some more surely placed than others. There remain half a dozen more that I cannot fit in, but cannot ignore since they complete the known Anglo-Saxon runic corpus. From the royal collection of George III the British Museum received a struck gold *solidus* with the legend **skanomodu**. It is quite early in date, possibly before *c*.610, but its provenance is unknown. So is its purpose; possibly a coin, possibly a medal or ornament – indeed it once had a loop for suspension. It *could* be Frisian, but it could perhaps be English. Indeed for a long time it enjoyed the prestige of being thought the earliest English text. The whale's bone casket now in Brunswick is put in the late eighth century. It is not firmly provenanced though it is often said to have come from Gandersheim. Discussion of where it was made has long been bedevilled by an absurd reading of its cryptic text which attributed it to Ely.

There is the additional complication that the Brunswick runes, which are cut on a copper-alloy plate curiously stuck to the base of the box, are of doubted authenticity.[20] Undated and unprovenanced save that it came from a Derby antiquary's collection is an inscribed bone slip of unknown purpose, commonly called the Derby bone plate. Neither runologist nor archaeologist can give a date to a bronze ring found at Cramond, Edinburgh. On historical grounds it is more likely to be in the later than the earlier group, though the Anglian occupation of Lothian began soon after 600. There are two very recent finds. The 1988 excavations at Thames Exchange, London, revealed a copper-alloy ring, perhaps the hilt-band of a knife, with curious runic/rune-like forms. It has yet to be dated.[21] From the river Yare at Keswick (Norfolk) comes a copper-alloy disc of unknown purpose, with a group of eight runes set radially round a central hole. There is no indication at what point the text opens, and the runic sequence makes no obvious sense.[22]

An important group of Anglo-Saxon inscriptions must be added to our lists, but not to our maps since they are outside Britain. Among early mediaeval names carved into the stone-work of the church at Monte Sant'Angelo, Gargano (Italy), are a few Old English examples, some of them in runes, and there is another disfiguring a fresco at the Cimitero di Commodilla, Rome.[23] These are the work of travellers, presumably pilgrims to Rome and to the Holy Land, who did as so many modern tourists do, carved their names on historic monuments – or had them carved by local workmen. These inscriptions are dated generally between the late seventh and the early ninth century. It is not unlikely there will be more such finds in the future.[24] The existence of these runes in Italy lends some credence to another Italian find, a runic alphabet, containing some Anglo-Saxon types mingled with Norse ones, cut on a fragment of the rim of a bronze pot. An American buyer found it in Rome early this century, and it is now somewhere in Chicago, though nobody

---

20 *The Making of England: Anglo-Saxon Art and Culture AD 600–900*, edd. L.Webster and J.Backhouse (British Museum 1991), no.138.

21 K.Gosling, 'Runic Finds from London', *Nytt om Runer* 4 (1989), 12–13.

22 J.Hines, 'An Inscribed Disc from the River Yare near Norwich', *Nytt om Runer* 12 (1997), 13–15.

23 Derolez and Schwab, 'Runic Inscriptions of Monte S. Angelo'; M.G.Arcamone, 'Una nuova iscrizione runica da Monte Sant' Angelo', *Vetera Christianorum* 29 (1992), 405–10. R.Derolez, 'Anglo-Saxons in Rome', *Nytt om Runer* 2 (1987), 14–15.

24 David Ganz has drawn my attention to a possible new Italian example which calls for investigation: A.Ferrua, *Inscriptiones Christianae Urbis Romae*, N.S. 6 (Roma in civitate Vaticana 1975), no.15966, B.6.

seems to know where. This piece has hitherto been viewed with suspicion, though a recent publication by Gösta Franzén gives it some credibility.[25]

Runic inscriptions are usually named after their find-spots even when, as in the case of the Mortain casket, it is a chance one telling nothing about the place of manufacture. There are a couple of exceptions. The whale's bone casket first recorded at Auzon is commonly called the Franks casket in honour of the great antiquary who gave it to the British Museum. It is common practice to refer to St Cuthbert's coffin rather than the Durham coffin, though some call it the Lindisfarne coffin after the place where it was made. Occasionally the Brunswick casket is named the Gandersheim casket. When there are two or more provenances suggested for an object it would be desirable to give them all. Examples are the Sandwich/Richborough stone, the Ash/Gilton pommel or the Bramham Moor/Harewood/Sherburn-in-Elmet amulet ring. I do this occasionally but the effect is clumsy, and it is convenient to choose one of the find-spots arbitrarily – as the Bramham Moor ring – even though it is a little misleading. Where there are two objects of the same nature from the same site I distinguish them by upper-case Roman numerals, reflecting the order they were found in; as the stones Maughold I, Maughold II, or Thornhill I, II and III; where the objects from one site are of different types I do not number, for it is easier in an introductory book simply to refer to, say, the Chessell Down scabbard mount, the Chessell Down bronze pail rather than distinguish them numerically. If one object has two or more discrete texts on it they are distinguished by lower-case Roman numerals. So, there are two inscriptions on the Great Urswick stone, Great Urswick i is the memorial text, Great Urswick ii the artist's signature. Lindisfarne II i denotes the first text on the second Lindisfarne stone.

[25] 'A Runic Inscription found in Rome', *Saga och Sed* (1986), 101–8.

3

The Anglo-Saxon Runic Letters

Altogether thirty-one distinct runic characters, some with major variants, appear in Old English inscriptions; and there are also one or two nonce-forms that occur in special contexts. Modern scholars, following their Anglo-Saxon predecessors, list the runes in a peculiar order called the *futhorc* (or some use the form *fuþorc*) after the values of the first six letters. This order derives from that of the primitive Germanic runic alphabet (the *futhark/fuþark*), but its ultimate origin is unknown.

For convenience of printing and for the benefit of language students unacquainted with the character, runologists usually transliterate their texts into roughly equivalent roman ones. For runic inscriptions of early times, and for later runes in Scandinavian contexts and on the Continent, **bold** letters are commonly used in transliteration, so that, for example, the maker's inscription on the wooden box from Stenmagle, Sjælland (Denmark) is represented **hagiradaR:tawide**, 'HagiradaR:made'; the personal name on the Harlingen (Frisia) solidus appears as **hada**. Note that lower-case letters are used throughout (there is no capital initial for the personal name) save for occasional special forms like **R** which represents a distinctive northern development of earlier /z/. In the case of Anglo-Saxon inscriptions there is some diversity of practice. In the 1930s the English runologist Bruce Dickins developed a convenient system of transliteration which gave each rune a lower-case roman (or more or less roman) equivalent which he set between single inverted commas to indicate it was a transliteration from runic. So, in his system the Kirkheaton stone inscription will be transliterated 'eoh:worohtæ', 'Eoh:made'; the moneyer's name on a group of early pale gold coins 'pada'. More recently I modified the Dickins system in a couple of ways, while retaining its essentials.[1] For distinctiveness I tried spacing the transliterated text, as 'e o h : w o r o h t æ' though that sometimes produces

[1] R.I.Page, 'On the Transliteration of English Runes', *Medieval Archaeology* 28 (1984), 22–45.

lay-out problems. Inevitably (knowing runologists) there are those who disagree with the Dickins-Page system, preferring to use **bold** for English
inscriptions too: as **eoh:worohtæ**. There are justifications for both systems of
transliteration. To use bold stresses a continuity of runic tradition from Germanic to Anglo-Saxon times, and so is useful, and indeed is used in this
book, in representing the very earliest English inscriptions. To use spaced
within single quotes indicates that the English developed a characteristic set
of rune forms distinct from those of Scandinavia and Continental Europe, and
so is useful in presenting the later Anglo-Saxon runic texts. The debate continues.

Transliteration simply replaces a graph of one writing system by a more
accessible graph of another; it is essentially graphemic not phonetic. So, it
can be misleading in that it requires a fixed one-to-one correlation between
runic and roman characters. It disregards the fact that runic may have its own
spelling conventions which differ from contemporary bookhand ones. It
cannot allow for diverse developments in the two scripts which render an
equivalent that is appropriate for one date inappropriate for another. Therefore we must always remember, when using a transliterated text, not to interpret it as if it were an original. For the original we must go back to the runes.[2]

For all that, the Dickins-Page system of transliteration is a useful and adequate tool, and I shall employ it in this book, certainly for the later inscriptions (reserving **bold** for some of the earlier, though I sometimes find it hard
to decide which to use). The English epigraphical runes, with roman equivalents, are then:

ᚠᚢᚦᚠᚱᚳᚷᚹᚻᚾᛏᛁᛉᛋᛣᛏᚻ
'f u þ o r c g w h n i j ï p x s'
1 2 3 4 5 6 7 8   9 10 11 12 13 14 15 16

ᛏᛒᛖᛗᛚᛝᛞᛟᚪᚫᚣᛠᚸᛣᛢ
't b e m l ŋ d œ a æ y ēa ḡ k k̄'
17 18 19 20 21 22 23 24 25 26 27 28 29 30 31

Few of the equivalent symbols need explanation. Students of Old English
will recognise 'þ', *thorn/þorn*, the symbol for the dental spirants [θ], [ð],
which Anglo-Saxon scribes borrowed from runic into bookhand; and two

---

2 Cf. my article 'A Note on the Transliteration of Old English Runic Inscriptions',
English Studies 43 (1962), 484–90; and my comments on recent misapprehensions
of the nature of transliteration, *Runes and Runic Inscriptions*, 92–3, 271–3.

vowel characters used in Old English manuscripts, 'æ' for the low fronted vowel and 'œ' for the mid-central rounded vowel, reflex of *o. . .i* (*o* affected by *i*-mutation), though only in some dialects. The symbol 'ɨ' is borrowed from the International Phonetic Alphabet to represent an ambiguous rune which sometimes has a vowel value in the neighbourhood of [i] but sometimes gives a voiceless palatal or velar spirant, perhaps [χ]. Also from the International Phonetic Alphabet is the symbol 'ŋ' which represents a voiced velar nasal [ŋ] – the sound represented by *ng* in modern English *singing*. Rune 28 is unique among epigraphical runes in representing a diphthong, and for this is used the unspaced 'ea', as opposed to 'e a' = two runes 'e' and 'a'. The superscript lines that distinguish 'ḡ' from 'g', and 'k̄' from 'k' I will justify when I consider how these particular runes are used.

Of the thirty-one runes listed five have major variants. 'c' has the common ᚲ and the rather rare ᚳ, and there seems to be an occasional English example of the primitive form ᚲ, ᚱ from which both derive. As has been seen, 'h' has an early form ᚺ and a later and more common one ᚻ. 's' is usually ᛋ, but ᛌ appears on runic coins and perhaps elsewhere, and there are a couple of rare early forms of the letter with multiple staves, ᛋ and ᛋ. There is another distinctive and fairly rare type of 's', ᚱ, which may have been borrowed from bookhand, though there is an alternative explanation. ᛄ 'j', has the variant ᛡ (transliterated 'j̄' to distinguish it) which appears rarely in inscriptions but is the common form in Old English manuscript accounts of runes. ᚩ is the common form of 'œ', but ᛟ appears occasionally epigraphically and rather more often in manuscripts. In addition to these there are a few very rare, and in some cases doubtful, variants. The Thames scramasax *futhorc* contains several odd forms, perhaps because of the difficult technique the smith was using; but it has two which may be genuine: ᛭ for 'j' and ᛦ for 'y'. In some inscriptions (and occasionally in manuscripts too) 'i' occurs, either accidentally or by design, as a rune of only half normal height.

All scripts show minor formal variations arising from individual preference, skill, training or experience. Epigraphical scripts vary according to the techniques and materials used, and Anglo-Saxon runes sometimes show the influence of roman lettering. In the figure above I have given the English runes in their classical form, made up of straight lines only. Scholars have traditionally claimed that the script was developed in the first place for cutting upon wood. Few early examples in this medium remain for it has poor survival qualities, but it is plausible that, in a society where pen, ink, paper or parchment were not easily come by but where everyone carried a knife, wood would be ideal for recording bargains, sending messages, declaring ownership, expressing orders and so on. Therefore, the argument goes, the Germanic runes, and the Anglo-Saxon graphs that derive from them, are designed for incising in such a soft, grained material. The characters are formed of vertical lines (verticals, stems) cutting the grain at right angles, and of sloping straight lines (twigs, arms) which, running at an angle to the grain, would be readily distinguished from it. These angled lines sometimes form pointed loops or bows. Horizontal lines (which might get lost in the grain) and curves, rounded loops and circles (hard to cut) would be avoided.

Even in early times, however, runes were not used only on wood. When rune-masters chiselled or punched their texts on stone, scratched them on metal or cut them in bone, the rationale for a straight-line script ceased, and forms with curved lines and rounded loops or bows appeared, as ᚠ for 'f', ᚢ for 'u', ᚹ for 'w'.

At first there was no recognised direction of writing. An inscription, and so its letter forms, could run from left to right or right to left, and some inscriptions mix the two. By far the most common direction for the Anglo-Saxon runes is from left to right. When they run in the opposite direction there is often a reason for the deviation, as with some of the coins struck from reversed dies, or in the base-line of the text on the front of the Auzon casket, which goes backwards to complete its square. (In a rigorous transcript it may be desirable to indicate a right-to-left text; which can be done by an arrow ←, as in ←'e p a', the retrograde legend on some examples of an Old English coin type). However, individual letters may be retrograde in an otherwise left-to-right inscription, so that 'n' can be either ᚾ or ᚾ, 'i' either ᛁ or ᛁ, 's' either ᛋ or ᛜ, and so on. Rarely we may come upon a rune that is cut upside-down. Here practical considerations may have prevailed – perhaps it was easier to fit an inverted form into the space available.

Sometimes we cannot be sure if a variant is intended or if it arises from a rune-master's incompetence or lack of care, or perhaps his sense of epigraphical style. For instance, inscriptions sometimes contain forms in which the stem projects above a twig or bow which ordinarily springs from its top, as ᚱ for 'r', ᛚ for 'l'. Obviously this could arise out of carelessness in forming the letters, but it occurs often enough in German inscriptions for Helmut Arntz to have thought it a local characteristic, even though there are examples enough from outside Germany.[3] Certainly some English rune-stones, from Maughold and Lindisfarne, for example, show this feature. In the case of 'd' the practice produced a commonly used variant type, ᛗ for ᛞ, while a few examples of ᚫ, ᚩ for 'a', 'o', suggest that they too were accepted as regular variants.

As well as the runes I have listed there are others which I prefer to call pseudo-runes. These never occur in inscriptions (for safety I should say have

---

3 Arntz and Zeiss, *Einheimischen Runendenkmäler*, 195.

not yet been found there) but are known from written accounts of the script from the eighth century onwards, the *runica manuscripta* which I deal with in chapter 5. In my opinion (which is not shared by all my colleagues) such manuscripts are the work not of rune-carvers but of runic antiquaries, of men fascinated by this declining script, of scholars who were more at home with the roman alphabet, of the immature who delighted in strange and cryptic alphabets. They produced their own variant rune types. ⟨ (the variant 'j' that I have listed tentatively above) and ⟨ (a variant for 'ḡ') are examples. Apparently they also invented new runes, either filling gaps they felt existed, or providing runic equivalents for roman letters or even letter groups not represented in the epigraphical *futhorc*: ⟨ 'q', ⟨ 'st', ⟨ 'io'. These were never, I think, intended for practical use and are therefore only curiosities in the history of runic studies, showing that the eccentricities of some modern runologists were anticipated when runes were still a living, or perhaps a dying, script.[4]

The Germanic rune-row, the *futhark*, had only twenty-four characters. Even the earliest epigraphical examples of it show that variant forms already existed, and I give below a couple of specimens (the letter shapes tidied up a little) to show the range of forms in it. There are also minor differences in letter order which we can ignore for the moment.

My first *futhark* is from a stone from a grave at Kylver, Gotland (Sweden) uncertainly dated on the evidence of grave-goods to the fifth century. It reads from left to right, though some runes are retrograde.

ᚠᚨᚦᚱᚱᚲᚷᚹᚺᚾᛁᛃᛈᛇᛋᛏᛒᛖᛗᛚᛜᛞᛟ

f u þ a r k g w h n i j p ï R s t b e m l ŋ d o
1 2 3 4 5 6 7 8 9 10 11 12 13 14 15 16 17 18 19 20 21 22 23 24

The second is from a bracteate found at Vadstena, Östergötland (Sweden) and assigned to the sixth century. Being punched through from the back of the disc it is retrograde, but I give it here in left-to-right form. The final letter, presumably a **d**-rune, is hidden by the pendant fastening.

ᚠᚢᚦᚨᚱᚲᚷᚹ᛫ᚺᚾᛁᛃ ᛇᛈᚱᛋ ᛏᛒᛖᛗᛚ ᛜᛟ

f u þ a r k g w . h n i j ï p R s t b e m l ŋ o
1 2 3 4 5 6 7 8   9 10 11 12 13 14 15 16   17 18 19 20 21 22 24

---

4   'st' graphs, in two variants, have been suggested on the Frisian Westeremden B stave, but the identification is uncertain and modern runic scholars have rejected

For comparison here is the Anglo-Saxon *futhorc* again.

ᚠᚾᚦᚨᚱᚲᚷᚹᚻᚾᛁᛃᛂᛈᛉᛋ

'f u þ o r c g w h n i j i̵ p x s'
1 2 3 4 5 6 7 8 9 10 11 12 13 14 15 16

ᛏᛒᛖᛗᛚᛝᛞᛟᚪᚫᚣ ea ᚸᚴᚳ

't b e m l ŋ d œ a æ y ea ḡ k k̄'
17 18 19 20 21 22 23 24 25 26 27 28 29 30 31

In this the Germanic runes are represented by Anglo-Saxon characters 1–3, 26, 5–24. Runes 4, 25 and 27–31 are English or Anglo-Frisian innovations. Of these 4, 25 have some connection with 'Anglo-Frisian' sound-changes; rune 27 with the later sound-change called *i*-mutation; and runes 29–31 are refinements of the script, apparently confined to the north of Anglo-Saxon England. The reason why rune 28 was invented to represent a diphthong remains a mystery.

It was long thought that the relationship between 4, 25 and 26 revealed how far sound-changes affected the script. The Germanic letter ᚨ had the value **a**, /a/, and seems to have had a rune-name **ansuz*, meaning 'god', cognate with the common Old Norse noun *áss/óss*. The creation of the new graphs 4, 25 is traditionally linked to developments affecting Germanic *a* that are common to Old English and early Frisian. WGmc *a* followed by *n* + voiceless spirant underwent a series of changes: nasalisation of the vowel, with subsequent loss of *n* and compensatory vowel lengthening, and in Old English and in Frisian rounding to *ō*. Thus WGmc **ans-* became OE *ōs*, a word rare as a simplex but quite common as the first element of a personal name such as *Ōswald*. In certain other contexts WGmc *a* underwent the change called fronting, becoming a low front vowel represented in later English manuscripts by *æ*, *ę* or in some dialects *e*. Old English and Frisian still needed a symbol for the low back vowel /a/ in those words where neither rounding nor fronting took place or where retraction neutralised the effects of fronting, and for the /a:/ which derived from Gmc *ai*, at any rate in Old English. Where the single symbol ᚨ had sufficed for Germanic, 'Anglo-

it; for example, A.Quak, 'Runica Frisica', *Amsterdamer Beiträge zur älteren Germanistik* 31–2 (1990), 365. There is apparently an 'st' rune incorporated in a pair of signatures cut in the margin of the St Petersburg/Leningrad Gospels, fo. 213r, but that presumably represents a manuscript tradition.

Frisian' needed three. In Old English the original type, ᚠ, was used for the fronted vowel, and received a new and appropriate name *æsc*, 'ash-tree'. For the low back vowel was invented ᚪ, which some have derived from ᚠ + ᛁ, **a** + **i**, and which was assigned the new name *ac*, 'oak' (Gmc **aik-*). These are runes 26 and 25 of the *futhorc*. The rune-name **ans-*, now *os*, retained the fourth place in the *futhorc* but with the form ᚩ which some have identified as a combination of ᚠ + ᚾ, **a** + **n**.

At first glance the hypothesis looks plausible. The two new runes ᚪ and ᚩ occur in only two areas of the runic world, Anglo-Saxon England and early Frisia. Since they appear to coincide with sound-changes that are common to English and Frisia, it seemed reasonable to assert that they were invented when these two languages were in close contact, in a 'period of Anglo-Frisian unity'. In recent years the full forces of Anglo-Frisian scholarship and of modern linguistic theory have been assembled to put this concept in doubt. Some scholars deny there ever was a 'period of Anglo-Frisian unity', suggesting instead that the close similarities of the two languages are the effect of convergence, possibly the effect of cultural interchanges between England and Frisia after the Anglo-Saxon settlement of this country. Others point to chronological difficulties, the circumstance that these sound-changes common to English and Frisian did not, apparently, take place at the same time or in the same order in the two languages. The rune-name *āc* is a further crux, for the recorded Frisian word for 'oak' is consistently *ēk*, yet Frisian runic texts use the *āc*-rune with the value /a/ as in England. Yet there is no doubt that, up to now, the graphs ᚪ and ᚩ have appeared only in English and Frisian inscriptions, and it is convenient to call them 'Anglo-Frisian', as long as inverted commas are used to signal the uncertainty.[5]

A third new rune, no.28, ᛠ, 'ea', is more problematic. It has not (yet) been found in Frisia. There seems no reason why anyone should have invented it, for its work in representing the diphthong *ea, æa* could have been done (and sometimes *was* done) by two already existing vowel runes, 'e a'. Yet in appearance it somewhat resembles the newly created ᚪ and ᚩ, and I have been inclined to regard it as an 'Anglo-Frisian' rune though I seem to be alone in that belief.[6]

When Old English underwent the sound-change known as *i*-mutation, perhaps in the sixth century, there were two effects on the *futhorc*. One was

---

5 Discussed several times recently, as in the articles A.Bammesberger, 'Frisian and Anglo-Saxon Runes: from the Linguistic Angle', *Amsterdamer Beiträge zur älteren Germanistik* 45 (1996), 15–23; D.Parsons, 'The Origins and Chronology of the "Anglo-Frisian" Runes', *ibid.*, 151–70.
6 R.I.Page, 'The Old English Rune *ear*', *Medium Ævum* 30 (1961), 65–79.

only a modification of usage. ᛟ had had the name *ōþil, 'family estate, native land', but in Old English this became œþil, later eþel; accordingly the graph began to represent o. . .i, leaving ᛟ for o unsusceptible to i-mutation. i-mutation of u produced the high central rounded vowel which Anglo-Saxon scribes give by y. For this new phoneme the rune-masters invented ᚣ, a form which obviously combines ᚢ + ᛁ, and to it they gave the arbitrary name yr.

Changes in the pronunciation of velar stop consonants /k/ and /g/ led to the creation of the last three runes, ᚳ ᛣ and ᚸ. To simplify, Old English seems to have diverged from Germanic in that it developed distinctive front and back allophones of these consonants. Writers of Anglo-Saxon manuscripts did not usually differentiate between the allophones in their spellings. Nor did some rune-masters. Others used the newly invented rune ᛣ, 'k', *calc*, for back k/c, and ᚸ, 'ḡ', *gar*, for back g. They retained the old ᚳ, 'c', and ᚷ 'g', for the fronted, palatal, consonants in virtue of their names *cen*, 'torch', and *gyfu*, 'gift, act of giving'. The Ruthwell cross rune-master seems to have produced a further refinement (though scholars differ as to its significance): ᚸ, 'k̄', appears on one side of the cross in contexts that require a back k/c followed by a secondary fronted vowel, as in a word like *cyning*. No manuscript records this rune so its name is unknown. These last three runes clearly derive formally from 'c' and 'g' respectively.

Of the twenty-four *futhorc* runes which descend direct from Germanic prototypes, nineteen retain what we may think of as the Germanic forms. These are 'f', 'u', 'þ', 'r', 'g', 'w', 'n', 'i', 'ï', 'p', 'x', 't', 'b', 'e', 'm', 'l', 'd', 'œ', 'æ', though 'p' is something of an unknown, for it is rare in early times and yet displays several variant though related shapes.

Germanic **k** was ᚲ apparently cut smaller than other characters. Variants, ᚴ, ᛣ developed early. English inscriptions (apart from the unique Watchfield ᚴ) suggest (for 'c') the series ᚲ (Loveden Hill), ᛣ (the two Chessell Down texts, apparently the **skanomodu** solidus if that is English), and the common ᚳ which contrasts with the usual North Germanic type ᚴ. **h** is something of a problem as we have seen. North Germanic inscriptions use the single-barred ᚺ. Most West Germanic ones use the double-barred ᚻ, but there is an increasing number of early English inscriptions known to have ᚺ. How the scatter of distribution came about we do not know. ᚺ is presumably the primary form. It is certainly the one recorded earliest, perhaps on the comb from Vimose, Fyn (Denmark) from the second century A.D. Germanic **j** was the curious ᛃ, ᛃ preserved, for example, on the spear-head from Øvre Stabu (Norway) and on the golden horn from Gallehus (South Jutland). Some early rune-masters seem to have resented the unorthodox appearance of this character and to have rearranged its elements to make it resemble other rune forms. Thus, the Vadstena *futhark* has ᛃ; one on a brooch from Charnay (Burgundy) ᛃ; one on a pillar from Breza (Bosnia) ᚾ; while a bracteate from Sjælland (Denmark) displays ✝ which is also a rare Anglo-Saxon form of the letter. The common epigraphical ✳ and the manuscript ✦ look like further examples of this rearrangement. Of the **s**-rune early inscriptions already show two types, one of three lines, ᛋ, ᛂ; the other made up of four or more lines as ᛌ, ᛍ. Anglo-Saxon has both sorts, though the second is uncommon and apparently early. It also has ᚱ (St Cuthbert's coffin, Kingmoor, the Thames scramasax and some *runica manuscripta*) which may be a simplification of ᚾ (ᚾ > ᚾ > ᚱ or ᚻ > ᚻ > ᚱ) though Dickins preferred to think it taken from the long *s* of Anglo-Saxon bookhand.[7] For the **ŋ**-rune early inscriptions show a variety of forms based on a small square or circle, as Vadstena ◊ and Kylver ◻. The invariable Anglo-Saxon form is ᛜ, not found outside England and presumably a local modification, bringing a small letter up to full rune height.

In discussing how the Anglo-Saxon runes were used it would be convenient if we could make precise statements: defining, for instance, the sounds that individual characters represented or the extent to which differences of letter form marked phonemic distinctions. I think this not possible partly because of our detailed ignorance of Anglo-Saxon pronunciation, but partly too because we have so few clearly and unambiguously comprehensible runic texts and they spread over a wide range of dates and places. Professional linguists will despair at my account because I do not use their advanced terminology and conventions of presentation. However, the only suitable way of defining Anglo-Saxon runic values is by demonstrating the letters in use (treating them as graphemes as my learned contemporaries would put it) and this I do tentatively in later chapters. Here, however, I must make a few general statements.

In most cases the Dickins-Page transliterations are useful pointers to the way rune-masters used their script. Apart from the graphs 'ŋ' for ᛜ and 'i̇' for ᛄ our transliteration system employs letters found in Anglo-Saxon scribal texts (at any rate as shown in printed editions), and there is a fairly general correlation between manuscript usage and that in the transliterated runic inscriptions. If the transliterated texts look strange to the general student of Old English it is partly because they are texts from early dates and unusual dialect regions. Only in small part is it caused by unusual spelling practices.

One point where runic spelling practices are important concerns the treatment of the sounds that developed from Gmc *k* and *g*. This brings in, not only the related rune forms 'c', 'k', and 'k̄', and 'g' and 'ḡ', but also 'j' and 'i̇'. As we have seen, some rune masters used 'c' and 'g' for both palatal and velar

---

[7] 'The Inscriptions upon the Coffin' in C.F.Battiscombe, *The Relics of Saint Cuthbert* (Durham 1956), 306.

stops; others, and they are exclusively in north-west England, developed the new symbols 'k' and 'ḡ' for the back consonants, restricting 'c' and 'g' to the fronted ones. 'k' occurs as far south and east as Thornhill and Bramham Moor, both in Yorkshire, 'ḡ' only at Bewcastle and Ruthwell in the very north-west, while the more subtle variant 'k̄' (for a back consonant preceding a front vowel) appears only at Ruthwell.[8] Palatalised *g* before stressed *i* could be represented also by the rune 'j', with an example again at Thornhill, but another in the south, on the Dover slab, as well as a couple at Westeremden in Frisia. 'i̵' seems originally to have been a vowel rune, giving a mid-front vowel in the region of *e* and *i*: hence Continental runologists sometimes transliterate it *ė* or *ï*. It still is a vowel on the Dover slab, whose inscription '*j* i̵ s l h ea r d:' records the personal name *Gislheard*. At Thornhill, however, 'i̵' appears for the palatalised *g* in 'ea t e i̵ n n e' (the personal name *Eadþegn-*), whereas at Great Urswick and Ruthwell it represents the voiceless velar and palatal spirants in 't o r o i̵ t r e d æ' (the personal name *Torhtred-*) and 'a l m e i̵ t t i g' (*almehtig*). This variety of values led Dickins to a compromise transliteration 'ȝ' which I have altered to 'i̵'.[9]

Anglo-Saxon runic and manuscript spelling practices also diverged in their ways of using doubled letters. In Scandinavia the rune-masters avoided doubling letters even when they wanted to record long or repeated sounds. If, to take an extreme case, a word ended with a letter which was also the first of the next word, a Scandinavian inscription would often have the character cut once only. The only likely example of this in an Anglo-Saxon runic inscription, 's e *t* t æ f t e r' for *settæ æfter* on one of the Thornhill stones, may be a carver's mistake, but certainly there are curious examples of single for double, and double for single letters in these texts: for instance, 'g i b i d æ þ' for *gebiddæþ*, 's e t æ' for *settæ*, and 'k r i s t t u s' for the Christ title, 'r i i c n æ' for *ricnæ*, 'g o o d' for *God*, and 'h i l d d i g y þ' for the personal name *Hildigyþ*. Sometimes there may be a pragmatic explanation for this. The carver tried to space out his inscription neatly and had to distort the spelling to do so. Sometimes, however, there is no obvious explanation for the practice, and it may be that the English rune-masters had in these cases no firm orthographic tradition.[10]

On occasion rune-masters – certainly those in Scandinavia – ligatured two

---

[8] All our evidence for 'k̄' comes from a single stone, Ruthwell (and moreover from one side only of it), which may be untypical.

[9] I give an extended discussion of this rune in my 'The Old English Rune *eoh, íh*, "yew-tree" ', *Medium Ævum* 37 (1968), 125–36.

[10] The evidence for this is in my 'The Use of Double Runes in Old English Inscriptions', *Jnl of English and Germanic Philology* 61 (1962), 897–907.

or more letters together, perhaps to save space or effort, perhaps (it has been darkly suggested) to control for magical purposes the total number of symbols that an inscription contained. The resulting conjoint runes are called bind-runes. Anglo-Saxon inscriptions occasionally contain bind-runes, usually two letters possessing a common vertical, though there are a couple of examples with three runes bound together: the Whitby comb and one of the Monte Sant'Angelo graffiti. For example, the word *gebiddaþ* on one of the Thornhill stones has its two *d*-runes bound thus ᛥ, represented in transliteration 'd͡d': the name of the moneyer Brother on Northumbrian stycas appears sometimes as 'b r o þ e͡r' with the bind ᛗᚱ: the Latin word *meus* occurs on the Whitby comb as 'm͡ æ u s', with ᛗᚠ. Some early and eccentric runologists seem to have been fascinated by bind-runes and to have identified them freely in Anglo-Saxon contexts. In fact they are fairly rare in England, uncommon enough in practice to make me suspect any reading that relies heavily on finding bind-runes in a text.

One more, fairly rare, transcriptional point needs mention. It occasionally happens that the runologist is unable to identify a character in an inscription, even though it is well preserved and clearly visible. The form may be ambiguous or simply unknown, perhaps a variant that we have no other example of, perhaps a rune-master's error that we may suspect but not be sure of. In these cases I represent the unrecognised character by an asterisk. An example is the verbal '* s e t e' on the Thornhill II stone, where I am not sure if we have a half-length inset 'i' making 'i s e t e' (for *gisette*) or a runemaster's mistake, beginning the stem of 's' too far to the left and then abandoning the cut.

All I have done in this chapter is give a general summary of English runic types and practices. I have hinted at some ways in which runic forms differ according to the material they are cut on or the date and place of cutting. This is an aspect of runes we would be glad to know more about, to trace how the script and its use changed in the hands of different rune-masters spread out over the land and over the Anglo-Saxon period. Unfortunately the corpus is too small, and any study of the palaeography of English runic inscriptions can only be crude and tentative, pointing out obviously early and archaic forms or noting clearly defined local variants. Until substantially more rune-inscribed objects are known, it is unlikely to advance far.

4

Condition, Preservation, and Record

Recording a runic monument involves more than reading and transliterating its legend. The runologist must also be aware of the non-linguistic aspects of his find, its archaeological, historical, social, political, economic and artistic contexts. On these it is wise to get expert opinion. To take an example, it is fascinating to see how the distinguished runic scholar, Wolfgang Krause, modified his dating pattern for early Germanic inscriptions when the distinguished archaeologist, Herbert Jankuhn, collaborated with him in the second edition of *Die Runeninschriften im älteren Futhark*, a work of the 1930s being dragged into the 1960s. Now in the 1990s it is equally fascinating to see how far the Krause-Jankuhn datings are being put to question. To turn to another field, it is impressive to watch numismatists using their technology to date, localise or interpret the Anglo-Saxon runic coins, to set them in sequences or judge their significance. Yet in this chapter I want to ignore these ancillary crafts, and to think only of the difficulties of approaching the runic inscriptions as records of the Old English language. Here the runologist must work in terms, not just of what he sees recorded on an object, but of what the rune-master may be supposed to have cut, or have intended to cut. He must keep in mind the tools and techniques available to the rune-cutter. Connected with this are such considerations as the state of preservation, whether the text survives completely or in part, whether the rune-master was careful or careless, whether he created his text or copied, more or less correctly, from an exemplar. Also whether what survives is typical of what was planned – when we see an inscribed stone, we have to accept the possibility that the artefact was intended to have its carved surface covered with a thin layer of plaster, indeed that the runes may originally have been painted, as in some surviving examples from later Scandinavia.

The best way to define the complexities is by giving examples. The first involves the two runic stones from Hartlepool, commonly associated with the monastery of *Heruteu*. There is neither detailed nor technical report of the discovery, but we know the rune-stones were revealed by foundation trenches

Fig.11. The Hartlepool I name-stone.

for new houses dug on the Hartlepool peninsula in 1833. The diggers broke in on an Anglo-Saxon burial field and found linked somehow with the skeletons, though how is not clearly or consistently described, a group of incised and inscribed stone slabs of small size. Two were runic and recorded personal names, presumably of the dead. One, now in St Hilda's church, Hartlepool, bears the name *Hildiþryþ*: the other, in the Museum of Antiquities, Newcastle-upon-Tyne, reads *Hildigyþ* (figs. 11, 12). Though very alike in size, shape, material and design, the two stones show different characteristics. The first is in immaculate condition, its surface showing little sign of weathering. Its design is a decorative cross incised within a border, with the Greek letters *alpha* and *omega* in the upper quadrants and the personal name divided into its two elements set in the lower ones: 'h i l d i ‖ þ r y þ'. The incisions remain clear and precise. The lay-out of the pattern is accurate. The

Fig.12. The Hartlepool II name-stone.

runic letters are carefully cut and elegantly seriffed, and though they increase in size towards the end of the text, they look neatly set out. Which might imply that the increase in size is intended not accidental; it was part of the carver's sense of design. The whole gives the impression of an expertly cut monument, preserved under unusually favourable circumstances. Indeed, the surface condition is so fine that we must assume not only was it prepared by a skilled craftsman, it must also have been protected for nearly all the period of its existence. The stone cannot have stayed long above ground and in the open, but must have been buried or covered, either purposely or by chance.

The second Hartlepool stone also has an incised decorative cross within a border. The upper quadrants are empty. The lower contain the deceased's name, but not divided into its two elements or conventionally spelled. The division is 'h i l d ‖ d i g y þ', with the 'd' doubled and the 'g' originally omitted and cut later above the line, with an insert point to show where it belonged. The letters are poorly spaced and not in line. The stone surface when found was heavily weathered, so it must have been above ground for some time, presumably during its early history. The effect is that details of the incisions are lost, though we can see that the letters are not seriffed and apparently were not so elegantly formed as on the first stone. We are left to wonder how closely we may properly compare the two monuments, similar but with distinct differences, from the same grave-field. This is relevant in determining how to treat the curious spelling 'h i l d ‖ d i g y þ', which is amended from 'h i l d ‖ d i y þ' on the stone itself. Stone I is well set out and neat: the wear on stone II makes this detail unclear, but it was apparently not so carefully prepared. Stone I could have had its pattern laid out, perhaps in chalk, before cutting. Is this likely to have happened with stone II? If so, would the carver have made his errors in the name form? Could he have chalked in 'h i l d ‖ i g y þ', have smudged his marks as he cut the first part of the name, and misread 'i g' as the similar 'd i'? Is the lay-out of the inscription too little symmetrical for such an explanation?

This is a simple case where an object's condition and lay-out affects how we interpret its text. It is also an example of how misleading it can be to work from a simple transliteration of an inscription, without being aware of its disposition on the object, or the condition in which it survives. The transliteration system we use needs to incorporate some way of showing such important aspects of the inscription. In practice, this is difficult. The more diacritics added to a system of notation, the less accessible it becomes save to specialists, and runic studies are a field where those who are not runologists have proper claims. However, there are some things we can do. In the Hartlepool case it was clearly important to show how the inscribed name was split into two by the shaft of the incised cross. The double vertical ‖ gave the line

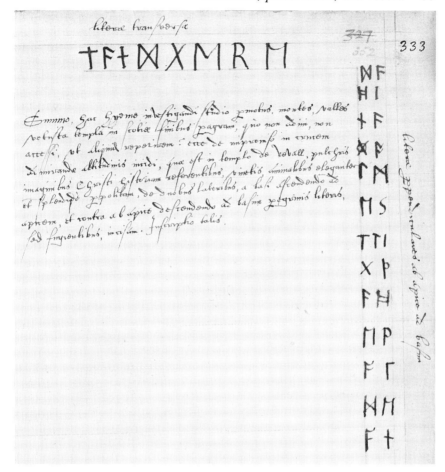

Fig.13. Reginald Bainbrigg's drawing of the Ruthwell cross inscription
(British Library MS Cotton Julius F.vi).

of division. We can use a similar symbol, the single vertical |, to record how a longer text is distributed over several lines. For example, the Kirkheaton stone inscription, set in two uneven lines, reads 'e o h : w o r o | h t æ'.

Much more important, indeed essential, is a means of showing when an inscription is so affected that letter forms are damaged or lost. For example, of the six rune-stones from Lindisfarne only one has its runes complete and readable. Three are weathered in varying degrees. Two are small fragments, and for representing their inscriptions our transliteration system needs a symbol to show that they break off abruptly because part of their stone is lost. For this I use an open square bracket. Thus I give the texts of Lindisfarne IV, two bits of compound names, one on each side of the stone: a first element 'a u d [' and a second '] l a c'. The bracket shows that something is lost, but the fact that the bracket is left open and not closed shows there is no way of knowing how much.

Often, however, a monument has not suffered as severely as this, and there is a range of ways of representing less serious damage to a text. Sometimes a rune is slightly worn or broken away, but most of its form remains so that there is no doubt about identification. In this case I italicise the transliterated rune. Thus, on Thornhill III the bases of all letters of the last line are lost because the stone base is broken away. All the runes are clearly to be read, but because they are damaged they are shown as '*þ æ r : s a u l e*'. Sometimes the damage to a letter is so severe as to mask its shape without however rendering it entirely unreadable or ambiguous: then we italicise the transcription and put it between square brackets [] to show that something has to be supplied here. There are other ways of supplying a badly damaged rune: perhaps the context makes clear what it must have been, or perhaps early drawings show the rune undamaged. For instance, numbers of pictures survive of the Ruthwell cross from the early seventeenth century onwards. We can use these (with critical caution) to supplement present-day readings, again employing italic letters within square brackets for the purpose. As an example, Reginald Bainbrigg drew part of the Ruthwell inscription that quotes *The Dream of the Rood* before reforming zeal threw down this cross as an 'Idolatrous Monument' in the seventeenth century (fig.13). Thus he recorded the beginning of the text which is now smashed away. Today the inscription starts, '[.] g e r e | d æ | h i | n æ | ḡ o | d a | l m | e ɨ | t t i | g'. From Bainbrigg's picture we can safely complete the first word as '[+ *o n d*] g e r e d æ' or '[+ *a n d*] g e r e d æ' (Bainbrigg could not distinguish between the similar graphs 'o' and 'a'), and note that this corresponds satisfactorily with *ongyrede* in the manuscript version of the same poem.[1]

Here in the case of these Ruthwell cross runes I admit another source for supplementing damaged words, the roughly parallel material of the poem in the famous codex known as the Vercelli Book (Vercelli, Chapter Library, MS CXVII). Now and again it is possible to draw on the Vercelli text to replace with some certainty letters almost completely lost from the stone, relying on the tiny bits that remain and the calculated space available. In my transcriptions I put such rare, replaced, letters within double rounded brackets (( )) and in italics. For instance, my rigorous transcript '[.] f | [.] *m* | [.] ea | [. *d*] u' can safely be completed '((*h* ea)) f | ((*d u*)) *m* | ((*b i h*)) ea | ((l)) [*d*] u' on the evidence of *heafdum beheoldon* in vv.63–4 of Vercelli and taking into

---

[1]   R.I.Page, 'An Early Drawing of the Ruthwell Cross', *Medieval Archaeology* 3 (1959), 285–8.

account this rune-master's spelling practice. This is a clumsy device, but the best I can think of with the technology available to me.

More often, however, there is no evidence on which to supply the missing runes of a damaged text. We may know that one or more are worn away, but we cannot be sure what they were. When this happens I indicate the gap by [.]. It would be useful if we could easily include some means of showing exactly how many letters are lost. If we could calculate, even approximately, how many are missing we could use some system such as [-5-]. Dickins experimented with a small open point [○] to indicate a single graph missing, reserving [.] for a gap of uncertain length, usually implying more than one. This particular distinction is unwelcome to those who produce camera-ready copy or a print-out for scanning since the two sorts of symbol are too alike. Moreover, there are probably too many cases where it is hard to calculate with any precision how many letters are lost, so it is more convenient to persist with a symbol [.] which records a loss in general terms, and to leave it to the detailed description of the monument to give an estimate of how many runes have been destroyed.

An example is the Overchurch rune-stone, with its damaged text in two lines (fig.14). The beginning of line 2 is worn or weathered away, and a mediaeval mason trimmed off the ends of both lines when he reshaped the stone for building use. What remains is:

> 'f o l c æ a r æ r d o n b e c [
> [.] *b* i d d a þ f o t e æ þ e l m u *n* [

The general sense is clear, and losses can be tentatively supplied, so that it becomes

> *folc arærdon becun:*
> *gebiddaþ fore Æþelmunde*

'The people erected a monument: pray for Æthelmund.' Plausible though this is, it is worth pointing to its uncertainties. I have suggested a form *gebiddaþ* rather than *biddaþ* because other rune-stones have the prefixed verb rather than the simplex, but of course Overchurch may have been an exception, and the space before '*b* i d d a þ' may have held a cross, or even the end of the previous line if the carver had not kept to his individual line lengths in arranging his lettering. If the prefixed verb was used, the form of the prefix could have been 'g e' or 'g i'. 'b e c [' is certainly the beginning of *becun*, 'monument', but we do not know how the word was spelled here: was it 'b e c u n', 'b e c n' or 'b e c o n'? The name 'æ þ e l m u *n* [' was in an oblique case after *fore*, but which? An accusative in *-mund*, dative in *-munde* or *-mundi*, or instrumental in *-mundi*?

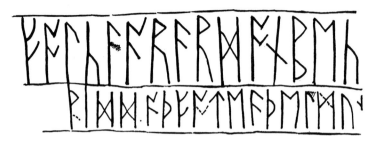

Fig.14. The Overchurch stone runes. (1:5)

There is a further problem. A comparison of my reconstructed text with what survives on the stone shows that I have made two emendations. The stone's 'f o t e' is a clear error for 'f o r e', the usual preposition in such a prayer formula. The group 'f o l c æ a r æ r d o n' also looks mistaken. A nominative *folcæ* is very odd, and a verbal form *æarærdon* equally so, though we know so little about the Old English dialect of the Wirral that we cannot be quite sure that in this respect the carver cut his text wrongly. Here we enter the realm of interpretation rather than record, a dangerous act.[2] It is essential to have a diacritic to distinguish an amended form, a reading that is different in one way or another from what is found in the inscription. I use the diagonal brackets < >: so, 'f o <r> e' on the Overchurch stone. But should we have a signal to indicate a superfluous letter which the editor would prefer to remove? I have suggested the use of hooked brackets, { } as 'f o l c {æ} a r æ r d o n', but I would use them sparingly.

The diagonal brackets can also be employed to distinguish a letter added by the editor because the rune-carver had omitted it, if we can identify such an error with any certainty. An example may be in the Thornhill I inscription:

'+ [.] þ e l b e | [.] *t* : s e *t* t æ f t e | r e þ e l w i n i : [.] r'

Possibly the final unstressed vowel of the verb has been lost, and we should rather read 's e *t* t <e> æ f t e r' or 's e *t* t <æ> æ f t e r'. There is no certainty that this emendation is correct – 's e *t* t æ f t e r' could be a rune-master's spelling for *settæ æfter*. The brackets serve to warn the reader that there has been editorial tampering with the text.

Finally, there are one or two refinements of transcription that can be mentioned here, though they need not be in common use. It may sometimes be desirable to distinguish a letter that was originally missed out by the carver and added later. This can be done by the use of single round brackets: so, the Hartlepool II inscription described above could be rendered 'h i l d ‖ d i (g) y þ'. In a few cases we can identify a clear correction in an inscription. Letters of the main Ruthwell cross texts seem to have been sketched in on the stone first and recut more boldly later. The recutting allowed the carver to correct errors he identified in the first attempt. For example, the 'œ' of the sequence 'l i m w | œ r i g | n æ' was first cut as 'g' and then amended. This could be signalled by the use of double square brackets: 'l i m w | [[œ]] r i g | n æ', if it were thought significant enough.

The supplementary details of transliteration that I have listed here leave a good deal to the editor's discretion. It is unlikely that any two scholars will produce exactly the same transcriptions from a group of texts that have suffered damage or loss. One may regard a letter as so severely ravaged that it must be reproduced between brackets: another may simply italicise. One may be prepared to supply a missing letter where another hesitates because he sees a wider range of spelling possibilities in the word. As a case in point it might be instructive to compare my text of the Ruthwell *Dream of the Rood* on p.147 below with that printed by Dickins and Ross in their popular edition of the poem or more recently by Michael Swanton.[3] All use Dickins's system of transliteration or something close to it, but there are numerous differences of detail. The comparison stresses that there is a subjective element in many examples of runic transliteration, and the student must recognise, accept and be on his guard against it. In return it is the runologist's responsibility to reduce the subjective element to a minimum.

There are pragmatic problems. The accuracy or precision of a record depends in part on the conditions available to the recorder. Is an inscription easily accessible? Can lighting be varied? Are technical aids such as the binocular microscope available and appropriate? Can an inscribed piece be moved, or is it fixed? Consider some examples. The Bewcastle cross stands in the open, unsheltered over the centuries, in a still-used churchyard where some reverence of behaviour is proper. Its inscriptions are weather-worn. Natural lighting varies with weather conditions and time of day. Elaborate artificial lighting is not convenient to instal nor will it always help. So it is easy to see how variant readings of the Bewcastle texts come about. The Ruthwell cross is within a church, but to reach some of its inscriptions the student must get ladder and scaffolding and permission to use them. For side-lighting to throw up fine distinctions of letter form additional lamps are

---

3   B.Dickins and A.S.C.Ross, *The Dream of the Rood*, 4th ed. (London reprinted 1963), 25–9; M.Swanton, *The Dream of the Rood* (Manchester 1970), 90, 92.

needed. Even when an inscribed object is in a museum there can be problems. A major museum may be expected to have available such equipment as the binocular microscope, the variable cold light source; though expectation is sometimes disappointed. A small local museum may not have any of these, and a runologist may have to bring his own portable and perhaps inadequate tools. Within a university context it may be possible to call on advanced technologies for image enhancement or to use sophisticated equipment like the scanning electron microscope to determine whether different texts on the same object are contemporary, cut by the same tools. Of course, earlier runologists will not have had access to modern technology, and this must be kept in mind when we criticise their work.

Hitherto I have written as though the inscriptions consist only of runes. In fact there are often other symbols too: perhaps a cross to mark the beginning, and several forms of punctuation mark, the point set at mid height, the colon, several points in vertical line, or in one case slashes. In transliteration all these are copied as closely as is conveniently possible, and are included within the single inverted commas that, in the Dickins-Page system, mark off the runic inscriptions. These inverted commas are always used when transliterating runes save for those that occur in inscriptions intermingled with roman characters. There the commas would be clumsy and obtrusive.[4] In dealing with a runic topic it is usual to transliterate roman characters by capitals, no matter what form of roman alphabet, majuscule or minuscule, actually appears in the inscription in question. So a mixed text would have the roman characters in capitals and the runes, easily distinguished from them, in lower case. Thus, the name on the Chester-le-Street standing stone is EADmVnD, with most of the letters in roman but 'm' and 'n' in runes (fig.15); the Llysfaen ring has the name ALHSTAn, again with only 'n' runic.

I have described methods of precise transliteration, when the runologist tries to represent his inscription as simply yet as completely as possible. However, this is not always what is needed. There are cases where we are justified in presenting a less precise transcript so as to stress some particular aspect of the material. Most obvious is where the reader wants to know the content of the text but is less concerned with the minutiae of its form and condition. Rune-masters often did not take the trouble to divide their sentences into discrete words nor did they bother to accommodate their words to the line-lengths available. The general Anglo-Saxonist usually wants the

---

4 B.Dickins and A.S.C.Ross, 'The Alnmouth Cross', *Jnl of English and Germanic Philology* 39 (1940), 171 announced this convention but Dickins himself strayed from it, with unhappy results, in publishing mixed texts from St Cuthbert's coffin and the Lindisfarne Gospels, in Battiscombe, *Relics of St Cuthbert*, 305–6.

Fig.15. The Chester-le-Street stone
inscription. (1:5)

editor to do the rune-master's work for him, and so to make the inscription
more accessible. Thus, a rigorous transcript of the Great Urswick memorial
verse is:

'+ t u n w i n i s e t æ | æ f t e r t o r o ɨ | t r e d æ b e k u |
n æ f t e r h i s b | æ u r n æ g e b i d æ s þ e | r s ‖ a u | l æ'

For general purposes it is enough to put:

'+ t u n w i n i   s e t æ   æ f t e r   t o r o ɨ t r e d æ   b e k u n
æ f t e r   h i s   b æ u r n æ   g e b i d æ s   þ e r   s a u l æ'

In this book I shall use both these styles, each as is appropriate to the particular context. The reader must expect me to appear inconsistent.

We cannot make the text more easily understood than this without interfer-
ing with its form, and we must then release it from its inverted commas and
admit we are producing not a transcript but an edited text. Then we can write:
+ *Tunwini setæ æfter Torohtredæ bekun æfter his bæurnæ: gebidæs þer
saulæ.* Thereafter, if we want to show it as a verse text, stressing its literary
rather than its linguistic significance, we can normalise:

Tunwini settæ   æfter Torhtredæ
becun æfter his bæurnæ: gebiddæs þer saulæ

By this time we have stopped thinking of Great Urswick as a runic text. It has
become part of the Anglo-Saxon poetic corpus.

5

Runica Manuscripta and the Rune-names

In an earlier chapter I drew the *futhorc* with a roman equivalent given for each rune, and in doing so I followed Anglo-Saxon precedent. From Anglo-Saxon and early post-Conquest times survive a number of manuscript records of runes, the letters arranged sometimes in *futhorc*, sometimes in ABC order. Their scribes drew the runic characters with more or less accuracy and usually added the roman value above or below the rune, and sometimes also the rune-name. Roughly contemporary with them – indeed, some of them surviving from rather earlier date – are Continental manuscripts which contain Anglo-Saxon rune-rows, apparently written by local scholars from English exemplars, often with added roman values or with rune-names whose forms are sadly distorted by foreign hands. All these are the *runica manuscripta* which the Belgian scholar, René Derolez, has examined in a monumental book which has eased the work of all later runologists.[1]

To our misfortune, one or two of the more important of these early accounts of runes survive on detached leaves or only in facsimiles made in the early modern period, and in these cases we know little of the context in which the runes were originally presented to the reader. But in others the context is clear, and it is interesting to see the runic script preserved in miscellanies of scientific knowledge, among computistical or mathematical lore, in company with etymological and grammatical treatises, or with lists of exotic alphabets, cryptograms and puzzles. To take two examples. St John's College, Oxford, MS 17 is a handsome twelfth-century codex, preserving material from an earlier date. The manuscript contains several scientific and mathematical texts, including works by Bede, Abbo of Fleury and Byrhtferth of Ramsey, and there are also a calendar, astronomical tables, annals, lists of propitious and unpropitious days, and grammatical, medical and geographi-

---

[1] R.Derolez, *Runica Manuscripta* (Brugge 1954) with addendum in *English Studies, Supplement* 45 (1964), 116–20; also '*Runica Manuscripta* Revisited' in Bammesberger, *Old English Runes*, 85–106.

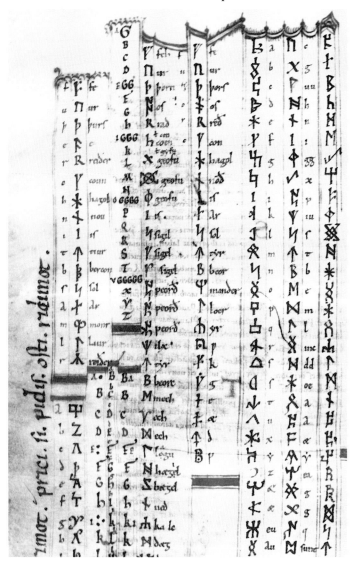

Fig.16. English and Norse runes on a page from St John's
College, Oxford, MS 17.

cal information. The runes are on fo.5v, an elaborately tabulated page most
recently dated, with remarkable precision, to 1110/1111 (fig.16).[2] It lists
several rune-rows, English, Scandinavian and mixed, arranged both as

---

[2] D.Parsons, 'Byrhtferth and the Runes of Oxford, St John's College, Manuscript
17' in Düwel, *Runeninschriften*, 441.

futhorcs and ABCs, as well as fictitious alphabets of 'Egyptians', 'Chaldeans' and of Nemnivus and Aethicus Ister. There are some elementary code alphabets which gain their mystery by disguising their vowels, and one which ingeniously replaces each letter by the one immediately following it in the ABC (a = B, b = C, c = D, etc.). There are four *rotae* to be used for computation, and finally, eight lines of cryptic writing based on primitive one-to-one codes, some with reversed letter order.[3]

Earlier is Vienna, National Library, MS 795, the main body of which was copied apparently in S.Amand, France, in the late eighth or early ninth century. It contains a number of works by the eighth-century Northumbrian scholar Alcuin (as well as a treatise on orthography conventionally ascribed to him) and writings of Augustine and other church fathers. Fos. 19 and 20 were originally left blank and, in the ?tenth century, filled with a group of alphabets, Greek and Gothic, as well as an Anglo-Saxon *futhorc*.

The compilers of these pages seem to have thought of English runes as just another curious script, perhaps a secret one and certainly an uncommon one. Such an attitude, though it may be near that of the carvers of some of the later, bi-alphabetical inscriptions in England, is obviously distant from that of the rune-masters who cut the early Anglo-Saxon runes. Consequently the evidence of the *runica manuscripta* is suspect, to be used only with caution. In the first place, some of them contain evident mistakes of detail. One of the scribes who contributed to the composite runic page of British Library MS Cotton Domitian ix confused the similar runes 'd' and 'm', and, trying helpfully to supply roman equivalents or names to the later and rarer characters of the *futhorc*, got them all wrong.[4]

More insidious than obvious errors like these is the likelihood that the *runica manuscripta* developed their own runic traditions, divorced and in some ways different from the epigraphical ones. Many runologists have missed this point, and have distorted the picture of Anglo-Saxon runes by trying to combine manuscript and epigraphical materials where they are in fact not supplementary but alternative. (This at any rate is my opinion, though it is not accepted by all students of the script.)[5] Despite this type of difficulty, we cannot do without the evidence of the *runica manuscripta* for

---

3   Derolez, *Runica Manuscripta*, 26–34 gives a detailed description of the manuscript's runes.
4   Derolez, *Runica Manuscripta*, 14–15.
5   An alternative opinion is given in R.Derolez, 'Epigraphical versus Manuscript English Runes: One or Two Worlds?', *Academiae Analecta* 45 (1983), 69–93. Also D.Parsons, 'Anglo–Saxon Runes in Continental Manuscripts' in Düwel, *Runische Schriftkultur*, 195–220.

they are the source of our system of runic-roman equivalents, and supply the main evidence for the Anglo-Saxon rune-names.

Each Anglo-Saxon rune had a name which was also an Old English common or proper noun. Usually the rune-name began with one of the range of sounds that the rune represented, as *feoh*, 'money', for 'f'; *hæg(e)l*, 'hail', for 'h'; and *dæg*, 'day', for 'd'. When, as sometimes happened, no suitable Old English word had the right opening, the system was satisfied with a rune-name containing the appropriate sound, as *Ing*, the name of a god or hero, for 'ŋ'. There is nothing specifically Anglo-Saxon about this, for the later Scandinavian runes had names too, and in many cases they were cognate with the English ones. If the Gothic material in Vienna, National Library, MS 795 is to be believed – and there is some question about this – letter-names of the Gothic alphabet descend from a related system, and it then looks as if the bulk of the Anglo-Saxon rune-names go back to common Germanic times.[6]

The Anglo-Saxon *Runic Poem*, once in British Library MS Cotton Otho B.x, formed the most detailed of the early accounts of the English rune-names to come down to modern times. It survives by great good luck. The 1731 Cotton fire destroyed much of the manuscript, including the *Runic Poem* folio. Fortunately Humfrey Wanley had already transcribed it for p.135 of section I of Hickes's *Thesaurus*, and the poem is known only from the printed version of this transcription (fig.17). The integrity of the Hickes text is suspect, for some of the material he prints with the *Runic Poem* derives quite clearly from another, still extant, Cottonian manuscript, Domitian ix. Whether Wanley conflated the two, or whether an earlier scholar transferred the Domitian ix material to Otho B.x, whence Wanley took it into the *Thesaurus*, is in dispute. What is clear, however, is that some of the prefatory runic information of our only text of the *Runic Poem* does not properly belong to it. Luckily this hardly affects what the poem tells us about the rune-names.

The poem has twenty-nine stanzas of alliterative verse, each from two to five lines long. Each begins with a rune whose name the rest of the stanza expounds, so that the whole comprises an elementary guide to the *futhorc*, presumably designed to help the memory. The Anglo-Saxon *Runic Poem* is not unique, for there are Norwegian and Icelandic parallels, suggesting that this was a common mnemonic verse type. However, these extant Scandinavian versions are considerably later than the English and are not all that close

---

6   A classic, sceptical, study of the Gothic letter-names is J.Blomfield, 'Runes and the Gothic Alphabet', *Saga–book of the Viking Soc.* 12 (1937–45), 177–94, 209–31. More recently M.-L.Rotsaert, 'Gotica "Vindobonensia": Localisation, Sources, Scripta Theodisca', *Codices Manuscripti* 9 (1983), 137–50.

F	ᚠ ᵖᵉᵒʰ	byþ fnofum. fina ȝehpýlcum. rceal ðeah manna ȝehpýlc. miclun hýt bælan. ȝif he pile. fon ðnihtne domer hleotan :.
u	ᚢ ᵘⁿ	byþ anmoð. 7 ofen hýpneð. fela fnecne. ðeon feohteþ. mið hopnum. mæ-pe mon rtapa. þ ir modiȝ puht :.
ᵟ	ᚦ ᵈᵒᵖⁿ	byþ ðeaple rceapp. ðeȝna ȝehpýlcum. anfen-ȝýr ýfýl. unȝemetun þeþe. manna ȝehpýlcum. ðe him mið perteð :.
o	ᚩ ᵒʳⁱ	byþ ondfnuma. ælcpe rppæce. pirdomer ppaþu. anð pitena fnofun. anð eopla ȝehpam. eaðnýr anð to hiht :.
ɲ	ᚱ ⁿᵃᵈ	byþ onþecýðe. þinca ȝehpýlcum. refte anð rpiþhpæt. ðam ðe ritteþ on-ufan. meaþe mæȝen heapðum. ofen mil paþar :.
c	ᚳ ᶜᵉⁿ	byþ cpicena ȝehpam cuþ on fýne blac anð beophtlic býnneþ ofturt ðæn hi æþelinȝar inne pertað :.
ᚷ̇	ᚷ ᵍʸᵖᵘ	ȝumena býþ ȝlenȝ anð henenýr. ppaþu 7 pýnþrcýpe 7 ppæcna ȝehpam an anð ætpirt ðe býþ oþna lear :.
uu	ᚹ ᵖᵉⁿ	ne bnuceþ ðe can peana lýt raper anð fonȝe anð him rýlfa hæfþ blæð 7 blýrre anð eac býnȝa ȝeniht :.
h	ᚻᚻ ʰᵃᵍˡ	byþ hpiturt copna. hpýnfct hit of heofoner lýfte. pealcaþ hit pinðer rcu-na. peopþeþ hit to pætene rýððan :.
n	ᚾ ⁿʸᵈ	byþ neapu on bneortan peopþeþ hi ðeah oft niþa beapnum to helpe anð to hæle ȝe hpæþne ȝif hi hir hlýrtaþ æpon :.
ı	ᛁ ⁱʳ	byþ ofen cealðunȝe metum rliþop ȝlirnaþ ȝlær hluttun ȝimmum ȝeli-curt. flop foprte ȝe populht fæȝen anrýne :.
ȝx	ᛄ ˢᵉⁿ	byþ ȝumena hiht ðon ȝoð læteþ haliȝ heofoner cýninȝ bnuȝan rýllan beophte bleða beopnum anð ðeapfum :.
eo	ᛇ ᵉᵒʰ	byþ utan unrmeþe tpeop. heapð bnuȝan fært hýnðe fýner. pýntnumun unðeppnepýð pýnan on eþle :.
p	ᛈ ᵖᵉᵒʳᵈ	byþ rýmble pleȝa. anð hlehten plancum ðan piȝan rittaþ on beop rele bliþe æt romne :.
ᚷ	ᛉ ᵉᵒˡʰˣ	reccaþ hæfþ ofturt on fenne. pexeð on patupe. punþaþ ȝnimme. bloðe bneneð beopna ȝehpýlcne ðe him æniȝne onfenȝ ȝeðeð :.
r	ᛋ ˢⁱᵍᵉˡ	re mannum rýmble biþ on hihte ðonn hi hine fepiaþ ofen fircer beþ oþ hibþim henȝert bninȝeþ to lanðe :.
ᛏ	ᛏ ᵗⁱᵖ	biþ tacna rum healðeð tpýpa pel. piþ æþelinȝar a biþ onfæpýlðe. ofen nihta ȝenipu. næfne rpiceþ :.
b	ᛒ ᵇᵉᵒʳᶜ	byþ bleða lear. beneþ efne rpa ðeah tanar butan tuððen. biþ on telȝum pli-tiȝ. þeah on helme hnýrteð fæȝene. ȝeloben leafum lýfte ȝetenȝe :.
e	ᛖ ᵉʰ	byþ fon eoplum æþelinȝa pýn. hopr hofum planc. ðæn him hæleþe ýmb. pe-leȝe on picȝum pnixlaþ rppæce. 7 biþ unrtýllum æfne fnofun :.
m	ᛗ ᵃⁿ	byþ on mynȝþe hir maȝan leof. rceal þeah anna ȝehpýlc oðpum rpican. fon ðam ðpýhten pýle dome rine þ eapme flærc eopþan betæcan :.
l	ᛚ ˡᵃᵍᵘ	byþ leoðum lanȝrum ȝeþuht ȝif hi rculun neþun on nacan tealtum. 7 hi ræ ýþa rpýþe bneȝaþ. anð re bnim henȝert bniðler ne ȝým :.
mȝ	ᛝ ᵘⁱⁿᵍ	pær æpert mið eart ðenum. ȝe repen recȝun. oþ he rið ðan eft. ofen pæȝ ȝepát pæn æftep pan. ður heanðinȝar ðone hæle nemðun :.
oe	ᛟ ᵉᵗᵉˡ	byþ ofen leof. æȝhpýlcum men. ȝif he mot ðæn. pihtep anð ȝepýrena on bnucan on bloðe bleaþum ofturt :.
ᚧ	ᛞ ᵐᵃⁿⁿᵘ	byþ ðpihtner ronð. beope mannum. mæpe metoðer leoht, mýnȝþ anð to hiht eaðȝum anð eapmum. eallum bnice :.
a	ᚪ ᵃᶜ	byþ on eopþan. elða beapnum. flærcer foðop fepeþ ȝelome ofen ȝanoter bæþ ȝaprecȝ fanðaþ. hpæþep ac hæbbe æþele tneope :.
æ	ᚫ ᵃᵉˢᶜ	biþ ofen heah. elðum ðýpe. rtiþ on rtaþule. rteðe pihte hýlt. ðeah him feohtan on fipar moniȝe :.
y	ᚣ ʸʳ	byþ æþelinȝa 7 eopla ȝehpær. pýn anð pýnþmýnð. býþ on picȝe fæȝep. fært-lic on fæpelðe. fýnð ȝeacepa rum :.
ιo	ᛡ ⁱᵒ ⁱᵃʳ	byþ ea fixa. anð ðeah abnuceþ. foðner onfalðan. hafaþ fæȝepne eapð. pætne bepoppen. ðæn he pýnnum leofaþ :.
eaɲ	ᛠ ᵗⁱʳ ᵉᵃʳ	byþ eȝle eopla ȝehpýlcun. ðonn færtlice flærc onȝinneþ. hnapcolian hnuran ceopan blac to ȝebeðban bleða ȝeðpeopaþ. pýnna ȝepitaþ pena ȝerpicaþ :.
cpen̄ð	ᛢ	
q		

ᛋᛏᚪᚾ Stan / ᚪᛏ / ᚥᚱ / ᛋ

Hos Characteres ᛈᚾᚻᛈᛇᚣᚹᛉᚷ *ad alia festinans Studioso lectori interpretanda relinquo.*

Fig.17. The Anglo-Saxon *Runic Poem*, from Hickes's *Thesaurus*.

to it, so they should be used only with great caution to illuminate the Anglo-Saxon poem.[7]

Typical stanzas are the three that begin the Anglo-Saxon *Runic Poem*, presented here in edited form.

> ᚠ (feoh) byþ frofur   fira gehwylcum;
> sceal ðeah manna gehwylc   miclun hyt dælan
> gif he wile for drihtne   domes hleotan.
>
> ᚢ (ur) byþ anmod   and oferhyrned,
> felafrecne deor;   feohteþ mid hornum
> mære morstapa;   þæt is modig wuht.
>
> ᚦ (ðorn) byþ ðearle scearp;   ðegna gehwylcum
> anfeng ys yfyl,   ungemetun reþe
> manna gehwylcun   ðe him mid resteð.

> *Feoh*, wealth, is a comfort to all men. Yet everyone must give it away freely if he wants to gain glory in the Lord's sight.
>
> *Ur*, the aurochs, a very savage beast, is fierce and has huge horns. A great roamer of the moorlands, it fights with its horns. It is a courageous brute.
>
> *Ðorn*, a thorn, is extremely sharp. Grabbing hold of it is painful to any warrior, uncommonly severe to anyone who lies among them.

There are interesting comparisons to be made between these three Anglo-Saxon rune-names and their recorded Scandinavian equivalents. In the case of the first, the Norwegian and Icelandic *Runic Poems* have *fé*, 'wealth', which confirms both form and meaning of the Anglo-Saxon name. As regards *ur*, both Norwegian and Icelandic poems support the form, but give diverse meanings. Norwegian has *úr*, which seems to mean 'slag' in the sentence *úr er af illu járne*, 'slag comes from poor iron'; Icelandic has *úr*, 'drizzle', defined as *skýja grátr ok skára þverrir ok hirðis hatr*, 'cloud's tears and hay's destroyer and herdsman's hate'. For the þ-rune the Norwegian and Icelandic verses have the name *þurs*, 'demon, giant', in the sentences *þurs vældr kvenna kvillu*, 'a giant causes women distress'; and *þurs er kvenna kvǫl ok*

---

7 The latest study of these three poems is M.Halsall, *The Old English* Rune Poem: *a Critical Edition*. McMaster Old English Studies and Texts 2 (Toronto 1981), but its versions of the Norwegian and Icelandic poems are admittedly taken from secondary sources and are outdated. A new edition of the Icelandic poem, adumbrating the problems in establishing a definitive text, is R.I.Page, 'The Icelandic Rune–Poem', *Nottingham Medieval Studies* 42 (1998), 1–37.

kletta íbúi ok Valrúnar verr, 'a giant is women's torment and crag-dweller and (?the giantess) Valrún's mate'. Here 'Gothic' has the three relevant letter-names *fe, uraz* and *thyth*. Clearly it is likely that a Germanic form of the first rune-name was **fehu* with a meaning 'wealth, property, possessions'. For the second Germanic had a form which could give OE *ur*, ON *úr*, but we can only speculate on its meaning. In the case of the **þ**-rune we know neither the Germanic rune-name nor its meaning. Either Old English or Old Norse (or both) has altered the meaning of the **u**-rune's name: either Old English or Old Norse (or both) has altered the form of the **þ**-rune's name.

At this point of the discussion we must note the dates of the earliest surviving rune-name forms. The oldest English name list (which is in a Continental manuscript) is from the late eighth or early ninth century. Linguistic evidence – such as it is – puts the Otho B.x manuscript of the *Runic Poem* not before the end of the tenth century; critics have suggested, on stylistic grounds only, that the poem goes back to the eighth or ninth. The earliest catalogue of Norse rune-names, without definitions, occurs in a ninth-century S.Gall manuscript in a piece of doggerel called the *Abecedarium Nordmannicum*, a mixed text for it is partly in Continental Germanic and it also contains some distinctive Anglo-Saxon runic types.[8] By the ninth century the Norse rune-row had been reduced from twenty-four to sixteen characters, so that only sixteen Scandinavian rune-names are recorded. The Norwegian and Icelandic *Runic Poems* are only tentatively dated, perhaps to the late twelfth/early thirteenth and the fifteenth centuries respectively, though the earliest records of both are later. Thus all of our rune-name material is comparatively late, giving plenty of time for both English and Norse rune-masters to have tampered with the names of their characters. But what would be the incentive to do it?

A theory often put forward to explain which words the Germanic rune-masters chose as letter-names links the script to ancient paganism. Some scholars have thought that runes were originally a cult-script, and so have assumed that the names record those aspects of Germanic experience which were of religious importance. The theory can be worked out in greater or lesser detail, with more or less extravagance and absurdity. Extreme are the attempts of C.J.S.Marstrander and Karl Schneider to build up pictures of the religious forces that influenced the formation of the rune-names.[9] More moderate, though still firmly committed to the link between the religion and the

8 Derolez, *Runica Manuscripta*, 78.
9 C.J.S.Marstrander, 'Om Runene og Runenavnenes Oprindelse', *Norsk Tidsskrift for Sprogvidenskap* 1 (1928), 85–188; K.Schneider, *Die germanische Runennamen: Versuch einer Gesamtdeutung* (Meisenheim am Glan 1956).

alphabet, are Helmut Arntz, Wolfgang Krause and R.W.V.Elliott.[10] More cautious again, as befits a scholar trained in the austere disciplines of historiography, is Lucien Musset, but even he accepts that religion or magic helped to determine the choice of names though linguistic considerations were more important.[11] The Germanic rune-masters would probably have picked for their rune-names words which were frequent in the language, and if paganism coloured everyday life we should expect some of the Germanic rune-names to refer to it. This is the position taken up by Edgar C.Polomé in a recent survey.[12] In contrast is the firmly sceptical pronouncement of Erik Moltke, 'Attempts to explain these names – as elements in a sacred or cultic system, for example – have been doomed to . . . failure . . . We may safely relegate them to the world of fantasy.'[13]

If a rune-name were openly and obviously pagan, of course, we might also assume that the introduction of Christianity would affect it. The Anglo-Saxon names are known only from Christian times, but the *Abecedarium Nordmannicum* recorded the Norse ones when much of Scandinavia was still heathen (though the manuscript it appears in is a Christian and learned one). Here lies the importance of the Norse evidence for us. To take an example: some scholars would assert, fairly plausibly, that ON *þurs*, 'demon, giant', represents the Germanic name of the þ-rune, and that OE *þorn* shows Christian replacement of the superstitious word 'demon' by the harmless 'thorn'. Some would go so far as to suggest that the Anglo-Saxon runic verse is an old *þurs* verse adapted to *þorn*: 'A giant is extremely fierce. Grappling with him is unpleasant for any warrior. They are uncommonly severe to anyone who lives among them.'

There is another more general reason why a name might change, or at any rate shift meaning. It might refer to an object or idea no longer common or current among the people. *Ur* is an example here. The aurochs or wild ox was hardly likely to be an everyday topic of conversation among Anglo-Saxons and Scandinavians, certainly not among the Icelanders of the later Middle Ages: hence in the Norwegian and Icelandic *Runic Poems* the more common concepts 'slag' and 'drizzle' replace 'aurochs'. Though 'aurochs' remains in the English *Runic Poem*, this does not mean that all Anglo-Saxons inter-

---

10 H.Arntz, *Handbuch der Runenkunde*, 2.ed. (Halle/Saale 1944), 188–229; W.Krause, 'Untersuchungen zu den Runennamen I–II', *Nachr. v. d. Akademie d. Wissenschaften in Göttingen* (1946/7), 60–3; (1948), 93–108; Elliott, *Runes, an Introduction*, 45–61: 2.ed., slightly modified, 60–78.
11 L.Musset, *Introduction à la Runologie* (Paris 1965), 136–41.
12 E.C.Polomé, 'The Names of the Runes' in Bammesberger, *Old English Runes*, 421–38.
13 *Runes and their Origin*, 37.

preted the rune-name in that way. How many of them would ever have seen an aurochs? At any rate some of Cynewulf's runic signatures to his poems seem to have the letter 'u' standing for the more common word *ur(e)*, 'our'.[14]

The discussion so far shows something of the uncertainty that surrounds the Anglo-Saxon rune-names. The name forms themselves are fairly well attested, for there is quite a large number of lists of rune-names, and we can cross-check. But we cannot assume that all go back to the earliest runic times in this country, nor can we expect the *Runic Poem* verses to be safe guides to the meanings of the English rune-names at all dates. Some verses retain old names in their original meanings, others may have old names with new meanings, others again new names; and in some cases the writer of the *Runic Poem* may, for all we know, have imposed his own interpretation upon a rare word. With this caution in mind we can now examine the rest of the rune-names.

4. ᚩ, os, The Anglo-Saxon poem calls this 'the origin of all speech, the prop of wisdom and the comfort of the wise, and a joy and consolation to every man.' The Norwegian poem has the name *óss*, its sense clearly 'river-mouth'. The Icelandic poem has *óss* = *áss*, 'heathen god' (though a few later manuscripts confuse this with *óss*, 'river-mouth'). Most scholars accept 'god' as the primary meaning, and it certainly suits the forms of the name in the several languages and may also account for the relationship between Anglo-Frisian 'o' and the Norse a-rune. Some have suggested a semantic restriction to 'the great god', that is Woden or Óðinn, to whom Norse writers attributed skill in speech and poetry. Otherwise they are embarrassed by a list of rune-names which, by their hypothesis, reflects pagan belief but omits the name of the high god. Dickins, arguing that it is unlikely that all human speech would be attributed to a single deity, prefers to take the Anglo-Saxon *Runic Poem*'s *os* as the Latin word for 'mouth', and Halsall (and most editors) agree with him in this.[15] But that, presumably, is a late introduction, not a natural development of a Germanic name.

5. ᚱ, *rad.* 'In the hall *rad* is pleasant for every warrior, and very energetic for the man who sits on the back of a powerful horse covering the mile-long roads', says the English *Runic Poem*. The Norwegian and Icelandic poems have *ræið*, *reið* apparently in the sense 'riding' (glossed in one case by the Latin *equitatio*, in another by *iter*). The English verse may hold this meaning and express a contrast: riding seems comfortable when you are sitting at

---

[14] See below, p.192.
[15] Kemble translated the *Runic Poem*'s *os* as 'mouth' as early as 'On Anglo-Saxon Runes', 340.

home, but turns out to be hard work when you are actually on a journey. Some have discovered another type of antithesis depending on different senses of *rad* in the two parts of the verse. In the first, *rad* may mean the change and variety of tone in the musical instrument (as in the compound *sweglrad*, 'modulation, music'), or perhaps it is related to ON *reiði*, 'equipment', in some sense like 'furnishings'. It is this meaning (or these meanings) that is 'pleasant to all warriors in the hall', whereas *rad* = 'horse-riding' is strenuous. If this interpretation is right the *rad* verse has something of the quality of an Anglo-Saxon riddle, misleading the hearer by dwelling on the diverse meanings the one letter sequence can have.

6. ᚳ, *cen*. This word, not otherwise known in Old English, can be interpreted from its *Runic Poem* context and from occasional use of the rune elsewhere as an ideograph. The *Runic Poem* says, *'Cen* is known to all living beings by its flame, pale and bright. Most often it burns where princes are staying.' From this is deduced a meaning 'torch' which is confirmed by the OHG cognate *chien, chen, ken* glossing Latin *facula* and perhaps meaning specifically 'torch of pine-wood'. The Norwegian and Icelandic poems have *kaun*, 'ulcer, sore', as the name of this rune, while the *Abecedarium Nordmannicum* has a spelling *chaon*, and the 'Gothic' letter-name is *chozma*. The variety of forms in the various languages makes it impossible to determine what was the Germanic name.

7. ᚷ, *gyfu*. There is no **g**-rune (and so no rune-name) in the shorter Norse *futhark*. The 'Gothic' letter-name appears as *geuua*, presumably Ulfilan Gothic *giba*, corresponding to the English rune-name. *Gyfu* has the primary meaning 'gift' but the *Runic Poem* uses it with the genitive plural *gumena* in the sense 'act of giving, generosity'. 'Men's generosity is a grace and an honour, a support and a glory; and a help and sustenance to the outcast who lacks any other.'

8. ᚹ, *wynn*, 'joy', though the *Runic Poem* manuscript apparently recorded a Kentish form *wen*. 'Joyful is the man who knows no miseries, affliction or sorrow, and who has prosperity and happiness and the wealth of great towns.' No Scandinavian name is recorded but the 'Gothic' letter-name *uuinne* sufficiently confirms the Anglo-Saxon. This has not stopped the speculative from suggesting quite different Germanic names for this rune, notably **wulþuz*, 'splendour, the god Ullr', for which there is no evidence whatsoever.

9. ᚻ, *hægl*, 'hail', supported by the *hagall/hagal* of the Scandinavian sources and by the 'Gothic' letter-name *haal*. 'Hail is the whitest of grains. It swirls

from the heights of heaven, and gusts of wind toss it about. Then it turns to water.'

10. ↑, *nyd*. The Norwegian and Icelandic *Runic Poems* have the cognate *nauðr* with the meaning 'constraint'. 'Gothic' has the odd letter-name *nooicz*. OE *nyd* has a range of meanings, 'need, oppression, affliction', and it is the latter which the *Runic Poem* defines. 'Affliction constricts the heart, but it often serves as a help and salvation to the sons of men, if they attend to it in time.'

11. ᛁ, *is*, 'ice', with the cognate *ís* in the Scandinavian sources, and *iiz* in 'Gothic'. 'Ice is very cold, extremely slippery. A floor made by the frost, fair to the sight, it glitters like jewels, clear as glass.'

12. Epigraphical ᛡ and (mainly) manuscript ᚼ, *ger*. (Not all scholars agree on this equivalence: I retain it here for convenience – the arguments on the two sides are too complex to summarise.)[16] The Germanic name of the rune was clearly **jēra-* whence ON *ár* with loss of the initial semivowel and a consequent change in the rune-value from **j** to **a**. ON *ár* (= NE 'year') often has the specialised meaning 'fruitful year' and so 'fertility, abundance', a quality which literature often attributes to the god Freyr. The Norwegian and Icelandic *Runic Poems* record this meaning in identical words, *ár er gumna góðe*, 'a fruitful year is a benefit to men'. The Anglo-Saxon poem has a related definition: 'a year of good harvest is a joy to men, when God, holy king of heaven, makes the earth give forth bright fruits for both men of rank and the needy'. 'Gothic' has a related letter-name *gaar*.

13. ᛇ, *eoh*, though a variant *ih/ih* occurs in some *runica manuscripta*. The Anglo-Saxon *Runic Poem* shows the meaning to be 'yew-tree', a word that elsewhere in Old English appears as *eow, iw*: it is 'a tree with a rough bark, hardy and firm in the earth, supported by its roots, the guardian of flame and a pleasure upon an estate'. The rune does not appear in the later Norse *futharks*, but the Scandinavian rune-masters attached the cognate name *ýr* to the rune which is usually represented as **R** (see under no.15 below). This may confirm that 'yew-tree' was one of the early rune-names though we cannot be sure which rune it belonged to.

14. ᛈ, *peorð*. This word is a mystery. There is an equivalent 'Gothic' letter-name *pertra* but no recorded rune-name from Scandinavia. *Peorð* (or *peord*

---

[16] D.Parsons gives a divergent view in 'Anglo-Saxon Runes in Continental Manuscripts', 200–5.

as it is also written) appears only as the name of an English rune, and its *Runic Poem* verse, as well as being defective in one place, is too general to give much clue as to precise meaning. '*Peorð* is a continual source of amusement and laughter for the great . . . where warriors sit cheerfully together in the beer-hall.' Scholars have been ready enough to suggest meanings, more or less delicate, to fit this vague context but none is convincing beyond reasonable doubt, and the gap in the text, revealed by its defective metre in one line, does not help.

15. Y, *eolhx*, with many variants such as *iolx, ílx, ílcs, ílíx* in *runica manuscripta*. This too is a baffling name. The equivalent rune of the Germanic *futhark* had the value /z/ found principally in inflexional endings. Old English had no need of such a rune, so some English rune-masters used the character as the equivalent of the roman letter <x>. Since this occurred only in texts of a learned nature, the rune is rare in Anglo-Saxon epigraphy usually appearing in Latin surroundings. The early Norse reflex of /z/ was the perhaps palatal liquid which philological texts record as *R*, and this was the sound the Norse equivalent rune ⋏ gave. Its name was *ýr* which is cognate with OE *eoh, íh*, 'yew-tree', and is defined in the Norwegian *Runic Poem* as 'the greenest of trees throughout the winter' and in the Icelandic poem as 'a bent bow' since bows were made of yew wood. If, as is likely, the Scandinavian rune-masters took over the name of the thirteenth rune for their ⋏, OE *eolhx* may be our only clue to the Germanic name of the fifteenth rune. Again the meaning is a problem. The *Runic Poem* which needs emendation at this point defines, not *eolhx*, but a compound *eolhxsecg*, some form of sedge-grass which 'usually lives in the fen, growing in the water. It wounds severely, staining with blood any man who makes a grab at it.' Elsewhere the same compound occurs glossing *papiluus* (?= *papyrus*). Possibly the rune-name was originally *eolh* to which was added the new value of the rune, *x*. *Eolh* means 'elk', and scholars have been quick to note that the second part of the *Runic Poem* verse could properly be applied to that animal. Some have found a rune-name 'elk' insufficiently profound, preferring to link the form with Gmc **algiz*, 'protection', with Gothic *alhs*, 'sanctuary' or with the brother gods whom Tacitus says the Naharvali worshipped under the title *alcis*.[17]

16. N, *sigel*, 'sun', with the parallel *sol* for the Scandinavian rune-name, and the dubious form *sugil* for the 'Gothic' letter-name. 'The sun is a continual

[17] *Germania*, xliii.

joy to seamen, when they take a sea-steed over the fish's bath until it brings them to land.'

17. ↑, *tir*. The Scandinavian rune is named after *Týr*, properly described in both Norwegian and Icelandic *Runic Poems* as 'the one-handed god'; the Icelandic version develops this by calling him 'the wolf's left-overs' (since it was the wolf Fenrir who bit off Týr's hand and left the rest of him).[18] The Old English equivalent of this god-name is *Tiw/Tig*, but for the rune-name the various Anglo-Saxon manuscripts have *tir, tyr* and *ti*. There is little doubt that the Germanic rune-name was that of the god, and it looks as though the Old English form was affected by the Norse, perhaps influenced too by OE *tir*, 'glory'. However, the meaning of the Anglo-Saxon name, if the *Runic Poem* is to be believed, is far from 'one-handed god'. '*Tir* is one of the guiding marks (*tacn*). It keeps its faith well towards princes. Above nights' clouds it is always on its path and never fails.' This is taken to be a guiding star or constellation perhaps named after the god.

18. ᛒ, *beorc*, 'birch-tree'. The 'Gothic' name is *bercna*, which reminds one of the Scandinavian rune-name *bjarkan*, 'birch-twig'. This the Norwegian *Runic Poem* defines as 'the bough with the greenest leaves'. The parallel Icelandic verse reveals a very confused tradition, but among its definitions are 'little tree', 'blossoming tree', 'little sprig', 'leafy wood', 'little branch', 'glorious wood'. There is an arboricultural difficulty about the English rune-name. The *Runic Poem* reads: '*Beorc* has no fruit (?flowers), yet without seeds it produces shoots. It is glorious in its branches, tall in its crown, beautifully adorned, spreading its leaves high, reaching to the sky.' Not all details are clear, but the text clearly describes a tree grown from root suckers rather than seed, and this cannot be a birch. Dickins therefore suggests 'poplar', *populus*, which *beorc* occasionally glosses, but it is curious that this verse, in defining the rune-name, should diverge from a meaning 'birch' which seems to have been far commoner. Botanical identification in Old English is notoriously difficult (incidentally the early sixteenth-century manuscript of the Icelandic poem has the added gloss *abies*, 'fir-tree', though an eighteenth-century version has *betula)*. But this English verse displays clear knowledge which we cannot ignore. Perhaps it is a learned revision of an earlier 'birch' stanza.

19. ᛖ, *eh*, 'horse'. There is no recorded Scandinavian name, and the 'Gothic' letter-name is *eyz*. 'The horse, the charger proud in its hoofs, is a prince's

---

[18] As told in Snorri Sturluson's *Prose Edda; Gylfaginning*, ed. A.Faulkes (Oxford 1982), 25, 27–9.

delight in the presence of fighting-men, when rich men on horseback discuss its points. For the restless it is always a means of relaxation.'

20. ᛗ, *man*, 'man, human being', supported by the Scandinavian *maðr* and by the 'Gothic' letter-name *manna*. 'In his mirth man is dear to his kinsman. Yet each is bound to fail his fellow because the Lord, by his decree, wishes to commit the wretched body to the earth.'

21. ᛚ, *lagu*, 'water'. The Norwegian and Icelandic *Runic Poems* have the confirmatory *lǫgr*, defined as 'a force tumbling from the mountain-side' and 'a swelling stream and great cauldron (*ketill*) and fishes' field'. The 'Gothic' letter-name is *laaz* which scholars have derived from Ulfilan Gothic **lagus*. Despite this agreement Krause would have us believe that the Germanic rune-name was **laukaz (= ON laukr)*, 'leek, herb'.[19] Most Scandinavian *runica manuscripta* confirm *lǫgr*, but a few early examples of the name form certainly resemble *laukr*. Arguing from the position that the rune-names reflected significant aspects of paganism, Krause points to the connection in Old Norse literature between the word *laukr* and pagan, particularly phallic, practices, and to the frequent occurrence of the word, apparently with mystical significance, in early Scandinavian runic inscriptions; together with the appearance of the l-rune in contexts where it may well be an abbreviation of *laukr*. OE *lagu*, ON *lǫgr* are then Christian replacements, necessitated by the strongly pagan connotations of **laukaz*. This case Krause argues with cogency and a good range of evidence, but whether you accept it or not depends on how closely you think that runes were connected with the old religion – Halsall regards Krause's proposal as 'unlikely'. There is at any rate no evidence that in English tradition the rune-name was anything other than *lagu*, 'water'. The Anglo-Saxon *Runic Poem* defines it: 'Water seems interminable to men if they have to venture on the rolling ship, and the sea-waves scare them out of their wits, and the surf-horse does not respond to its bridle.'

22. ᛜ, *Ing*, 'the hero Ing'. The Scandinavian name is unrecorded: the 'Gothic' letter-name is *enguz*. 'Ing was first seen by men among the East Danes until he travelled east (reading *est* which some scholars amend to *eft*, 'back') across the wave. His chariot followed on. This is what the Heardings (or perhaps 'the warriors') called the hero.' A hero Ing is unknown to Anglo-Saxon tradition but his name forms the first element of *Ingwine*, 'friends of Ing', as *Beowulf* sometimes calls the Danes. The Ingwine are surely the

---

[19] 'Untersuchungen zu den Runennamen I'.

Ingaevones (?for Inguaeones) whom Tacitus singles out as the Germanic tribal group living nearest the sea. Elsewhere Tacitus mentions an island people who cultivated a goddess Nerthus who had a sacred car or chariot in which she progressed among her devotees.[20] *Nerthus* is etymologically identical with the name of the Norse Njǫrðr, a deity of wealth and fertility who was the father of the more famous god of riches, peace and fruitful seasons, Freyr. In a later Norse tradition Freyr progressed through the land in a car, and the thirteenth-century Icelandic historian, Snorri Sturluson, noted that he had the second name *Yngvi* and that his descendants were Ynglingar. The Eddic poem *Lokasenna* records the name *Ingunar-Freyr* for him. These various facts link circumstantially to suggest that Ing was a Germanic fertility god whose cult involved a cart or chariot, the *Runic Poem* demoting him to a hero.[21]

The *Runic Poem* continues with the verses for *eþel* and *dæg*, but I list them in the more common reverse order.

23. ᛗ, *dæg*, 'day'. The Scandinavian name is unknown. 'Gothic' has the letter-name *daaz* which bears the same relationship to *dæg* as *laaz* has to *lagu* and *haal* to *hægl*. 'The day, dear to men, is the Lord's gift (*sond*, perhaps 'messenger'), the Creator's glorious light. It is a joy and solace to rich and poor, and useful to everyone.'

24. ᛟ, *eþel*, 'land, ancestral home, landed property'. Elsewhere the name appears with rounded initial vowel, as *oeþil*, *oeþel*. The Scandinavian name is unrecorded. 'Gothic' has a letter-name *utal*. 'The ancestral home is dear to every man, if in his house there he can enjoy what is right and decent in continual prosperity.'

The last five verses define a group of rune-names, most of which are of later creation.

25. ᚪ, *ac*, 'oak-tree'. The verse divides, riddle-like, into two sections, the first defining the tree, though allusively (by way of the acorn) rather than directly, the second an oak-timbered ship. 'On land the oak feeds (the pig) for meat for the sons of men. It often journeys over the gannet's bath. The ocean tests whether the oak keeps faith honourably.'

---

[20] *Germania*, xl.
[21] E.O.G.Turville-Petre expounds the range of references to Ing in *Myth and Religion of the North: the Religion of Ancient Scandinavia* (London 1964), 170–1.

26. ᚫ, *æsc*, 'ash-tree'. 'The ash, precious to men, is very tall. Firm on its base it keeps its place securely though many men attack it.'

27. ᚣ, *yr*. As the new rune 'y' represented, both in form and value, *u . . . i*, so the name probably originated as an *i*-mutated form of *ur*. Its meaning is elusive, and the *Runic Poem* definition does little to help. '*Yr* is a piece of battle-gear. It is a pleasure and an adornment to all princes and fighting-men, fine on a horse and firm on a journey.' On the basis of this slender and unhelpful description scholars have suggested meanings like 'horn', 'saddle' and 'saddle-bow', while Dickins noted the form *æxe yr(e)* in the *Anglo-Saxon Chronicle (E)* for 1012, where it seems to mean 'hammer of an axe'. The most tempting interpretation (though it fits the verse only indifferently) is 'bow', for this links the word to a Scandinavian name for the final rune of the *futhąrk*, *ýr*, which the Icelandic *Runic Poem* glosses, though fitfully, 'bent bow'.

At this point in the series the *Runic Poem* interposes the letter ᛡ which coincides with the epigraphical form of 'j'. The *Runic Poem* gives its name as *iar* though other manuscripts have a form *ior* and a value *io*. The verse defines *iar* as 'a river-fish (amending Hickes's genitive plural *ea fixa* to *eafix*; Halsall retains the reading, though as a compound noun with adjectival value here: *eafixa*, 'of or belonging to the riverfish'), yet it always takes its food on land. It has a fine dwelling-place surrounded by water where it lives in happiness.' The word is not otherwise known and no satisfactory etymology is supplied for it. But the verse, if rightly amended here, suggests a meaning 'eel', perhaps 'newt' or even 'beaver'. Schwab and, following her, Looijenga put forward the alternative that here *iar/ior* = 'boat', which takes its cargo from the land while dwelling on the water. They point to ON *jór*, 'horse', in verse kennings for 'ship'.[22] There is no shortage of interpretations here. Some think that the formal resemblance between this graph and epigraphical 'j' makes it unlikely that the similarity in names, *iar/ior* and *ger*, is coincidental; but what the link is between *iar/ior* and its verse definition or why it was thought necessary to provide a rune for the diphthong *io*, I do not know.

---

22 U.Schwab, *Die Sternrune im Wessobrunner Gebet*. Amsterdamer Publikationen zur Sprache und Literatur I (1973), 69; T.Looijenga, 'Runes around the North Sea and on the Continent AD 150–700; Texts and Contexts'. Doctoral Dissertation, Groningen 1997, 77. Even an interpretation 'hippopotamus' has been suggested for this rune-name.

28. ᛡ, *ear.* Its final verse gives the *Runic Poem* a dying fall. '*Ear* is hateful to every man, when the flesh, the pallid body, begins inexorably to grow cold, to choose the earth as its consort. Prosperity fades, joys pass away, covenants lapse.' The meaning is clearly linked with the idea of 'death', and elsewhere I have argued in detail that *ear* in this verse must mean 'earth' and hence 'grave', cognate with ON *aurr*, 'wet clay', *eyrr*, 'gravelly bank near water', and Gothic **aurahjons*, 'tomb'.[23]

Outside the Anglo-Saxon *Runic Poem* four rune-names are recorded. Two can be dismissed fairly readily, for they are the names of manuscript runes which have not yet appeared in epigraphical contexts: *stan*, 'stone', for 'st', and *cweorþ* for 'q'. The latter is a word of unknown meaning, probably formed as a rhyme for *peorð* which would immediately precede it in a runic ABC. Neither of these is part of the runic tradition proper. Two names are given for new epigraphical runes of the north and north-west, ᚷ, 'ḡ', is called *gar*, 'spear'; ᛣ, 'k', is *calc* which I take to be a Northumbrian form of OE *cealc*, 'chalk', though others have preferred to identify it with OE *calic*, 'cup, goblet', or *calc*, 'slipper, sandal'. These are learned loan-words, and the rune may be an invention of a learned rune-master.

There are sixteen cases where we can compare English and Scandinavian rune-names. In eleven the names in the two tongues agree adequately in form and meaning, and for two names *os/óss* and *eoh/ýr*, there is a less clear correspondence. One, *ur*, compares satisfactorily in form but not in meaning. Only two runes, *þorn/þurs* and *cen/kaun*, have distinct names in the two languages. It is usual and reasonable to assume that, where the Scandinavian name confirms the English one, the two represent Common Germanic, though Krause's taut argument asserting that the Germanic l-rune was called **laukaz* (contrasting with OE *lagu*, ON *lǫgr*) shows up the flimsiness of the assumption. In general (and despite the late date from which our records of the rune-names derive) it seems likely that most of the sixteen names we can check go back to Germanic ones, and the same probably applies to the names we cannot check. It seems therefore that some twenty rune-names represent aspects of early Germanic life important enough to be kept in mind when letters were named.

This point has excited some runologists who see here a chance to gain entry to an otherwise unrecorded area of Germanic culture. In particular it has tempted amateurs of Germanic paganism who have thought to find some clue to the nature of that religion. It is easy to see why. The rune-names

---

[23] Page, 'The Old English Rune *ear*'.

include two names of gods, *Tiw* (*tir*) and *Ing*; the general word for god, *os*, perhaps used here in the sense of 'the great god Woden'; and the general word for 'demon' if *þurs* gives the Germanic name of the þ-rune. For some investigators *man* refers to the god *Mannus* whom Tacitus mentions among the Germani, and some think that *rad* could be translated 'cart, chariot', and so refer to a cult-waggon of some sort. *Ger*, 'good season, prosperity', may be linked to the god Freyr and to the divine kings of early Germania who were responsible for their peoples' harvests, and, more speculatively, *feoh*, 'wealth', to the rich god Njǫrðr. Speculating in a different way, some connect the animal names *eolh*, *ur* and *eh* with theriomorphic gods the Germanic peoples may have cultivated, and *eoh* and *beorc* with trees they treated as sacred. Among natural phenomena important in early cult are *lagu*, 'water', and *sigel*, 'sun', and its accompanying *dæg*, 'day'. Contrasting with them are destructive forces like hail, *hægl*, and ice, *is*, the two perhaps linked to the idea of constriction and oppression expressed in the neighbouring rune *nyd*. Enclosing the twenty-four-letter rune-row are the two important concepts of *feoh*, 'wealth won or earned', and *eþel*, 'inherited property'.

How far we pursue this idea depends on how imaginative or how sceptical our minds are. There is no reason to reject out of hand some picture of Germanic belief such as the *futhark* presents, but every reason to doubt the extreme efforts of some runologists to read mystic significance in every rune-name. The words *hægl* and *is* are simply weather words but some would extend their sense to 'malicious and destructive forces' and assert they have such meaning in magical runic texts. *Gyfu* means 'gift' but Krause understands it as 'religious offering'. Arntz claims that the meaning of *ur* developed from the fierce and powerful animal to that of 'ferocious strength'. Such extensions of sense were not in the mind of the compiler of the *Runic Poem* who seems to have been a simple and literal-minded man, but we must always keep in mind the possibility that, at some dates and under some circumstances, rune-masters may have understood the rune-names in different and wider senses from those recorded in the poem.

Even in later Anglo-Saxon times rune and rune-name could remain intimately linked, with the effect that a rune could be used to represent the word that supplied its name. The clearest evidence for this is in manuscripts where, for example, ᛟ, ᛗ, ᛞ occur as convenient abbreviations or representations of *eþel*, *man* and *dæg*. To take examples: ll.520–1 of *Beowulf* on fo.141v of British Library MS Cotton Vitellius A.xv, have *ðonon he gesohte | swæsne · ᛟ ·*, 'thence he sought his native land'; 1.23 of *The Ruin* on fo.124r of the Exeter Book is *meodoheall monig · ᛗ · dreama full*, 'many a meadhall full of human delights'. ᛗ and ᛞ are quite common for *man* and *dæg* in the glosses to the Durham Ritual and the Lindisfarne Gospels, sometimes even being

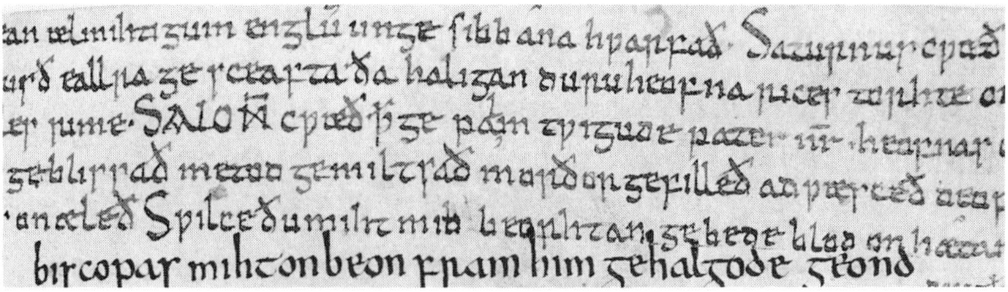

Fig.18. The abbreviated name of *Solomon* in the Corpus Christi College,
Cambridge MS 41 text of *Solomon and Saturn I*.

given inflexional endings, as ᛜ *ges* (= g. sg. *dæges*) and · ᛗ · *no* (= acc.sg.
monno). In the Corpus Christi College, Cambridge, MS 41 text of *Solomon
and Saturn I* the name of the first character is sometimes given as *SALO* ᛗ
(fig.18). Only a few of the individual runic graphs have so far been recorded
as used in this way; but, as I indicate in chapter 14, this is a field that calls for
further study.

If a rune can express its name-word in a manuscript text there is no reason
why it should not do it too in an epigraphical one. This is hard to demonstrate
conclusively from English material but there are certainly inscriptions from
Scandinavia, and probably from Continental Germania too, where runes are
used as ideographs/*Begriffsrunen/begrepsruner* or *symbolruner*. For instance,
a massive gold neck-ring found at Pietroassa (Rumania) along with a great
treasure in gold and gems, has the inscription **gutaniowihailag**. Parts of this
text are immediately clear: **gutani** must be some form of the tribal name
'Goths', and **hailag** an early Continental Germanic equivalent of OE *halig*
meaning 'holy, inviolable'. The central section is difficult but it is now commonly thought that the **o**-rune is a symbol for **oþala* (related to OE *oeþil,
eþel*, 'hereditary possession'). The whole text then divides and becomes
Gutanī ō(þal) wī(h) hailag, 'hereditary treasure of the Goths, holy and sacro-
sanct'.[24] A Scandinavian instance is on the stone of Stentoften, Blekinge
(Sweden). This has a group of related inscriptions, part magical. One section
runs **hAþuwolAfʀgAfj**, obviously beginning with the personal name *Haþu-
wulfaʀ*, ON *Hálfr*. The sequence **gAf** is the verbal form, 'gave', and **j** must
then provide the object of the sentence. Scandinavian runologists take it as
PrON **jāra*, ON *ár*, 'year', in the sense of 'fertile year, fertility'.[25] The sentence then records Hálfr's skill at bringing fruitfulness, prosperity and wealth
to men. An English epigraphical example is the coin legend wBERHT,

[24] Krause and Jankuhn, *Die Runeninschriften im älteren Futhark*, 91–5.
[25] Moltke, *Runes and their Origin*, 103.

recording the name *Wynberht* for a moneyer of Alfred and Edward the Elder, but here the inspiration was probably from manuscript texts since epigraphical runes hardly exist in Wessex. Old English runic inscriptions proper contain no examples of *Begriffsrunen* as convincing as the Continental ones I have mentioned, but I suggest a few possibilities in chapter 7 below.

6

The Divided *Futhorc* and Runic Codes

The only complete epigraphical *futhorc* we possess is that of the tenth-century Thames scramasax. This weapon, which was recovered from the river Thames near Battersea in the nineteenth century, is a one-edged sword some 72 cm (28.5 inches) long. Its blade is elegantly decorated with line patterns, the personal name *Beagnoþ* in runes, and the twenty-eight letters of a *futhorc*. The smith who adorned the blade had a difficult task, for he had to cut matrices in it for his lines and letters and then fill them with contrasting metals: silver, copper and bronze. To the difficulty of inlaying we may ascribe the curious or careless forms some of his letters took, notably 'd' and 'œ'. But he was also an indifferent runic scholar and he made mistakes, probably in a couple of the strange graphs, certainly in his omission of 's' (which had to be squeezed in later) and in the order he gave to the later letters of his *futhorc*. He cut 'f u þ o r c g w h n i j ï p x (s) t b e ŋ d l m œ a æ y ea', an order which is in the main orthodox, but in the sequence 'ŋ d l m œ' is not paralleled elsewhere (fig.19).[1]

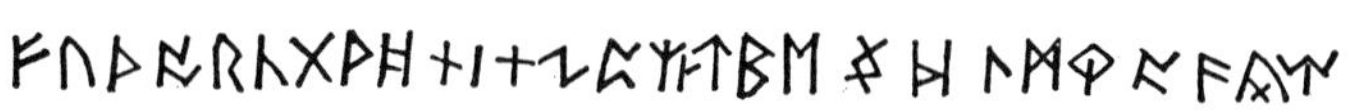

ᚠᚢᚦᚨᚱᚲᚷᚹᚺᛁᛄᛇᛈᛉᛏᛒᛖᛜᛞᛚᛗ ᛟ ᚺ ᛗᛗᚩ ᚱ ᚠᚪᛁᛁ

Fig.19. The Thames scramasax *futhorc*. (1:2)

A second epigraphical example, part of the *futhorc* only, appears on the rounded head of a pin, of a type usually found in pairs, from a Middle Saxon context at Brandon, Suffolk. It records the first sixteen letters (a number

[1] V.I.Evison, reviewing my publication of the scramasax *futhorc*, gives a detailed archaeological account of these runes (*Antiquaries Jnl* 45 (1965), 288). Her comment, that I had looked carelessly at the inscription's lay-out and so fallen into error of interpretation, is a proper warning to the philologist to take note of the archaeological aspects of runic material.

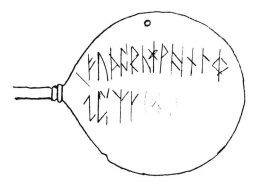

Fig.20. The part-*futhorc* of the Brandon pin-head. (4:3)

which may be significant): 'f u þ o r c j w h n i j̄ | i̇ p x s' followed by some scratches which are unlikely to be the rest of the *futhorc* (fig.20). Here the letter order is orthodox enough, but putting 'j', ✳, rather than 'g' in seventh place and ⸙, 'j̄' (the common manuscript variant of 'j') in twelfth is idiosyncratic.

In Scandinavia and the Continent, in contrast to England, epigraphical *futharks* are fairly frequent. Their general agreement shows there was a fixed order for runes to be put in. It was **fuþarkgwhnijïpzstbemlŋdo**, with perhaps **od** as an acceptable alternative arrangement of the last two. It seems that this letter order goes back to early runic days. At any rate the Anglo-Saxon one derived from it, but with the necessary differences the peculiar English (or 'Anglo-Frisian') developments required. For the Anglo-Saxon order the evidence is not the suspect Thames scramasax or the incomplete Brandon pin but the number of early *futhorcs* drawn in Anglo-Saxon manuscripts or in Continental manuscripts of Anglo-Saxon inspiration. These confirm that the first twenty-four runes were:

'f u þ o r c g w h n i j i̇ p x s t b e m l ŋ d œ'
    5   10   15   20   24

also with the possibility of a reversal of the last two letters. The order of the additional runes is less clear, and is bedevilled by the fact that manuscript *futhorcs* admit also the pseudo-runes 'io', 'q', and 'st'. Nos 25–8 are nearly always 'a æ y ea' which may represent an early expansion to a twenty-eight letter rune-row, but more probably shows that these were the only additional runes known generally in England. Thereafter occur a variety of arrangements and types for rune 29 and after: 'io q k st ḡ'. 'k q io st ḡ', 'ḡ q st k', and so on. Clearly at this point we can deduce no certain order, nor do we know where the epigraphical rune 'k̄' fitted in to the *futhorc*.

From quite an early date Scandinavian rune-masters divided their *futharks* into three groups of eight letters each. Seventeenth-century Icelandic runic scholars called these groups *ættir* which coincides with the Icelandic word meaning 'families', though as used in runic studies etymologists prefer to connect it with the word *átta*, 'eight', and so to translate it 'groups of eight'. The earliest examples yet found of this division are on two bracteates, dating 450–550, from southern Sweden. The Vadstena, Östergötland, example (which has a duplicate struck from the same die, found at nearby Motala) has the groups cut off from one another by pairs of points in vertical line: the Grumpan, Västergötland, bracteate marks off the divisions by rows of dots. The Scandinavians continued to divide their rune-row into *ættir* even in later times when it had been reduced from twenty-four to sixteen characters, and when the *ættir* held six, five and five runes respectively.

In contrast, the Thames scramasax *futhorc* is undivided, and so are those drawn in most of the Anglo-Saxon manuscripts that describe runes. The Brandon pin holds the first two *ættir*, undivided but separated from the third *ætt* if indeed that was on the lost matching pin. The scribe who drew the *futhorc* contained in British Library MS Cotton Domitian ix put a single point between individual letters, but two in vertical line before 'h' and three before 't', showing that he too recognised the *ættir*.[2]

At some unknown date rune-masters developed a cryptographical system based on a *futhark* of fixed letter order, split up into three groups of eight. In such an arrangement each rune can be represented by two figures. The first will give the number of the group where the letter occurs, the second its position within the group. So, the *ætt* beginning 'f' can be numbered 1, that beginning 'h' 2, and the one beginning 't' 3. 'c', the sixth letter of the first *ætt*, can be given as 1/6: 'i', the third letter of the 'h' *ætt*, would be 2/3: 't', the first letter of the third group, is 3/1, and so on.

A Latin runological treatise preserved in five latish manuscripts (the earliest is from the ninth century) shows this code system applied to the *futhorc*.[3] This treatise is usually known as the *isruna* tract, named after one of the methods of representing the two significant figures each rune needs. It assumes a division of the *futhorc* into *ættir*, though they are called here *versus* or *ordines*; and it describes several ways in which the group number and rune number can be drawn. The first is called the *isruna* method, from the word *is*, 'ice', the name of the rune 'i'. It uses small forms of 'i' to give the group number, and big ones for the rune number. Thus 'c', the sixth letter of the first group, is ⏐⏐⏐⏐⏐. Similar is the *lagoruna* method, which uses in the same

2   Derolez, *Runica Manuscripta*, 10.
3   Derolez, *Runica Manuscripta*, 89–137.

way forms of the rune 'l' whose name is *lagu*. Thus 'c' is ⌐↑↑↑↑↑. A related system of *stopfruna* employs dots set in horizontal line: thus 'i', the third rune of the second group is ∷. or ∴. The *hahalruna* system represents each rune by a vertical stem, with arms to its left giving the group figure and arms to the right the rune figure: 'i' is ↑.

Though this cryptographical system is obviously a secondary development, something of an antiquary's toy, yet rune-masters did sometimes use it for their inscriptions. It was in Scandinavia that the method of encoding runes reached its greatest elaboration, applied to the later, sixteen-letter rune-row whose *ættir* are conventionally given as **fuþąrk:hnias: tbmlʀ**. To mystify further Scandinavian rune-carvers reversed the natural numbering of the groups, calling the **f**-*ætt* 3 and the **t**-*ætt* 1. They developed many ingenious and sometimes absurd ways of indicating the two numbers that identify each rune. Some are closely related to the *hahalruna* system, giving each rune by the number of twigs, or semicircles, or short dashes on each side of a vertical stem. Others are more picturesque. The earliest manuscript of the Icelandic *Runic Poem*, AM 687d 4° in the Stofnun Árna Magnússonar, Reykjavík, has, drawn in to follow the text of the poem, a series of cryptic rune types, often with their technical names: there are *fiskrúnar*, 'fish-runes' where the twigs are fins on either side of a fish: *svínrúnar*, 'pig-runes', with bristles on either side of a pig's body; *skialdrúnar* where the twigs decorate shields; *skiprúnar* where they decorate stem and stern of a ship; *knífrúnar* on the blades and hafts of knives and so on.

Code runes based on this principle are not purely antiquarian inventions. They occur in Scandinavian inscriptions. So, a rune-carver might incise, for each rune, a crude human figure with outstretched arms, specifying his letter by the number of vertical lines hanging beneath each arm. Or he might cut a series of male heads with forked beards, the number of hairs on each side of the fork giving the rune value (fig.21). There may indeed have been a certain amount of oneupmanship in being able to write in such a secret way. In one of the mediaeval Norwegian inscriptions cut in the prehistoric burial mound at Maeshowe, Orkney, the carver boasted that his inscription was cut by the man who knew most about runes west across the ocean: for the phrase 'these runes', **þisar runar**, he used cryptic forms.[4]

Only one English rune-stone uses this general code system, that of Hackness. It is a badly damaged piece. Two stone fragments now remain, apparently bits of the same large standing cross or pillar from the eighth or ninth century, and carved in high relief with scrollwork, interlace, and probably

---

4 M.P.Barnes, *The Runic Inscriptions of Maeshowe, Orkney*. Runrön 8 (Uppsala 1994), no. 20.

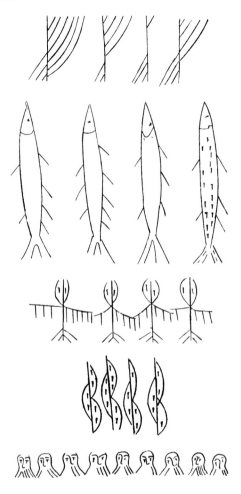

Fig.21. Norse cryptic rune types from Bergen.

human figures on a large scale. One local tradition says they were found in the pond nearby, though the earliest find-report puts them in the outbuildings of Hackness Hall. Whatever the truth, they are severely weathered, with much of the stone surface worn clear away so that many of the incised letters are unidentifiable. There are two Latin inscriptions in roman capitals, readable in part and referring to one Oedilburga in words which suggest she was abbess of the monastery of *Hacanos* which Bede tells of.[5] The runic section consists of two lines of ordinary runes, partly identifiable but not making any

---

5   *Historia Ecclesiastica*, iv.23. For the reconstruction of these damaged texts see P.Grosjean, 'L'inscription latine de Hackness', *Analecta Bollandiana* 79 (1961),

Fig.22. The cryptic runes of the Hackness stone.

obvious sense, followed by three and a half lines of *hahal*-runes and then
three roman capitals, perhaps ORA finishing the inscription (fig.22). The
stone breaks away at the bottom, taking with it the bases of all letters on the
final line, and the *hahal*-runes are very badly worn and may have been cut
shallower than the ordinary characters that begin the text. This makes things
hard for the investigator. If part of an ordinary rune is lost the original graph
can often be identified from what remains. The forms of *hahal*-runes are so

340–3. Defined most recently in J.Lang, *York and Eastern Yorkshire*. CASS 3
(British Academy 1991), under Hackness.

alike that conjectural identification of this sort is impossible. Despite recent claims that the enigma has been solved by computer technology, we must at present admit the Hackness graphs are unreadable, being satisfied merely with accepting them as *hahal*-runes similar to those defined in the *isruna* tract. From what remains it looks as though they are based on a *futhorc* of four *ættir*, the third having at least nine letters. This suggests a late, thirty-three-letter manuscript type, perhaps with rearrangement of the *ættir*.

Some scholars have seen a Celtic basis to the cryptographic system of the *isruna* tracts. They relate it to the early Celtic script called ogam, which also has an alphabet of fixed letter order subdivided into smaller letter groups within which each letter is defined by number. Late manuscripts, notably those of a treatise commonly known as *Auraicept na nÉces*, 'The scholars' primer', describe elaborate cryptic systems based on ogam and similar to these runic ones. And it is perhaps significant that one of the Hackness stone fragments bears an unread text in a cryptic script which looks something like ogam though it clearly is not.[6] As a whole the Hackness monument, with its Latin and its codes, looks as though it was made for a closed community with esoteric and presumably learned scripts of its own, and the *hahal*-runcs fit comfortably into this picture.

There is only one other Anglo-Saxon artefact which certainly uses code runes, though of a different sort from these described so far. This is the Auzon or Franks casket. The top and three sides of this box have inscriptions in the common rune forms with some roman characters as well. But on the right side is a cryptic text, not yet adequately read, surrounding and describing a group of carved scenes, not yet adequately identified despite numerous efforts. The consonant runes of this text show the usual types, but the carver replaced most of the vowel runes by arbitrary forms whose derivation can be conjectured and whose values deduced from the contexts.

In encoding only the vowels of his text the Auzon rune-master followed a fairly common practice of Anglo-Saxon manuscripts, for quite a number of written works use simple substitution codes for the vowels. In the glosses in Boulogne-sur-Mer MS 189, for instance, a vowel is sometimes replaced by the consonant following it in the alphabet, so that *lusaþ*, 'goes astray', becomes *lxsbþ*, and *tigle*, 'tile, sherd', appears as *tkglf*;[7] while in Corpus Christi College, Cambridge, MS 178 the personal name *Coleman* is written

---

6   G.Calder, *Auraicept na n-Éces: the Scholars' Primer* (Edinburgh 1917), 288. The Hackness cryptic runes are illustrated in Lang, *York and Eastern Yorkshire*, pl.457.

7   H.D.Meritt, *The Old English Prudentius Glosses at Boulogne-sur-Mer* (Stanford 1959), nos.192, 243. There are several other examples of this code system in the Boulogne glosses, and it is occasional elsewhere in Anglo-Saxon glosses.

cplfmbn. St John's College, Oxford, MS 17 lists a series of cryptograms, including substitutions which depend on the vowel's position within either the alphabet or the rune-row: so, a vowel is replaced by the Roman number which records its alphabetical position (a = I, e = V, i = IX, o = XIIII, u = XX), or by a number of Gs giving its position within the vowel-row (a = G, e = GG, i = GGG, etc.). A vowel may take the place of the one before it in the vowel-row, so that the Latin *miles in arma fremit* becomes *molis on erme frimot*. Quite common in manuscripts are the *notae Bonifatii* in which points or dots appear instead of vowels (a = ·, e = :, i = :· etc).[8]

In principle the use of cryptic vowel runes on the Auzon casket is the same as all these. The forms its carver cut in place of the usual rune types are ᚷ for 'e', ᛡ for 'o', and ᛋ, ᛈ and minor variants of these for 'i'. Two other symbols, ᚻ and ᛇ occur, and these must represent 'a' and 'æ', but it is not clear which is which or even if the carver distinguished competently between the two. Christopher Ball has ingeniously suggested that what the rune-carver did was take the name of each vowel rune and use the last letter of its rune-name as a basis of his vowel form. So, representing 'o' (*os*) is a graph derived from 's'; for 'i' (*is*) a derivation from a variant 's'; 'a' (*ac*) and 'æ' (*æsc*) take their forms from variant *c*-runes. Only 'e' (*eh*) presents difficulty, and here Ball has to assume a derivation from 'g', which requires an unorthodox spelling of the rune-name.[9]

Why the Auzon casket carver chose to put this text, and no other, in code I do not know. With the Anglo-Saxon manuscript code texts there is often a clear requirement of secrecy or at least furtiveness – they are vernacular glosses or cribs on Latin words which the master may well have wanted to conceal from his pupils – and the Auzon rune-master may also have had something to hide. The cryptic inscription, as far as we can understand it, describes the mysterious scenes carved on its side of the casket. They are still, in my opinion, unidentified, but seem to refer to an early, apparently pagan, story.[10] Indeed, one of the figures may be a pagan deity or priest.

---

8   On these codes W.Levison, *England and the Continent in the Eighth Century* (Oxford 1946), 290–4; J.M.Clark, *The Abbey of St Gall as a Centre of Literature and Art* (Cambridge 1926), 107–8.
9   C.J.E.Ball, 'The Franks Casket: Right Side – Again', *English Studies* 55 (1974), 512.
10 However, the most recent attempt at identification, L.Peeters, 'The Franks Casket: a Judeo-Christian Interpretation', *Amsterdamer Beiträge zur älteren Germanistik* 46 (1996), 17–52, particularly 18–34, links the carving to the biblical *Book of Daniel*.

Perhaps the pagan element of the tale was too obtrusive (or offensive to some believers) to be openly referred to on a box which may have had Christian use and which certainly used Christian and learned material in its decorative scheme.

7

Runic or Rune-like

Even a cursory glance at the *futhorc* will show that its letter forms are not exclusively or diagnostically runic. In a few cases – 'r' and R, 'i' and I, 'b' and B, 'g' and X, 'e' and M – runic and roman character coincide (more or less), which could be embarrassing in interpreting mixed runic and roman inscriptions. In a coin legend which is otherwise in roman characters, an inverted L may look like 'l', or an overcut M may approach to 'm'. Potentially more troublesome, however, are confusions that arise from the simple shapes of some runes and the decorative shapes of others. Some runic graphs are so elementary that accidental scratches or cuts may resemble them, as in the cases of k, X, †, I, ґ, ſ. Since runes themselves are often carelessly or casually scratched they sometimes look like chance surface marks. An effect of these similarities is that in the past archaeologists, antiquaries and amateurs have spotted runes where we would now find plough-marks on stones once buried, weathering cracks on stones in the open air or cleaning scratches on metal objects dug from the earth. Or they may have been identified on an object which shows marks of use that look like runes, as do some spinning whorls. Or where the crude casting of a lead object produces the effect of rough graphs. Or where a die-cutter's attempt at copying a coin legend for a new die is less than successful. Or where we may suspect some idle or pretentious Anglo-Saxon of wasting his and our time in meaningless scribbling. Most runic scholars will have been presented with bits of metal, stone or wood with marks on them, and asked whether they are runes. Unfortunately we cannot always be sure whether they are or not.

A clear case in point is a cremation urn from Lackford (Suffolk). Roughly marked in its surface before firing is a group of lines too irregular to be decorative, yet certainly man-made. At the beginning is something like 'g', then perhaps though doubtfully 'a', after which the lines flow into an apparently meaningless squiggle (fig.23). Runes are indeed occasionally found on cremation urns as we shall shortly see, so these could be an attempt at a runic text, or an attempt at giving the appearance of a runic text. But they could

Fig.23. Marks on
the Lackford urn.

also be accidental lines made in the clay surface during the preparation for firing. I doubt if we shall ever be sure. The hanging bowl found at Cleatham presents a different type of problem. It has a group of scratches running more or less parallel with one edge. By ignoring some of them (as being 'intrusive') the rest can be made to say 'e d i h' with perhaps a couple of letters before them.[1] But how justified are we in ignoring 'intrusive' lines?

Some runes have elegant, sometimes symmetrical, shapes such as form the bases of incised geometric patterns: ∧, ✕, ᚺ, ✶, ᚻ, ↑, ✕, ᛗ, ᛉ. If one or two of these occur on an Anglo-Saxon object in the absence of indisputable runes, we are again faced with a difficulty of identification. Are we in fact dealing with runes or with ornamental patterns? A good illustration of this problem involves one of the non-regal Anglo-Saxon coins. There is a *sceat*/penny type whose obverse has a bust or head, before it the moneyer's name 'w i g r d' (*Wigrœd*) and below it ✕. Describing this piece some years ago the numismatist Philip Grierson identified the runes as 'w i g u d', and the lines beneath the head as 'ŋ', perhaps interpreting it as the patronymic suffix *-ing*.[2] In fact, related coins show that the complex of lines is not a rune 'ŋ' at all but part of the ornamentation divorced from its proper context (fig.24). Here we are lucky in having comparative examples to help us decide, but this is unusual.

Fig.24. *Sceat* of Wigræd
with, below the head,
the ambiguous ✕. (3:2)

A more typical example of this problem concerns a sixth-century bronze cruciform brooch from a cemetery at Sleaford. Though this was found a

---

[1] This and some other of the 'runic inscriptions' in this chapter are discussed in J.Hines, 'The Runic Inscriptions of Early Anglo-Saxon England' in Bammesberger and Wollmann, *Britain 400–600*, 437–55, particularly 449–52.

[2] *Sylloge of Coins of the British Isles*, 1. *Fitzwilliam Museum Cambridge* (London 1958), nos. 235–6.

century ago it has only undergone close examination fairly recently. This revealed ⋈ scratched on the brooch face, below the bow. If this is decoration it is very crudely applied and does not look very decorative. If it is the rune 'd' what does it mean? A parallel may be the form ᚫ, 'æ', scratched inside the base of a bronze bowl from Willoughby-on-the-Wolds.[3] Here, however, the symbol can hardly be decoration: it is an irregular shape and is not displayed prominently on the bowl. I rather think that these examples are runes, but as to their significance I can only make guesses. They may be owners' marks, as we still sometimes scratch our initials on our property. They may be more than initials. The rune-names are *dæg* and *æsc*, both of which are quite common Old English personal name elements. Perhaps the Sleaford brooch was owned or given by someone called *Dæg . . .* or *. . . dæg*, the Willoughby bowl the possession of someone called *Æsc . . .* or the simplex *Æsc*.

If these interpretations bear any truth we have here possible examples of runes used as ideographs, representing the words which are their rune-names. The same may apply to a group of cases which display the symbol ↑, apparently the rune 't'. The rune-name refers, indirectly perhaps, to the god Tiw about whom English sources are reticent. His cognate Týr in the Old Norse material is more famous, for he is known to be the one-handed god who tricked the terrible wolf Fenrir, which bit off his hand in revenge. Týr is brave, a doughty fighter, taking on the hound Garmr in the last battle of the old gods at Ragnarǫk. Snorri Sturluson, writing in the thirteenth century, defines his qualities:

> He is very bold and stouthearted, and he is largely in control of victory in battle. It is useful for men of valour to cultivate him. It is a saying that a man who surpasses others and does not hesitate is Týr-valiant. He is wise too, so that it is also said that a man who is very wise is Týr-wise . . . He is not considered a god of reconciliation.[4]

A reference to him in the Eddic poem *Sigrdrífumál* is both baffling and suggestive. Speaking of the different ways of using runes the valkyrie Sigrdrífa tells the hero Sigurðr of those which bring success in war: 'Victory-runes you must know if you want to gain victory, cutting them on the hilt of

---

3   A.G.Kinsley *et al., Broughton Lodge. Excavations on the Romano–British Settlement and Anglo-Saxon Cemetery at Broughton Lodge, Willoughby-on-the-Wolds, Nottinghamshire 1964–8.* Nottingham Archaeological Monographs 4 (1993), 27 and fig.34.

4   *Edda: Prologue and Gylfaginning*, ed. Faulkes, 25.

your sword: some on the . . . and some on the . . . . and name Týr twice.'[5] The
gaps in the translation are because at these points the poem uses words for
parts of the sword whose exact meaning I am unsure of. In detail the verse
may be obscure, but the general sense is not in doubt.

The stanza can be related to a late sixth- or early seventh-century sword-
pommel from Faversham (Kent), on each of the two sides of which occurs the
pattern |↑| engraved and blackened with niello.[6] These could be decorative
but equally they could represent a two-fold naming of Tiw. It is perilous to
work from the Old Norse to the distant and much earlier English situation,
but there seems a remarkable coincidence of a two-fold invocation to Týr for
victory in the Scandinavian poem about runes and swords, and a two-fold
cutting of what may be the rune *tir/Tiw* in the English find of a sword-hilt.
Again I incline to think the English example to be runic rather than ornamental. If I am right, similar symbols elsewhere are likely to be runic. There is
another case of a 't'-like form on a sword-pommel from Kent, this time from
Ash/Gilton: Perhaps a thorough examination of the inventory of early sword
furniture would reveal others. In an iron spear-blade from the seventh-century
cemetery of Holborough (Kent) the pattern ↟ is inlaid in contrasting metal.
V.I.Evison has suggested that this too may refer to Tiw as a war-god, and
again the smith who forged the blade may have wanted to invoke him for its
success in fight.[7]

Several funerary urns from the heathen period have 't'-like forms cut or
stamped upon them. Again these may be decorative, or may be intended to
give the dead to Tiw's care. Significant examples are from Caistor-by-
Norwich, where the form is stamped round the circumference of the pot, and
from Loveden Hill, where an urn has a series of 't' forms angled round its
shoulder. Both Caistor-by-Norwich and Loveden Hill are places where runes
were used. From one of the Caistor pots comes the well-known runic astragalus, and there is also an inscribed brooch from the nearby cemetery at
Harford Farm. Loveden Hill is even more important for one of its urns has a
quite long runic inscription, not yet interpreted despite several efforts, but
which makes it certain that a community linked to this grave-field knew
runes. Another Loveden Hill pot has a curious 'crackle-ware' pattern cut
round it which rather looks like an attempt by someone who did not know the
script to produce something that looked like a runic inscription. There is,

---

5   *Sigrdrífumál* v.6 (*Edda*. ed. G.Neckel, 3.ed. revised H.Kuhn, Heidelberg 1962),
    191; *Vǫlsunga saga*, ed. R.G.Finch (London/Edinburgh, 1965), 36.
6   Hawkes and Page, 'Swords and Runes in South-east England', 7.
7   V.I.Evison, 'An Anglo-Saxon Cemetery at Holborough, Kent', *Archaeologia Can-
    tiana* 70 (1956), 97–100.

then, some evidence to support a runic interpretation of the ↑ forms of these particular urn-fields. Whether we can go further and explain as runic the wide range of other rune-like forms which adorn cremation urns both in England and the Continent is more doubtful. Patterns such as ✳, ⚹ and ✕ are quite often cut on them before firing, but there is the strong probability that these are not runes at all but decorative motifs which happen to coincide with runes.

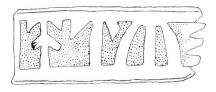

Fig.25. The Spong Hill 'mirror-runes'. (3:2)

One of the traps we can fall into is illustrated by the group of urns from Spong Hill. These use an unusual type of stamp, which certainly looks something other than decoration. Indeed it appears to present a sequence of three graphs. At first glance these look doubtfully runic, or runic by someone not in full control of the medium (fig.25). The graphs are ↑↑⋔, which I first took to be decorative or confused attempts at **tiy**, perhaps indicating the god-name *Tiw, Týr*. It was the German scholar Peter Pieper who drew our attention to another possibility, which indeed is a probability. He pointed to occasional evidence elsewhere of what he calls *Spiegelrunen*, 'mirror-runes'; that is, rune-forms that are doubled by mirror images of themselves.[8] Thus ↑↑⋔ are doubled forms of ᚨᛚᚢ, **alu**; a group that is common enough in magical or at least mystical contexts in early Norse practice. If this is the correct interpretation the Spong urn-maker had devised a revolutionary technique for reproducing runic messages in a soft material, by cutting them in relief in ?wood and printing them on the unfired pots.

Different again is an openwork swastika brooch, sixth-century in date, from Hunstanton. On its face, roughly spaced out round the circumference of its disc, is a series of deeply cut symbols. Some look like 'u', others are zigzags that could at a pinch be 's'. One is the very odd complex ✕ which might be a reversed 'g͡l' or 'g͡æ'.[9] These are not obviously decorative, but they do not look very informative either. I have not the least idea if they are runes or not; if they are runes I have not the least idea what they mean. But the appearance of a bind-rune 'g͡æ' twice (in a cryptic context) on the Undley

---

8 P.Pieper, 'Spiegelrunen' in *Runor och Runinskrifter*. Kungl. Vitterhets Historie och Antikvitets Akademien, Konferenser 15 (Stockholm 1987), 67–72.
9 Hawkes and Page, 'Swords and Runes in South-east England', 23.

bracteate may be thought to support the runic identification. There is something similar cut on the back of a copper alloy disc-brooch found at Boarley. A group of incisions cut between framing lines has some forms that are certainly rune-like, though others are more doubtful. No satisfactory reading has as yet been presented.[10]

Another case is a silvered bronze bracteate preserved fragmentarily, from the excavations of the monastic site at Whitby. Here it looks as if the craftsman tried to give the effect of a legend but was not literate enough. He produced a sequence of letter-like forms, some of which could be runic.[11] The result is like that on a number of early coins where an attempted or ill-copied legend produces occasional rune-like characters. Finally, a couple of examples on bone. From a cemetery at Barrington (Cambridgeshire) is a piece of polished bone with a number of scratches cut in rows upon it. One or two of them have forms which have been thought to supply convincing evidence of their 'pseudo-runic character'.[12] Somewhat similar is a bone comb-case from York, with a sequence of incised lines which nineteenth-century enthusiasts decided were runes.[13]

There are enough cases here to point the problem. Many individual runes are not distinctive enough in form to be identifiable without a clear context. They may not even have been distinctive enough for some Anglo-Saxons to have known what they were copying. Craftsmen who cut them may have confused decoration and letter. This is particularly hard to assess when approaching an object which appears within a runic milieu, as the Harford Farm brooch. Its added runic text confirms that it came from a community in which the script was known. Amidst the decoration that encircles its backplate are several examples of ᛗ. Is this the rune 'd' or not? Significant characters may have become decorative patterns in the hands of illiterate workmen, or decorative patterns reinterpreted as runes by semi-educated ones. It looks as if there will remain a group of monuments which are possibly but not certainly runic, where we must suspend judgment. This leads to a further problem for the runologist. Of course the most important aspect of his work is recording and interpreting runic inscriptions. But even an uninterpreted one has its significance, for it gives another point plot to a distribution map. It is this which makes it essential for us to try to find out if the examples I have quoted are in fact runic, even though their meanings may always evade

---

[10] D.Parsons, 'German Runes in Kent?', *Nytt om Runer* 7 (1992), 7–8.

[11] Sir Charles Peers and C.A.R.Radford, 'The Saxon Monastery of Whitby', *Archaeologia* 89 (1943), 53 and figs. 10, 13.

[12] Hines, 'Runic Inscriptions of Early Anglo-Saxon England', 452.

[13] Stephens, *Old-Northern Runic Monuments*, vol.3, 37.

us. Most of them are early – from the fifth and sixth centuries – and most are from southern or eastern England, from Kent, Norfolk, Suffolk, south Lincolnshire and Nottinghamshire. Adding them to a distribution map will increase the weight of early evidence for runes in the south and east. Missing them out will weaken our impression of the importance and popularity of the script in those areas. This is the problem but I confess myself at a loss as to how to solve it.

8

How to Use Runes

The flames which in 1955 destroyed much of Bryggen, the old Hanseatic quarter of Bergen, gave Norwegian archaeologists an unprecedented chance to dig a mediaeval mercantile town. Being Norwegians they seized it, and the results for runologists were astounding. Well over 500 new runic objects came to light, almost as many as were known before from the whole of Norway. The Bergen ones are relatively late in date (from *c*.1200 to the fifteenth century), but of high value for the picture they give of life in a Scandinavian trading town of the Middle Ages.

Luckily the earth of the site had the property of preserving wood and bone, so that from Bergen appeared types of inscription that were largely unknown until then.[1] Some are simply owners' marks, either on portable property or on traders' tallies securing their wares, and there are other commercial documents, records of payment or debt, advice and tax notices. Less formal are the bits of verse, and the magical incantations, amulets and charms, some of them for serious purposes like the one to help a woman in childbirth, others more trivial like the wooden stick with the magical *futhark* accompanied by the hopeful prayer, **ost:min:kis:mik**, 'kiss me, love'. Less solemn again are fragments of bone or bits of wood such as accumulated on the floors of ale-houses. Here we find comments like that on a rib-bone which a customer fished out of his stew, **nu er skøra mykyl**, 'now there is a lot of brawling'; or the boast on a small slip of wood, **inkebiǫrk uni mer þa er ek uar i sþafakri**, 'Ingebjǫrg loved me when I was in Stavanger'. And the wistful desire, **mynta:ik:myklu:opdar miǫþ:ranci koma nala**, perhaps 'I'd

---

[1] A convenient preliminary discussion is A.Liestøl, 'Runer frå Bryggen', *Viking* 27 (1963), 5–53; also published separately (1964) in slightly expanded form. The inscriptions are being gradually published in fascicules of *Norges innskrifter med de yngre runer*, vol.6. Further, though rather schematically expressed, in A.Haavaldsen and E.S.Ore, *Runer i Bergen: foreløpige resultater fra prosjektet 'Databehandling av runeinnskrifter ved Historisk Museum i Bergen'*, 2.ed. (Bergen 1995).

like to be able to get to a pub much more often.' Two inscriptions engraved on the one stick speak straight to the heart of modern man. The first of them is an order which an errant husband seems to have got from his wife: **gya:sæhir:atþu kak hæim**, 'Gyða says you are to go home.' Apparently Gyða's man had the nerve to reply, for there follows a second message cut by another hand. The writer was a little muddled as would be natural enough in a tavern. At any rate his answer makes no sense to us, and perhaps it did not to Gyða either. Confused though some of its runes are, this piece of wood with its command and retort, trivial in themselves, is important evidence. It shows the script used for passing everyday messages as a practical means of communication, and its implications for mediaeval literacy are profound.

A group of letters from Bergen provides clearer evidence on the same theme. One is a royal and official one, from Sigurðr lávarðr, son of King Sverrir, calling on a ship for the king's use, apparently in the 1190s.[2] Another one, obscure since we do not know the context of the correspondence, deals with some political matter, for it mentions one Óláfr hettusveinn, one of a group of rebels who fought against King Magnús Erlingsson *c*.1170. There are merchants' letters, one to a man Eindriði asking him to collect and dispatch some corn owed to the writer, and another from a certain Þórir to his partner Hafgrímr complaining of difficulties in getting a consignment of fish and ale. In the main such letters are on long sticks of wood, rectangular in cross-section. The sides of the stick are smoothed to carry the runes which run the length of each in turn. This method of correspondence is a practical one. The materials for writing were ready to hand: wood and a knife. The writer could correct errors as he went simply by cutting away the wrong runes and replacing them by the right ones. Once written the letter was sturdy and not soon damaged or lost. When finished with it was easily disposed of, for it could be used as kindling wood.

Runic sticks of this sort have long been known from the Icelandic sagas, where they are called *rúnakefli*. To take a single example, in *Grettis saga* the hero ventures into a troll's cave beyond a waterfall, and there kills the fierce occupant after a harsh struggle. Within the cave he finds the bones of two of the monster's victims. He puts them into a bag and brings them back to the church at Eyjardalsá. There he leaves them in the porch, with a *rúnakefli* on which are cut verses describing his achievement and an account of how he picked up the bones. This explanation was needed, for by the time the Eyjardalsá priest came upon them, Grettir was back in his lodging at Sandhaugar, some way away.[3] Though saga writers often referred to *rúnakefli*, compara-

2 A.Liestøl, 'Correspondence in Runes', *Mediaeval Scandinavia*, I (1968), 17–27.
3 *Grettis saga* (Íslenzk fornrit 7), ch.66.

tively few had been found until recent decades, and many runologists were inclined to think them a literary device, or at least to suspect that the writers exaggerated the extent of their use. The Bergen finds did a lot to correct this suspicion, partly by their proof that letters were in fact cut in runes and on wood during the Middle Ages, partly by showing how extensively mediaeval Norwegians used the script: on what a wide range of occasions, official, commercial, personal and magical.

Forty years on the Bergen finds can be fitted into a wider context. Urban archaeologists have now probed the mediaeval foundations of a number of Scandinavian towns, exploiting the conditions in which wood and bone survive. Places like Trondheim, Oslo and Tønsberg in Norway, Lund and Lödöse in Sweden, and Ribe in Denmark have all yielded exciting and sometimes amusing discoveries.[4] From Trondheim, for instance, an advertisement: **kliba bræstotir bylar þer**, 'Kleppa priest's daughter serves you (beer)'; from Tønsberg a scandalous verse: **þau:ero:bæþe:ibuþ:saman:klauua:kare:ok: kona:uilialms:** 'they're shacking up together, Klaufa-Kári and Vilhjálmr's wife'. Within the British Isles the only town with anything like this to show, so far, is Dublin, where the excavations of the 1970s and 1980s in the heart of the city threw up large quantities of wood and bone fragments, several with runic inscriptions, though they are neither so rich nor so informative as those from, say, Bergen and Trondheim.[5]

The Dublin finds are comparatively early – from the later Viking Age – and therein lies their importance. Most of the finds from Scandinavia itself are from the post-Viking Middle Ages, specifically from the twelfth to fourteenth centuries. Can we use them to throw light on runic usage in earlier times? The late Aslak Liestøl, a Norwegian scholar of immense experience in practical runology, thought that we could.[6] In 1971 he pointed out that, though *rúnakefli* from the Viking Age are rare, yet they do sometimes appear, regrettably hard to interpret. In addition to the Dublin material there is the

4   A splendid exhibition held in Stockholm's Medeltidsmuseum in 1994 had an accompanying volume which includes much of this material: *Runmärkt: från Brev til Klotter* (Stockholm 1994). Trondheim material is published in J.R.Hagland, *Runefunna: ei Kjelde til Handelshistoria*, 2.ed. (Trondheim 1990); Tønsberg in K.Gosling, 'The Runic Material from Tønsberg', *Universitetets Oldsaksamling, Årbok 1986–8*, 175–87; Lödöse in E.Svärdström, *Runfynden i Gamla Lödöse*. Lödöse – Västsvensk Medeltidsstad IV, 5 (Stockholm 1982).

5   The Dublin inscriptions are published in M.P.Barnes *et al.*, *The Runic Inscriptions of Viking Age Dublin*. Medieval Dublin Excavations 1962–81, Ser.B.vol.5 (Dublin 1997).

6   A.Liestøl, 'The Literate Vikings', *Proc. Sixth Viking Congress* (Uppsala/London 1971), 69–78.

wooden stave with an obscure verse text from the eighth- or ninth-century level at Staraya Ladoga, the trading town that Norsemen called *Aldeigjuborg,* in northern Russia. From Hedeby, South Jutland, come two ninth-century *rúnakefli* (as well as a third wooden fragment with runes), one of which could be the record of a commercial deal. On the evidence of such inscriptions and of the occasional contemporary literary reference to letters written by Vikings, Liestøl put forward the theory that many Vikings were runically literate, and claimed that they used the script for a range of purposes, prosaic and poetical, magical and practical. This is where the Dublin runes come in. Though it is hard to make much sense of most of them, there is a wooden paddle that probably had an owner's inscription, and a sentence inscribed on an antler that seems to record where it was found, perhaps as a claim to legal ownership. Again a practical use of the script.

Liestøl's thesis encourages the further question: if many of the Vikings could and did read and write in runes, what about the other Germanic peoples? In particular, from our point of view, what about the Anglo-Saxons? The difficulty in answering lies in the dearth of evidence. Most of the important inscriptions from Bryggen – those that Liestøl based his argument on – are on wood, a material that rarely survives long in the earth. He could argue from these mediaeval Bergen *rúnakefli* back to the Viking Age, both because the distance in time and space was not too great and because the Viking Age did produce a few runic monuments similar enough to the Bergen ones to sustain the argument. But it is a farther cry to Anglo-Saxon England, from which there survive only two cases of runic texts on wood, those on the York spoon and the (Lindisfarne) coffin of St Cuthbert, and neither of these is relevant to the point under discussion.

In fact, outside the North Germanic world only one area has preserved wooden objects in some numbers, and that is the northern coastal region of the Netherlands. The Dark Age dwellers of Frisia lived an amphibious life, supported on artificial mounds or *terpen.* In modern times archaeologists and compost-makers have cut into these, and found pieces of wood (and bone as well, occasionally metal) buried in them.[7] Four of these, coming from a wide date range, are of interest here. From Westeremden, pr. Groningen, come two sticks with runes cut along them, rather like the Norse *rúnakefli* in general appearance, with a third specimen found in Britsum, Friesland. In a *terp* at Arum, also in Friesland, there was a small wooden sword, elegantly shaped

---

7 The Frisian inscriptions are examined critically in *Frisian Runes and Neighbouring Traditions,* edd. T.Looijenga and A.Quak (= *Amsterdämer Beiträge zur älteren Germanistik* 45. 1996), many of whose articles contain detailed and up-to-date bibliographies of the material.

and inscribed in runes. Frisian runic texts are notoriously hard to interpret, and by now the student will know enough about the subject not to be surprised that various scholars have suggested various meanings for these four. One of the Westeremden sticks (A), which has been seen as a weaving slay, has the simplest of the inscriptions: **adujislu:mejisuhldu**. Though the noun endings cause concern the two personal names are clear, and a reading 'for Adugisl and Gisuhild' or something like that is likely. The second Westeremden rune-stick (B) has letter sequences so baffling that scholars have called them magical, working on the well-known epigraphical maxim that whatever cannot be readily understood must be sorcery. The Britsum staff is also baffling, though partly because some graphs are not certainly identified. More interesting for our purposes is the Arum sword. Archaeologists have placed it in the sixth or seventh century on the perilous criterion of the sword shape. Its inscription, in 'Anglo-Frisian' runes, is **edæ:boda**. This could be a personal name, but the second group of letters seems to contain the root *bod-*, 'announce', occurring in such words as OE *bodian*, 'tell, proclaim', and *boda*, 'herald, messenger'. The wooden sword is carefully shaped, its point charred in the fire, so it could be an object of ritual or formal significance. A tempting theory is that it was a signal of approaching war, carried from place to place as a warning that attack was imminent, and perhaps authorising the messenger who bore it to call up men for defence. Another takes the first element of the text, **edæ**, to mean 'oath'. It then identifies the sword as a ceremonial object on which public oaths were sworn. In either of these cases the Arum sword is a sign of office. To that extent it is an example of a public declaration cut in runes on wood. But this is some distance from the Scandinavian *rúnakefli* and can hardly confirm a general contention that the West Germanic peoples sent messages in runes inscribed on sticks.

For these numbers of runologists have welcomed support from a passage in a verse epistle by the sixth-century bishop of Poitiers, Venantius Fortunatus: *Carmina* vii. 18. Venantius was writing to a friend, Flavus, from whom he had not recently heard. He complained of the neglect and suggested some methods and scripts Flavus might use if he were bored with the roman ones. He could draw Persian or Hebrew characters, write Greek, employ papyrus or carve and colour runes on a *kefli*.

> Barbara fraxineis pingatur runa tabellis,
> quodque papyrus agit, virgula plana valet.

> Let the barbarous rune be painted on tablets of ash-wood,
> and what papyrus can do, that a smoothed stick is good for.

Here then, think some, there is direct evidence of runes cut on bits of wood to send messages; but such readers completely miss the quietly sardonic tone of Venantius's writing. He is suggesting scripts that Flavus, as an educated Christian, might know of but would be unlikely to use. Runes were presumably as exotic in the bishop's setting as Persian or Hebrew. If anything, the verses demonstrate how unlikely it was that Venantius knew much of runic correspondence. Though they certainly imply there was some sort of runic writing on sticks. Just as they indicate writing on papyrus; but by whom? And when?

The only evidence for English *rúnakefli* comes in a poem in the Exeter Book, known either as *The Husband's* or *The Lover's Message* according to the editor's attitude to the proprieties. It is not an easy work to follow in detail, for it comes near the end of its manuscript where the vellum is burned and holed so that the text has gaps. Moreover, opinions differ as to where the poem starts, since the Exeter Book's scribe neither titled the works he copied out nor marked clearly where one ended and the next began. Yet the narrative line is clear.

The poem is presented as spoken by an inscribed piece of wood which carries a message from its lord to his lady, who is a prince's daughter. Hostility had driven the man overseas where he rose above his troubles and rebuilt his fortune. The two lovers had pledged mutual faith, and now came the opportunity for the woman to escape across the waters to join her man.

> Hwæt. þec þonne biddan het, se þisne beam agrof
> þæt þu sinchroden sylf gemunde
> on gewitlocan wordbeotunga,
> þe git on ærdagum oft gespræcon,
> þenden git moston on meoduburgum
> eard weardigan, an lond bugan,
> freondscype fremman.

> See here! The man who engraved this slip of wood bade me tell you, bejewelled lady, to keep close within your heart the words of promise that the two of you repeated so often in days gone by, when you could live together in festive halls, walk the same land, let friendship flower.

Nowhere does the poet quote precisely the text of the message. He lets the *rúnakefli* paraphrase it: 'make your way to the sea, to the gull's home, board your ship, sail south along the sea-lanes to meet your man, to the land where your prince awaits your coming'. Finally the writer quotes a group of runes, 's', 'r', 'ea', 'w' and 'm' or 'd', since these bear the authority of the message. They were to testify that 'as long as he lived the prince would fulfil the pledge, the faith given between friends, that the two of you repeated so often in days gone by'.[8]

As evidence *The Lover's Message* is not much, though the obliquity of its reference to a rune-inscribed stave implies that the audience were used to such an object, at least in a literary setting, and could recognise it from an allusion alone. I am not sure what can be built upon such a frail foundation. The characters of the *futhark* were suitable for incising on wood, indeed perhaps designed with that in mind. The sixth-century Venantius Fortunatus had heard of letters being cut in runes on wooden tablets or squared sticks, though the practical applications of his knowledge are less certain. The Arum sword bears a message inscribed on wood from about the same date. Occasional wooden *rúnakefli* survive from the Viking Age and larger numbers of them from later mediaeval Scandinavia. Here is a skeleton of runic practice through the Dark Ages. *The Lover's Message* might suggest – but not prove – a similar tradition of writing on wood which lasted for some time in Anglo-Saxon England, even though all the examples, the English *rúnakefli*, have long since perished. Such a suggestion could lead to fruitful speculation (which will be examined in more detail in a later chapter). There may have been numbers of Anglo-Saxons who were generally literate in runes, perhaps dependent upon their belonging to an appropriate social, geographical or economic grouping: hence some of our surviving inscriptions whose nature is not obviously learned. Many English runic monuments, virtually all the rune-stones, are memorials, and I have often wondered what was the audience the commemorative inscriptions was supposed to serve. The theory suggested here – that there were numbers of Anglo-Saxons who were runically literate – would supply a suitable reading public.[9]

The Bergen, Trondheim and indeed the Dublin runes I have referred to were cut quickly and freely, without epigraphical style or decoration. In effect they are cursive, a script for business or personal use. A few English inscriptions have something of the same quality, and also in their content distantly echo the Bergen, Trondheim and Tønsberg specimens. The York spoon and the Whitby disc, with their short runs of simple characters, apparently bear their owner's marks, and so may the Sleaford brooch and the Willoughby-

---

8   For the runic forms of these and other Exeter Book poems see the facsimile, *The Exeter Book of Old English Poetry* (Exeter 1933): introduction by R.W.Chambers, M.Förster and R.Flower.

9   Anglo-Saxon runic literacy has been much discussed in recent years: as in R.Derolez, 'Runic Literacy among the Anglo-Saxons' in Bammesberger and Wollmann, *Britain 400–600*, 397–436, and D.Parsons, 'Anglo-Saxon Runes in Continental Manuscripts' in Düwel, *Runische Schriftkultur*, 195–220.

on-the-Wolds bowl with their single runes. The Harford Farm brooch has a run of plain rune-forms scratched on its back, with an unambitious message, recording 'l u d a : g i b œ t æ s i g i l æ', 'Luda repaired the brooch' – and indeed it does show a crude repair.

The personal name, *Luda*, is in larger characters than the rest, which suggests a naive self-pride. The Whitby comb has the remains of a more elaborate text in letters slim and elegant but again undecorated. It asks for God's help for someone, and if, as is likely, it was for the man/woman whose comb this was, it constitutes a rather upmarket sort of owner formula. If runic began as a practical script, invented for day-to-day purposes, these examples may develop the original practice.

From them may derive inscriptions of a different type but in a similar style of lettering. An obvious example is St Cuthbert's coffin, with its runic titles to some of the carvings, for this, like the *rúnakefli*, is of wood and its runes are appropriately simple. Perhaps here comes the Mortain casket with its prayer for its maker, and perhaps too the runic legends on coins, recording moneyers' names.

A second use of English runes I have just touched upon, the monumental. However this began – and there could have been wooden monuments, commemorative pillars, in Anglo-Saxon England – it survives to our day in stone. Here we are dealing with a craftsman rather than simply a literate Anglo-Saxon. Working mainly in a granular rather than a fibrous material gave the rune-master scope for varying his letter forms. He could use different techniques, for the letters could be chiselled out in a hard stone, cut out in a soft one, or the mason could use a punch to peck away the surface of a slab in a series of chips that would form the rune-staves. He could drill or punch out stave ends to form elementary serifs. He was released from any bondage to the straight line, and could cut curves with equal facility. Since his work was to be public and permanent, and not just a private message or memorandum, his patron or his professional pride might encourage him to formality and elegance in letter shape or in lay-out.

The effect of all this is to increase the possibilities open to the carver of runes. Since he was a trained craftsman he had skills other than those of a rune-master. Often, it seems, he knew roman script as well as runic, and techniques appropriate to the one were applied to the other. Thus the serifs he had been taught to add to roman letters he also put on runes, as the elegant letter forms of the Hartlepool I, Lindisfarne I and IV, and Monkwearmouth II stones show. Side by side with them simpler letters survive, as on Hartlepool II, Lindisfarne V and Monkwearmouth I. It is presumably from the monumental tradition that there descend the neatly cut and seriffed runes of some portable objects from later times, as the Kingmoor amulet ring, the Derby

Fig.26. Variant letter forms, seriffed and unseriffed: 'o' from Lindisfarne I, Maughold I, Bramham Moor and Ruthwell; 'r' from Hartlepool I, Ruthwell, Overchurch and Thornhill III.

bone plate and the Thames silver fitting. Using another technique, that of cutting away the background and leaving the characters standing proud, are the Bramham Moor and Manchester rings, where the effect is heightened by filling in the interstices with niello (fig.26).

Of the two uses discussed so far, the monumental is presumably secondary. As an argument for the existence of extensive correspondence in runes during Viking times Liestøl adduced the fact that there is a quite early Scandinavian practice of putting up runic memorial stones. This, he thought, would be pointless without a largely literate people to read them.[10] His argument is simplistic. It is now commonly thought that one reason why a memorial stone was erected in Scandinavia was to report a death legally and publicly so that heirs could take over. Or was a record of land-holding or transference of property.[11] This could explain why many Norse (and English) monuments give the name of the person who raised the stone equal importance to that of the deceased whose memory is being piously preserved. And also why, in the Scandinavian tradition, the memorials are often set up on prominent sites, beside main roads, or at river crossings, or at moot-places. Legal documents require, not a general reading public, but professionals specially trained to expound them, and this may be what the early Norse monumental tradition implies.

---

[10] 'Literate Vikings', 75.

[11] S.B.F.Jansson, *Runes in Sweden*, trans. P.Foote (Stockholm 1987), 97–100; R.I.Page, 'Scandinavian Society, 800–1100: the Contribution of Runic Studies', *Viking Revaluations*, edd. A.Faulkes and R.Perkins (London 1993), 149–50. Most recently, B.Sawyer, 'Viking Age Rune-stones as a Source for Legal History' in Düwel, *Runeninschriften*, 766–77.

However that may be, I have no doubt that in England monumental runes are late, are not the primary usage from which others derive. Here the chronology seems decisive. All surviving datable memorial inscriptions are late and Christian, and all early inscriptions occur, in simple runic forms, on portable objects, sword furniture, grave furniture, ornamental metalwork and the like.

That the monumental use is secondary does not in itself prove the day-to-day business or personal one primary. An alternative explanation of why runes were invented has attracted many scholars, and perhaps more non-scholars. This shows the Germanic peoples using the script in close connection with magic ritual, with lot-casting and divination, and probably with their pagan religions or superstitions. Elsewhere I have examined the Anglo-Saxon evidence for such an intimate link between runes and supernatural powers and concluded that English sources give little support to the theory.[12] It is enough here to sum up the arguments on both sides of the case.

The most recent studies of runes date the earliest extant examples to the second century A.D. or even a little before.[13] They are all from Scandinavia or Schleswig-Holstein/northern Germany. Clearly the inventors of runes cannot have worked later than the first century A.D., and they are usually placed somewhat earlier. We are then faced with an apposite question: what purpose would a Germanic script serve at so early a date, when it is fairly unlikely that the Germani would need one for administrative, mercantile or legal purposes? To this the proponents of rune magic have a ready answer: the Germanic peoples wanted a script for various cult purposes. They often adduce a passage from Tacitus, *Germania*, x, which describes how the Germani set about consulting their oracles.

> There is a simple procedure for casting lots. They lop a branch from a fruit-tree and cut it into slips, marking them with distinctive signs (*notis*). They scatter the bits of wood at random on a white cloth. Then the official priest (if it is a matter of public interest) or the head of the household (if it is private) prays to the gods, and looking up to the sky picks up three sticks, one at a time, interpreting them according to the signs already stamped upon them.

Writing at the end of the first century A.D. Tacitus used the general word *notae* for the distinguishing marks cut on the divination sticks, but this has not stopped many from asserting that he must have meant runes. The more cautious are less sure. If the *notae* were indeed runes, the passage would supply us with our first reference to the script, which was by this time already applied to prognostication and the appeal to the supernatural.

Certainly many of the extant early runic inscriptions of Scandinavia survive in contexts which are religious or magical in some way, though the details often escape us. For instance, a scabbard-chape from Torsbjerg has the complex **owlþuþewaʀ** which seems to mean or contain 'servant of (the god) Ullr'. On a buckle from Vimose are a pair of letter groups which contain **asauwija**, interpreted as *ā(n)sau wī(h)ia*, 'I dedicate to the god'. A spear-shaft from Kragehul, Fyn, has the rune-master's name and what seems to be a magical formula with the repeated group g͡a, plausibly (though not universally) explained as a standard phrase for good fortune, *gibu auja*, 'I give good luck'. Various objects bear magic words (by which is meant words that make no obvious practical sense in their contexts) like **alu** and **laukaʀ**. A bone from Lindholm, Skåne, has a long sequence of gibberish, **aaaaaaaaaʀʀʀnnn [.] bmuttt:alu**. It looks meaningless so it is interpreted as magic, and therefore the whole piece is identified as an amulet of some sort. Obviously in early times runes were used for occult purposes, but the question arises whether the supernatural power lay in the runes themselves or in the words they formed, whether runes were a magical script or just a script that happened to be used for magic.[14]

Proponents of the theory that runes were in themselves magical cite three sorts of supporting evidence: from etymology, archaeology and literature. The English word 'rune' derives directly from late Latin, but the Latin itself is a loan-word from Germanic, represented in Old English by *run*. Cognates survive in several Germanic languages, and the root is shared with Celtic and borrowed into Finnish. The Germanic words have meanings embodying the ideas of mystery and perhaps secrecy.[15] Gothic *runa* glosses Greek μυστηριον in references to the divine mysteries, and a related Gothic *garuni* means 'consultation, counsel'. Old High German uses *runa* and *giruni* in the same way. There is a group of related verbs, OE *runian*, OS *runon*, OHG *runen*, 'whisper'. The ON plural *rúnar* sometimes implies 'secret lore, mysteries'. Old Irish *run* means 'secret', and Middle Welsh *rhin* 'magical charm'.

---

[14] There is detailed, if rather indigestible, discussion of 'magical' runic inscriptions in S.E.Flowers, *Runes and Magic: Magical Formulaic Elements in the Older Runic Tradition*. American University Studies, ser.1, Germanic Languages and Literature 53 (New York 1986) with a listing of these mysterious objects.

[15] C.E.Fell discusses these meanings of the Old English word in 'Runes and Semantics' in Bammesberger *Old English Runes*, 205–16.

Finnish has *runo*, 'song', perhaps originally 'incantation'. OE *run* has corresponding meanings. It translates *mysterium* in contexts dealing with spiritual mysteries. It can mean 'council' or 'counsel', pairing or contrasting with *ræd* in alliterative lines. It carries a sense of secrecy, of isolation, sometimes of esoteric knowledge and even perhaps of secret scripts, symbols or messages. With its cognate *(ge)ryne* it can mean 'symbol, type' on occasion. On the other hand *run* never certainly means 'runic character'. For that the usual Old English word is *runstæf*, 'rune-stave'.

For a more explicit link between *run* and magic we must turn to compound words surviving largely in learned works or glosses. Here occur forms like *burgrune, helrun, hellerune, heahrun*, glossing words such as *furiae, pareas, pythonissa, divinatricem*. *Heagorun* is used to paraphrase *necromantia*, while a word *leodrunan* appears in a charm in the sense of 'evil magic' or perhaps 'sorcerer'. The difficulty in these compounds is in knowing whether the idea of magic and the supernatural is in the first or the second element. It is at least possible that *-run(e)* in all these cases means no more than 'one skilled in mysteries, one possessing esoteric lore'. With a first element *helle-* the compound is 'one who knows the mysteries of the dead or of hell' and so 'necromancer' or 'demon'. The first elements of *heahrun* and *heagorun* may be related to those of OE *hægtesse*, 'witch', and *heagotho* which glosses Latin *manes*, 'shade, spirit'. It is tempting to relate *leodrunan* to OE *leoð*, 'song', whose ON cognate *ljóð* occasionally means 'charm'. The sum of this brief investigation is to show that OE *run* often has the sense of mystery, perhaps secrecy or indeed isolation, but it is not clear that it expresses magic or the supernatural.

By archaeological evidence I mean those cases where the contexts in which the runes occur, archaeological or art historical, suggest rune magic. An early example is the Kylver slab. This has a *futhark* followed by an uncertainly runic symbol, possible of magical import, and then the palindrome **sueus** which has no known meaning (perhaps a duplication of the mysterious sequence **eus**, forms of which occur elsewhere in runes). The stone formed part of a grave lining. The early reports are contradictory so we do not know how the slab fitted the grave, but the runes seem to have been turned towards the corpse. Since there is no obvious sense to be made of the letter groups, and since they were not to be read once they had been placed in the grave, scholars suggest plausibly that the runes summoned supernatural powers, perhaps to protect the body or to prevent it walking again and disturbing the living.[16]

---

16 Jansson, *Runes in Sweden*, 12–13.

Something of the same sort is a wooden stave from Frøslev, south Jutland. This was taken from a mound, but not during controlled excavation, so the circumstances are obscure and its date uncertain. It has six symbols set between points. The first may not be runic; the other five apparently form a palindrome **RiliR**, again meaningless to us. Archaeological context (in so far as we know it) and obscurity of sense combine to suggest a magical use of runes.

Rather different are two texts inlaid in spear-heads, the one from Dahms-dorf, the other from Kovel. In each case the runes make perfectly good sense, and have been taken as spear-names: the first **ranja**, perhaps 'the weapon that makes them run' or 'assailant', the second **tilarids**, probably 'attacker'. In both cases the runes are set on the blades amidst symbolic patterns, the circle with a dot at its centre, the crescent, the swastika, the triskele and the like.[17] Since these almost certainly had sacral importance, it seems probable that the runic weapon-names also invoked hidden powers to help the warriors who fought with the spears.

Of course there is a large speculative element in this sort of evidence. We have no way of finding out the motives of the rune-masters who cut these inscriptions, and our assessment of them may be wrong. Sometimes we suggest – innocently – that such runes are magical because we cannot think what else they can be. Nevertheless the suggestion can be convincing, and there are a few such cases from Anglo-Saxon England. For example, the Loveden Hill urns were specially made to hold the cremation remains, so their design ought to reflect the fact. One of them has a runic inscription, not yet read, or rather read in so many different ways as to give rise to scepticism (see above, p.11). Others seem to have the **t**-rune, possibly representing the god Tiw. Another has a scribble of lines that look a bit like runes. All these imply a belief that runes were somehow appropriate to an object on close terms with death. The potter who made a group of cremation urns dug up at Spong Hill employed a stamp with rune-like characters on it, characters that have been plausibly interpreted as doubled forms of **alu**, a magical word common in Scandinavia. Again, if S.C.Hawkes's account of the Chessell Down scabbard-plate is right, a craftsman added this simple piece of silver to an elaborate scabbard-mount shortly before it was buried with its owner. The plate bears seven runes. Scholars have not yet found a satisfactory interpretation of them though they have been studying them for years. Yet again the script seems to have been determinedly brought into contact with the dead.

In the final instance, however, it is the literary evidence that bears the

---

[17] See Arntz and Zeiss, *Einheimischen Runendenkmäler*, pls. 1, 2.

burden of proof of the theory of rune magic. Mediaeval Scandinavia supplies a mass of information on rune magic, but the difficulty is in sifting it, in deciding how much is genuine, how much literary convention. A synopsis of rune magic is in *Sigrdrífumál*, one of the heroic poems of the Codex Regius of the *Elder Edda* and also surviving, in somewhat different form, in the *Volsunga saga*.[18] The great warrior Sigurðr wakes a valkyrie, Sigrdrifa, whom Óðinn has put into a charmed sleep. In return she imparts to him *speki*, wisdom, and *ráð til stórra hluta*, advice on matters of importance. This is partly proverbial lore, partly that of spells and charms. She teaches him different sorts of runes and when to use them: *sigrúnar*, victory-runes for incising on a sword. *brimrúnar*, surf-runes for cutting on ship or tackle to secure it in a dangerous sea; *málrúnar*, speech-runes to protect a man from malice at a legal assembly; *olrúnar*, luck-runes which save man from woman's treachery; *bjargrúnar* which give woman a safe childbirth; *limrúnar*, twig-runes which cure sickness; *hugrúnar*, mind-runes which give wisdom. *Hugrúnar* are specifically ascribed to Hroptr, one of Óðinn's nicknames.

A more detailed tale linking runes and Óðinn is reported in the rambling and shapeless poem *Hávamál*, also in the Codex Regius. The poem's central figure is the great god himself, who appears as a stranger entering a great house and warming himself by the fire. He is portrayed as a repository of traditional learning, as a deceitful and deceived lover, a god of wisdom, a sorcerer, and as the hanged and stabbed god sacrificed on a tree in his search for new powers.

> I know that I hung on the windswept tree
> Nine whole nights, wounded with the spear,
> Given to Óðinn, myself to myself,
> On the tree that sprang from roots
> No man knows of.
>
> They gave me neither bread, nor drink from the horn.
> I peered down.
> I took up runes, howling I took them,
> And then fell back.[19]

The stanzas are allusive ones, but it seems that the great god learnt the power of runes as a result of a mystic, perhaps a shamanistic, sacrifice of himself, hanged on a tree and thrust through with a spear as Óðinn's victims

---

18 *Sigrdrífumál* vv.6–13; *Volsunga saga*, ed. Finch, 36.
19 *Hávamál*, ed. D.A.H.Evans. Viking Society for Northern Research Text Series 7 (London 1986), vv.138–9.

traditionally were. Thereafter in the poem Óðinn boasts of his magical practices, which include necromancy.

> This twelfth (skill) I know. If in a tree-top I see
> A noosed corpse swaying,
> I cut and paint runes
> So the man will walk
> And talk with me.[20]

The early poetry of Scandinavia gives various other hints about the powers of runes, and its mediaeval prose takes up the theme enthusiastically. In *Grettis saga*, for example, evil runes bring the great outlaw to his death. He barricades himself in the fortress island of Drangey, but a witch takes a rooted tree, cuts runes on it, reddens them in her blood and chants a spell over them. Then she shoves the stump out to sea, bidding it float to Drangey and bring Grettir to destruction. It fulfils its mission.[21] The hero of *Egils saga* finds himself in bad company at the home of the unfriendly farmer Barðr. The wicked queen Gunnhildr, who is a fellow guest, arranges for Egill to be offered a horn of poisoned ale. He takes hold of the vessel, cuts runes on it, pierces his hand with his knife and uses the blood to colour the letters. The horn shatters and the poison runs harmlessly away.[22]

It is clear that mediaeval Scandinavia – or perhaps I should specify mediaeval Iceland – had a tradition that associated intimately runic letters and magical or supernatural powers. The difficulty is in tracing this back to earlier times, and linking it with practices outside Scandinavia. As they survive, the Norse sources are late. *Grettis saga* dates from *c*.1300. *Egils saga* is thirteenth-century work though the runic passage cited is based on a verse which, if rightly attributed to Egill Skallagrímsson, must be tenth-century. The Codex Regius of the *Elder Edda* is late thirteenth-century, but many of the poems are much earlier. Critics usually put both *Hávamál* and *Sigrdrífumál* in the Scandinavian heathen period, but even then they cannot go back in their present form beyond the eighth century, though they may incorporate older material. The plentiful Norse evidence for rune magic is fascinating and suggestive. No doubt some mediaeval Norsemen believed that cutting runes gave a man access to supernatural powers. But this does not prove that runic magic existed in Germanic times, and that it passed from there to the Anglo-Saxons.

The English literary evidence is slight. Scholars usually quote a story from

---

[20] *Hávamál*, v.157.
[21] *Grettis saga* (Íslenzk Fornrit 7), ch.79.
[22] *Egils saga* (Íslenzk Fornrit 2), ch.44.

Bede's *Ecclesiastical History* iv.20, which they seem to value highly perhaps because it is all they have. The tale is of a young man called Imma who was taken prisoner after a battle between Northumbrians and Mercians but could not be tied up since bonds always fell from him. As Bede explains, the reason was that Imma's brother was an abbot, who thought him dead and kept singing masses for his soul. At every celebration Imma's bonds were freed. His captors were not surprisingly baffled at the phenomenon and suspected Imma of sorcery. Their leader asked whether he had about him *litteras solutorias, de qualibus fabulae ferunt*, 'releasing *litteras* such as are told of in stories'. In the best-known Old English translation of this passage the man asked Imma *hwæðer he ða alysendlecan rune cuðe, and þa stafas mid him awritene hæfde, be swylcum men leas spel secgað and spreocað*, 'whether he knew the releasing *rune* and had about him the *stafas* written out, such as men tell idle tales of'. Elliott translates this as 'whether he knew loosening runes and had about him the letters written down',[23] but this seems to me to beg the question. As we have seen, *run* does not usually mean 'runic character', while *stafas* need not mean '*runic* characters'. Elliott's version is based on a combination of *rune* with *stafas* and *litteras*. Bede's *litteras* need not mean 'letters, characters' but could be 'letter, document, parchment'; even if it did mean 'characters' it need not be 'runes'. The translator's *rune* may mean 'charm, secret document, esoteric practice'. Bede's captor may be asking if Imma had a piece of vellum with a magical formula on it that stopped him being tied up. The translator's captor may wonder if Imma knew some secret or magical way of remaining unbound and had the appropriate spell on him. The spell need not be in runes, and indeed, if surviving Old English charms are anything to go by, would not be, for rune magic is most rare in them though several other scripts are employed for magical purposes.

Suggestive is a variant reading of the passage, less well-known than the one quoted above, and now surviving only in a single manuscript, Corpus Christi College, Cambridge, MS 41. Here the captor uses wording significantly different, asking *hwæðer he þa alyfedlican rune cuðe and þa stanas mid him hæfde be swylcum . . .*, 'whether he knew permitted *rune* (?secrets) and had the stones with him, such as men tell idle tales of'. If this translator was fully aware of what he was putting, he must have had in his mind something rather different from a magical written text.

More important than the original story is the use the later homilist Ælfric made of it when he composed a sermon on the efficacy of the mass. Ælfric told the story wrong, getting the protagonists on the wrong sides in their

---

23 *Runes, an Introduction*, 67; 2.ed., 81.

battle. When he came to the victorious leader's question he put it *hwæðer he ðurh drycræft oððe ðurh runstafum his bendas tobræce*, which we can only translate 'whether he shattered his bonds by sorcery or by runes'.[24] Whatever Bede and his translator thought, Ælfric knew of rune magic; the casual way he referred to it implies also that his audience could follow his meaning without explanation. But we do not know *what* Ælfric knew of rune magic. When he wrote, *c.*1000, Danish influence was strong in England and it is possible that a Scandinavian belief in rune magic lies behind Ælfric's wording. Rejecting it as irreligious, he nevertheless thought it likely that earlier generations of Anglo-Saxons had shared the superstition and so put it into a tale of events three centuries earlier. Certainly, Ælfric's Wessex is devoid of epigraphical runes, nor is there any trace of a living runic tradition there, though the script occurs not infrequently in West Saxon manuscripts.

This group of texts provides the only clear reference in Old English to rune magic. The few other examples that scholars have adduced from time to time – *Solomon and Saturn I* and the *Nine Herbs Charm* for instance – are inconclusive at best and misleading at worst. Relevant is the negative evidence, the almost complete absence of runes from Anglo-Saxon manuscript charms which survive in large numbers. In these circumstances it is dangerous to assert that the Anglo-Saxons in general believed they could call up supernatural powers by cutting, painting or naming runes; but not more dangerous than to claim, on the evidence available, that many of them used the script in their business and personal correspondence.

In fact there are a few examples of runic inscriptions from England which are certainly magical, though the magic may rest not in the graphs but in the words or groups they form. Three amulet rings with closely linked inscriptions have been found (figs. 27, 28). Two are of gold: the first, from the neighbourhood of Bramham Moor, reads 'æ r k r i u f l t ‖ k r i u r i þ o n ‖ g l æ s t æ p o n t o l', the other, from Kingmoor, '+ æ r k r i u f l t k r i u r i þ o n g l æ s t æ p o n | t o l'. An agate ring, probably from Linstock Castle, has the rather different but related '✱ ✱ e r y · r i · u f · d o l · y r i · u r i · þ o l · w l e s · t e · p o t e · n o l'. Dickins observed that the letter group 'æ r k r i u' appears as *ærcrio, aer crio* in two versions of a charm for stanching blood, and the same spells contain occasional other echoes of the ring texts.[25] What we have here is magical gibberish. The rings are clearly amulets. The runes may have

24 *Ælfric's Catholic Homilies: the Second Series. Text*, ed. M.Godden. EETS, SS5 (Oxford 1979), 204.
25 'Runic Rings and Old English Charms', *Archiv f. d. Stud. d. neueren Sprachen* 167 (1935), 252.

Fig.27.
The Bramham Moor amulet ring.

Fig.28.
The Kingmoor amulet ring.

added their own witchcraft, but there is a further possible source of magical strength. The Kingmoor ring has thirty runes, twenty-seven outside the hoop and three inside. The Bramham Moor ring has thirty also, divided by decorative symbols into three groups of nine, nine and twelve. Three and its multiples are common magical numbers, appearing often in manuscript charms. Part of the power of the amulet rings may reside in the individual characters cut on them, and there could be a link with the number magic some have detected in Scandinavian inscriptions.

Also connected with the control of occult powers is one of the inscriptions of the Thames scramasax. As we have seen, this is an elaborate and expensive weapon, with two texts and a series of decorative patterns cut along the length of the blade, the incisions filled in with contrasting metals. One inscription is the personal name 'b ea g n o þ', probably the owner's, though it could be the smith's mark. The other is the twenty-eight-letter *futhorc* for which I know no practical explanation outside magic. Early *futhark* inscriptions have generally been considered magical: otherwise, the pertinent question asks, what is their purpose? It cannot be decorative, for in some of the early inscriptions – Kylver is a case in point – there is no context for decoration. Presumably, then, the Thames *futhorc* has some link with rune magic, but what? It is anomalous. Its letter order is odd and occasional rune forms are unusual, even unique, and probably erroneous. Judging from its mistakes the competence of the magician who designed it must be called in question. To me it rather looks as if the Thames scramasax, a tenth-century weapon, is a late survival. The practice of inscribing magical runes on swords was an archaic one, known from earlier specimens that had survived or descriptions of them. Perhaps by the tenth century there was no longer much knowledge of runes in Kent, and no living belief in their magical powers. The man who ordered the Thames scramasax wanted an old tradition followed for prestige purposes, so his smith bodged up a *futhorc* for him.

The Thames scramasax is a tentative and indirect piece of evidence for English rune magic. There is another type of evidence, even more tentative and indirect, and yet equally suggestive. If forming a rune gave the runemaster access to mysterious powers, if being inscribed with runes gave an object supernatural qualities, it follows that the very act of cutting the letters of might was significant. Once they had been incised their magic was active, and it did not matter in the least whether they were elegantly shaped and neatly set out or not, nor need it matter if there were slight malformations or ambiguities; the primary intent of cutting the runes had been fulfilled.

If this argument is valid we would expect to find, among our early runic inscriptions, cases where the rune-cutting is rough even when applied to carefully made objects. This could support the rune magic theory by showing that the master's intent was not to match a fine object with a finely laid-out text, but to add to an object's usefulness by an act that released power. In fact this is what we do find. S.C.Hawkes's study of the Chessell Down sword and scabbard has shown how carefully it was assembled. The hilt has a plate of fine filigree work in gold. The scabbard mouthpiece is richly decorated. Yet the master scratched the runes in quite roughly on the added plate, apparently with an error where his graver slipped as he was forming the fifth letter. The silver-gilt pommel from Ash/Gilton has quite elaborate niello decoration, but its runes are crudely shaped and mixed with lines that seem not to be runic at all, but only scribbles. Rough too is the single rune on the Sleaford brooch and the few letters that survive on the gold fragments from Selsey and on the bronze-gilt pommel from Sarre. All these are apparently secondary, additions to a finished object, which may be significant.

Perhaps the most telling example is the Loveden Hill funerary urn with its inscription of fifteen runes divided into three groups. Here the master was working in a plastic material, for the runes were cut before the pot was fired. It would have been easy for him to correct mistakes or inelegancies, but he did not. The runes are poorly shaped and spaced, and uneven in size (fig.29). The writer began the second rune too near the first, so that when it was completed they almost ran together. He could easily have rubbed out and started again. Perhaps his work was complete once the runes were cut.

Here I have suggested three purposes for which runes were used: monumental inscriptions, practical correspondence and general use, witchcraft. The first predominates in the surviving comprehensible texts; evidence to support the second has increased in recent years; the third is implied rather than recorded. Yet I think it probable that the Anglo-Saxons used runes quite extensively in all these three ways, and that the dominance of the monumental among surviving comprehensible inscriptions is archaeological accident. Perhaps rune magic belongs largely to the earlier period, and possibly the rather late use of monumental runes in the north is something of an antiquarian fashion. For how long runes were a practical and everyday script is a matter for conjecture only.

Clearly it is hard to generalise about the Anglo-Saxons' use of runes, and what their attitude towards the characters was. Something can be found by

ᚣᛁᚦᚠᛒᚨᛘᚾᛁᛁᛈ/ᛋᛈᛁᛁᛘᚱᚠᛉ

Fig.29. The Loveden Hill urn runes. (1:2)

comparing runic and roman as epigraphical scripts. Apart from the distinctive magical use of runes such as appears on the Thames scramasax, there seems to be no property which is peculiar to that script. Indeed, one could even deny that the Thames *futhorc* is distinctive in view of the roman alphabet and part-alphabet inscriptions that have emerged in recent years.[26] On coins they record moneyers' names and occasionally royal names and titles just as roman letters do. On portable objects they give owners' names and marks, owner formulae, artists' signatures, comments on repair, descriptive titles to sculptural subjects. Further, on stones they give personal names of the commemorated dead, of those who commissioned and made the monuments, with commemorative prayer and maker formulae. For all these purposes the Anglo-Saxons could equally well use roman characters, and there are even bi-alphabetical inscriptions, as on the Falstone 'hogback' where almost identical texts occur side by side in the two scripts, and inscriptions which mix the two alphabets, as on the Manchester ring. For much of the Anglo-Saxon age runes and roman served similar ends, and there is no need to draw distinctions between them and no justification for deducing the nature of a text from the type of lettering it is written in.

Finally, the word 'rune-master'. As I have used it in this chapter, indeed as I use it in general, it means little more than the man who carved the runes on an object under survey. But of course the word will have different implications in respect of the different uses of runes I have discussed. In some cases the rune-master would be simply a monumental mason accustomed to cutting inscriptions on stones and mastering runes as one of the scripts appropriate to his trade. In others he might be a literate Anglo-Saxon who found it convenient to express himself in runes. In others again a die-cutter who copied runes from an exemplar, a coin, another die, possibly a drawing presented him by his employer. But if in early times runes were intimately connected with magic, a rune-master then would be a more awesome figure. By his use of the

---

[26] The standard catalogue of Old English non-runic inscriptions is E.Okasha, *Hand-List of Anglo-Saxon Non-Runic Inscriptions* (Cambridge 1971) with its supplements, *Anglo-Saxon England* 11 (1983), 83–118 and 21 (1992), 37–85. Inscriptions giving the roman alphabet are her nos. 178, 186, 190, 192.

symbols he would be in command of supernatural powers, enticing hidden forces into his service. It is this type of rune-master that has attracted and misled many scholars, and perhaps only this type truly deserves the title 'rune-master'.

9

Runic Coins

A major group of Anglo-Saxon runic texts appears on coins. These are important not for their content, which consists almost entirely of personal names, but for the fact that they can often be dated and localised precisely. This is why, in treating the different genres of runic inscription, I place them first though they are not the earliest. Numismatists have brought their study to a high degree of efficiency, and can place most (though indeed not all) Anglo-Saxon coins within narrow time limits and assign them to localities if not always to specific towns. Consequently those pieces with runic legends provide a scatter of provenanced and dated runes which may assist our study of other inscriptions that are less securely provenanced or less precisely dated. In the last decade or so the metal detector has increased dramatically the number of individual coins discovered, and attributions and datings are continually being questioned or refined. Much of what I wrote on this topic in the first edition of *An Introduction to English Runes* now needs revising and expanding, and this revised discussion is based on the discoveries of the new generation of numismatists.[1]

Throughout most of the post-migration age the Anglo-Saxons struck coins. They began ambitiously in gold, some time in the first half of the seventh century, say in the 620s. There followed a fairly rapid degeneration through electrum to silver, which remained the common metal for currency from c.680 until the fourteenth century. Occasionally base metal served, as in

---

[1] This work is summed up in an essential article by M.Blackburn, 'A Survey of Anglo-Frisian and Frisian Coins with Runic Inscriptions' in Bammesberger, *Anglo-Saxon Runes*, 137–89, and supported by the discussion and illustrations in P.Grierson and M.Blackburn, *Medieval European Coinage with a Catalogue of the Coins in the Fitzwilliam Museum, Cambridge*, vol.1 (Cambridge 1986). D.M.Metcalf has produced a major survey of material, *Thrymsas and Sceattas in the Ashmolean Museum Oxford*, 3 vols. Royal Numismatic Society Special Publication nos. 27A, B, C (London/Oxford 1993–4) which gives an impressive survey of the problems involved in studying these early coins.

the copper coinage (known as *stycas*) of ninth-century Northumbria. Four groups of coins concern runic scholars: an early gold one which seems to be mainly from the south of England; the type formerly known as *sceattas* (sg. *sceat*), now called pennies by numismatists, from the period *c.*675–750 (at the beginning of which the change from gold to silver took place), these concentrated in the south-east and east of the country; the silver 'broad pennies' of the late eighth and ninth centuries; the Northumbrian *stycas* of the first half of the ninth century.

Few early gold coins survive, and their runic legends are troublesome. The *sceattas*/pennies are much more common, though they have not many different runic legend types. These record personal names, now often assumed (though the evidence is slight) to be those of the moneyers who issued the coins on their own authority and whose integrity guaranteed their weight and purity. The broad pennies and the *stycas* are regal, or in a few cases episcopal.

Of the organisation of coinage in early times we know little. In the later Anglo-Saxon period coining was a royal prerogative giving the king part of his revenue. Naturally, he controlled it carefully, and consequently each coin bore the king's name and title, usually on the obverse. The officials who acted as intermediaries between king and people were the moneyers. In this later period the moneyer was a man of importance and wealth, with the privilege, which he paid for, of receiving the royal dies and issuing the royal coinage; and the responsibility, which was a heavy one, of ensuring the official weight of the new coin and the quality of its metal. Properly, therefore, his name and title and sometimes the mint-town occurred on the coin, usually on the reverse.[2]

At the time of the early broad pennies and *stycas* the moneyer was already a royal agent. Presumably the king kept general control over him, but how far at this earlier date he supervised the dies from which the coins were struck and so kept a close watch on the design of his coins is less clear. Of the organisation of the non-regal coinage we know practically nothing, though we can guess a little. Here the moneyer was not directly the servant of the king, but more a freelance, working perhaps by royal permission. His position was close to that of the merchant who dealt in weighed units of precious metal, and to the gold- or silversmith who worked it. Presumably it was he who determined the design of his coins and the legends they should bear.

Right through our period men made coins by the process developed in antiquity, which would continue in use in England until the milled coinages

---

[2] The moneyer's status in Anglo-Saxon England at various dates is considered in Metcalf, *Thrymsas and Sceattas*, vol.1, 10–25.

of the sixteenth and seventeenth centuries. The craftsman produced coin blanks of the appropriate metal and weight. He hammered the blank between two forged steel dies, each bearing in reverse the pattern of one side of the coin. Of course the dies were hand-cut, and so no two dies would be identical. Hence Anglo-Saxon coinage has little of the mechanical uniformity of appearance of modern currency.

Since we are concerned not primarily with the coins themselves but with their legends, it would be helpful to know who supplied the lettering for the coin; that is, who told the die-cutter what was needed and who supervised the spelling, script and format of what he produced. In late Anglo-Saxon times it seems that dies were often cut centrally and therefore under close regal inspection, and were sent out at fixed intervals to the mint-towns where the moneyers worked. Under these conditions we could expect consistency and accuracy of legend cutting.

Things were different in the earlier period. The first broad pennies show distinctive regional styles in coin design. Clearly the dies were of local manu-facture, and presumably moneyers had greater freedom in choosing their types. Possibly, too, the die-cutter had a say in what he produced, and letter and name forms may reflect personal preferences.

In the early non-regal issues there is a further complication. These coins would have no royal protection. If a particular coin type proved popular and useful, it could be imitated, design, legend and all, by anyone who wanted to. In the first instance the moneyer's name on a coin assured a recipient that he was getting full weight of pure metal. The name and the coin design were his guarantee. To convince, a coin must look like a coin. Hence later coin-makers, striving to produce convincing types, might imitate coins of the first moneyer, even to adding his name. This certainly happened in the *sceat*/penny series, as blundered legends copied from damaged or badly struck pieces show. In such cases the validity of the legend is in doubt.

The most notable examples of this are runic pennies struck in the Nether-lands in imitation of English ones. These often have a distinctive and local reverse design centred on a cross between pellets, but the obverse is a direct, though sometimes very rough, copy of a common English type which shows a crowned head facing right, and before the face the runic legend giving the personal name *Epa* or *Æpa*. As well as the head Netherlandish die-cutters copied the runes, but their attempts are often so barbarised as to be indeci-pherable. Occasionally, however, their runes are well-formed and we are then faced with the question: does this count as a genuine runic inscription, or is it a group of characters cut, accurately but without understanding, by a careful craftsman? The problem is made more piquant when, as sometimes hap-pened, a Continental die-cutter replaced the Anglo-Saxon 'a', ᚠ, by the rare but distinctive Frisian variant ᚠ, suggesting that he comprehended the significance of his letters.

Something like a hundred different types of early Anglo-Saxon gold coins survive, though few have runes on them. The coins divide into two groups according to weight. By far the more common is the *tremissis* (sometimes called *thrymsa*, though that term is rather outmoded), whose weight is roughly 1.3 grammes and whose diameter is about 13 mm. Very rare is the larger *solidus*. Theoretically this was three times the weight of the *tremissis* though no clear weight standard is deducible from the few surviving Anglo-Saxon specimens, and it must always be kept in mind that these pieces may have been intended as jewels rather than coins; to be mounted as pendants as Roman coins so often were. Keeping to a weight standard may not have been important.

The English die-cutters drew their inspiration from two main sources, from contemporary Merovingian pieces and from Imperial Roman coins of the third and fourth centuries. Their prototypes had legends in the roman character, and these the English workmen sometimes copied or imitated. The earliest runes on coins often appear in context with these copied legends, as additions to or replacements of roman letters. It may be that they were not always designed with any meaning, but were simply letter sequences which gave the coin a convincing appearance, since all coins ought to have a superscription. This would be a convenient though unimpressive explanation of the difficult letter groups that we sometimes meet with. Examples are a retrograde sequence, formerly read **delaiona** but now thought likely to be **desaiona**, on three *tremisses* (all from the same pair of dies) found at St Albans and Coddenham (Suffolk) and deriving from a coin of the Emperor Crispus; and the confused legend, something like **benu:tigo** or **benu:+:tid** which occurs on four or five related specimens, with provenances recorded at Dorchester (Oxfordshire), Eastleach Turville (Gloucestershire) and Amiens (fig.30).[3]

It is not until we get to the coins of Pada that we are on firmer ground.[4] This is a *sceat*/penny coinage on the module of the *tremissis*, beginning in the

---

3   C.H.V. Sutherland, *Anglo-Saxon Gold Coinage in the Light of the Crondall Hoard* (Oxford 1948), nos. 17–18, 27, supplemented by Blackburn, 'Anglo-Saxon and Frisian Coins', 144, and by Metcalf, *Thrymsas and Sceattas*, vol.1, 31–2.

4   The classic study of the early pennies/*sceattas* is S.E.Rigold, 'The Two Primary Series of Sceattas', *British Numismatic Jnl* 30 (1960–1), 6–53, with addenda and corrigenda in vol.35 (1966), 1–6. This has been expanded and developed in more recent times, as in Rigold's 'The Principal Series of English Sceattas', *British Numismatic Jnl* 47 (1977), 21–30, and most notably in Grierson and Blackburn, *Medieval European Coinage*, 164–89 and Metcalf, *Thrymsas and Sceattas*.

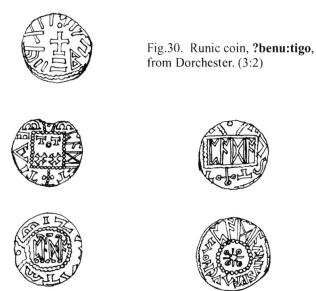

Fig.30. Runic coin, **?benu:tigo**, from Dorchester. (3:2)

Fig.31. 'p a d a' types. (3:2)

second half of the seventh century, *c*.655–70, and carrying through perhaps until 685. Pada's was an ambitious issue – over thirty specimens are known, with known provenances mainly in Kent, also in Suffolk and the London area. On this basis the coinage is thought to be Kentish. Technically it started as gold, though even at its finest the metal was alloyed with considerable amounts of silver, being at the best no more than *c*.20% gold. Before it came to an end it had degenerated to a silver one and so indicates a transition to the later *sceat*/penny coinage.

Pada took the designs for his pieces from Roman prototypes of the fourth century. The obverse always has a right-facing bust, wearing helmet, laurel or diadem, with the blundered remnant of a roman superscription. There are several reverse types bearing the moneyer's name, almost always in the form 'p a d a', clearly and neatly cut (fig.31). The earliest – at any rate a group which occurs in base gold only – derives from Roman reverses showing the imperial standard with the votive legend VOT XX·. The main feature has declined into a beaded rectangle with a 'fantail' representing the original standard top and a cross representing its staff. In some coins the votive text remains, more or less recognisable, with the moneyer's name set sideways along the edge of the standard, the rest of the reverse occupied with ill-shaped roman characters. In others 'p a d a' fills the standard to the exclusion of the votive legend. A second reverse type has a beaded circle with the name set horizontally within it and between two punched lines, only the 'fantail' remaining outside the circle to suggest the standard. Yet another type has a central cross between annulets, surrounded by a beaded circle round whose circumference runs 'p a d a' amidst yet another group of blundered roman letters. *Pada* is a monothematic masculine name. Formerly it was linked to the kings Penda of Mercia (d.654) and his son Peada (d.656), but scholars now recognise in it the moneyer responsible for the coins. The name does not occur elsewhere independently in Old English (though *Padda* does) but it is quite commonly identified as an element in place-names such as Padfield (Derbyshire), 'Pada's field', and Padiham (Lancashire), 'the village of Pada's people'.

Pada's coinage was short-lived. It was quickly and quite drastically deval-ued, and with it died regular Anglo-Saxon issues in gold. The next runic coins were silver *sceattas*/pennies, struck in the last years of the seventh century and the first quarter of the eighth and eagerly if crudely copied by Netherlandish mint-masters. They bear only moneyers' names: *Æpa/Epa, Til-berht, Wigræd*. Again we depend upon the numismatist's expertise and judg-ment to determine where probably the coins were minted. The earliest of these issues, in the name of 'æ p a' or 'e p a', are found scattered through southern and eastern England, and so are usually ascribed to Kent. The later coins, from *c*.720–50, are more or less confined to East Anglia.

The workmanship of these runic *sceattas*/pennies is fairly rough and it deteriorates with the later issues. The obverse shows a right-facing bust with radiate crown, and the reverse is usually an attempt at the imperial standard with its votive legend sadly distorted, though alternative designs comprise a saltire between pellets or a cross between annulets. This time the runic text is on the obverse, put radially before the crowned head, with the letter bases usually inwards but occasionally outwards (fig.32). The coins were often copied, and so it is common to find garbled versions of the legends. So, 'æ p a' or 'e p a' could deteriorate into what looks like 's p i', while 'e p a' com-bines with the distorted remnant of a roman T that appears on the prototype coin to produce a group resembling 'l e p a'. The die design may be reversed, producing retrograde letter forms, or the legend may be only partly copied, giving 'e p' or 'p a'. And there are even a few specimens with confused rune-like groups that seem to derive from a totally different original.[5] Presumably *Epa* and *Æpa* are forms of the same hypocoristic personal name using 'e' and 'æ' as equivalent graphs, as would be natural enough in the Old English

---

5   Illustrated in Metcalf, *Thrymsas and Sceattas*, vol.III, 514–15.

Fig.32. 'e p a' and 'æ p a' types. (3:2)

dialect of Kent and the neighbouring counties.[6] *Epa* seems not to be found elsewhere in independent use, but again may be the first element of a number of place-names, as for instance Epworth (Lincolnshire), 'Epa's homestead'.

Two other moneyers from the early period, Wigræd and Tilberht, appear to have worked in East Anglia. Wigræd's name appears in three forms: as 'w i g r æ d'; in a corrupt or abbreviated spelling 'w i g r d' (sometimes looking like 'w i g u d'), and as the shortened 'w i g r'. Both name elements are common though the compound *Wigræd* seems to have been rare; again it occurs occasionally in place-names, as Wyrardisbury (Buckinghamshire), 'Wigræd's manor', and there are Old Norse and Old Saxon cognates. Epa and Wigræd issued a rich coinage; in contrast Tilberht's coinage is rare and only recently has it been identified, in East Anglian contexts. Only one die (three specimens) has the clear form 't i l b e r h t'. Another seems to have the variant spelling 't i l b e r ᛇ t' with the rune *eoh* for the voiceless spirant [χ]. Perhaps from this developed the corrupt 't i l b e r l t' found on a third type.[7]

The last series of runic *sceattas*/pennies in the south is also fairly sparse. In 1991 Blackburn noted nineteen known specimens, and a few more may have appeared since.[8] The find-spots of these coins are in the south-east and East Anglia, with occasional examples from the Low Countries; on this basis they have been attributed to Kent or the Thames Valley, and dated on the evidence of their metal content *c*.715 and later. The obverse shows a severe deterioration of the helmeted head design that Pada had used, for here it has become an almost abstract arrangement of lines which numismatists satirically liken to a porcupine. The reverse holds the moneyer's name *Æthiliræd* in three different forms. It is divided into its two elements which are set, one upside down with respect to the other, on either side of a line that runs dia-

[6] I argue this case in 'A Note on the Transliteration of Old English Runic Inscriptions', *English Studies* 43 (1962), 1–6.

[7] Blackburn, 'Anglo-Saxon and Frisian Coins', 155. Further on this series in Metcalf, *Thrymsas and Sceattas*, vol.III, 518–23.

[8] Blackburn, 'Anglo-Saxon and Frisian Coins', 157–8; Metcalf, *Thrymsas and Sceattas*, vol.I, 120–4.

Fig.33. 'æ þ i l i r æ d' types. (3:2)

metrically between the coin's beaded borders (fig.33). Most of the specimens read clearly 'æ þ i l i | r æ d', which is acceptable though the final -*i* of the first element is unusual and probably archaic. There is also the occasional example with 'æ þ i l . | r æ d' and a corrupt and retrograde form 'æ + i l i | r æ d'. Some of the pieces have the unusual 'd' form ᛣ. These were presumably copied from imperfect coins of this issue, which were poorly centred on the flan so that the second stem of the last letter missed it. Until fairly recently the Æthiliræd of these coins was confidently identified as the Mercian king of that name, son of Penda, who ruled from 674 to 704. Metcalf still accepts this as a chronological possibility,[9] but other numismatists remain sceptical, taking *Æþiliræd* to be the name of the moneyer responsible for the issue.

A *sceat*/penny coinage persisted only in the north of England. There inscribed silver *sceattas*, non-runic however, began in the early eighth century and continued to be made into the 790s.[10] Thereafter, in the reigns of Eanred, Æthelred II, Redwulf and Osberht royal and archiepiscopal moneyers struck the small and undistinguished pieces which numimatists call *stycas*. They are mainly of copper, though some of the earlier specimens have a silvery appearance which links them to the *sceattas*. Apart from the occasional rune in mixed contexts on issues of Ælfwald I (779–88), runes occur on coins of Northumbrian kings in the 840s to 860s. These are official issues, so their designs, elementary though they are in the main, incorporate two names, that of the king or prelate together with his style, and the moneyer's name. These are set radially surrounding some insignificant central feature like a cross, group of pellets or annulet, the royal or archiepiscopal name on the obverse and always in the roman character, and on the reverse the moneyer's name. Often the die-cutter used roman letters for this too, but sometimes he cut runes, or mixed runes with roman characters. From this it looks as though there was some discrimination between the scripts. For the official name and title roman was proper, but runes could serve for the moneyer.

[9] Metcalf, *Thrymsas and Sceattas*, vol.I, 68.
[10] Grierson and Blackburn, *Medieval European Coinage*, 295–303.

Fig.34. Runic *stycas* of Brother and Wihtred. (3:2)

Eanred (*c*.810–?40) had three moneyers using runes. One, Dægberht, made coins which have a silvery appearance and so probably belong to the early stage of Eanred's currency. Two others, Brother and Wihtred, were later officials, working in the last few years of the king's reign. Dægberht never used runes alone, but occasionally put a runic 'g' in an otherwise roman form, as +DAEgBERCT, +DAEgBERC, though he also displays an occasional odd form that might be transcribed +dEbeɨt or +dEBeɨt. Brother and Wihtred sometimes used runes only, as ' + b r o þ e r' or with a bind-rune '+ b r o þ e͡ r'; '+ w i ɨ t r e d' or the corrupt '+ w i h t r r' (fig.34). But they also mixed the scripts producing forms like +BROAþer, +wihTrr. Wihtred continued to act as moneyer to Æthelred II (*c*.840–?48), and again he used occasional runes for his name, as did two new men, Cynemund and Leofthegn: so, we get forms such as +VIHtRED, +CVNEMVnD, +LEOFDEgN, +LEOF-DEGn. One of Osberht's moneyers, Wulfsige, has occasional runes in the curious spelling +VVLFSIgt. One runic letter, 'l', tends to intrude often into otherwise non-runic names. Since this is the only runic character to find a place on the obverses of *stycas* it is likely that the die-cutters confused it with inverted L. For example, Æthelred II's name appears in such forms as EDIlRED, EÐElRED, and in moneyers' names 'l' occurs in +lEOFDEGn, +VENDElBERHT and EDElHElM.

In more southerly parts of England there was created a new type of currency which was to endure long, the silver broad penny. These were first minted towards the end of the eighth century, but between the last of the *sceattas* of southern and eastern England and the first of its broad pennies numismatists place a couple of issues of intermediary coins. The first is a group struck in the name of a king called Beonna or Benna. No Old English source records him, but he is identified with the mid eighth-century East Anglian king whom Florence of Worcester calls *Beorna* or *Beornus*, and Symeon of Durham names *Beanna*. He seems to have ruled jointly with a king called *Alberht* who has recently made his way also into the numismatic record.

In 1973 only five coins of Beonna were known. With the discovery of occasional new specimens and of a considerable hoard at Middle Harling

Fig.35. Beonna types. (3:2)

(Norfolk) in late 1980 the number of specimens rose dramatically, and in 1985 stood at 76. At that date Marion Archibald wrote an authoritative survey, which more recent finds from East Anglian excavations have rendered somewhat out of date.[11] Beonna's coinage was certainly carefully controlled, and issued from more than one mint. Three moneyers present their names on the coins, Efe, Wilred and Werferth. The obverses have the royal name and title, set radially round a small central feature, pellets or a cross (fig.35). Occasionally this is fully in roman, +BEONNAREX. More often it is mixed runic and roman (though in the case of the letters B, R one cannot always be sure which script is intended): +BEOnnaREX or BEnnaREss/ BennaREɨs (the last two graphs are of uncertain identification). There are a few examples entirely in runes: '+ b e o n n a r e x', as well as a considerable number that have the royal name in runes followed by an arbitrary symbol Ⴤ which presumably stands for the title *rex*, invented to fit in the space available on the flan: '+ b e n + n a Ⴤ'. As for the moneyers, Efe gives his name in roman, save that in some instances the consonant looks more like the runic 'f' than the roman F. Wilred, who was responsible for the fully runic issues with the arbitrary royal title symbol, has his name always in runes '+ w i l + r e d'. He also uses a slightly odd variant of 'd', ᛟ (fig.36). Werferth also appears only in runes: '+ w e r f e r þ'.

The single example known so far of a coin of Beonna's contemporary Alberht/Æthelberht was unearthed at Burrow Hill (Suffolk). Both royal and moneyer's names are in runes, and there is no royal title. The obverse text, divided into four quadrants, reads 'e þ ‖ æ l ‖ b e ‖ r t ‖', the reverse has '* i ‖ æ l ‖ r e ‖ d ‖', perhaps an odd form of *Ceolred*.[12]

More ambitious in design is the second of these intermediary groups,

[11] M.M.Archibald, 'The Coinage of Beonna in the Light of the Middle Harling Hoard', *British Numismatic Jnl* 55 (1985), 10–54.

[12] M.M.Archibald and V.Fenwick in *British Museum Magazine* 13 (1993), 19; in more detail in 'A Sceat of Ethelbert I of East Anglia and Recent Finds of Coins of Beonna', *British Numismatic Jnl* 65 (1995), 1–19.

Fig.36. Beonna coin by Wilred, with
the unusual 'd' rune. (3:2)

which comprises coins attributed to the King Æthelberht of East Anglia
whom Offa of Mercia beheaded in 794. They derive obviously from classical
prototypes. The obverse shows a diademed bust facing right, and above it
two names differentiated by script, 'l u l' and EÐIlBERHT. The reverse has
a beaded rectangle containing the figure of the she-wolf feeding the twins
Romulus and Remus. Above is the title REX and below a rather ragged
pattern of dots. There can be little doubt that the word REX is to be linked
to the name EÐIlBERHT, both being in the roman character. 'l u l' then represents the moneyer's name – a Lul strikes in East Anglia over the next few
years – and the distinction of the scripts is functional.

Anglo-Saxon broad pennies were larger and thinner than *sceattas*. Those
of Offa of Mercia, for instance, are between 15 and 19 mm in diameter, and
have weight standards around 1.25 and 1.3 grammes. Broad penny coinages
seem to have begun with issues by Kentish kings *c.*775, but they first became
important and abundant under Offa some years later, and thereafter continued, with variations in size and weight, as the only currency for most of
England for some five hundred years. Not many Anglo-Saxon broad pennies
have runic legends. There are no runes on the few surviving specimens from
the Kentish kings, nor on West Saxon pennies, which were first struck in the
early ninth century. On the other hand, Mercian pennies have a few runes in
moneyers' names of the late eighth and early ninth centuries, and East
Anglian pennies of the ninth century have occasional individual letters of the
script. As C.E.Blunt's extended study shows, Offa of Mercia's coinage was
rich, diverse and artistically exciting, and it was the product, largely or
entirely, of mints in Kent and East Anglia working in his name though presumably not under his immediate control.[13] The penny issues of this and later
kings are too elaborate and numerous for anything like an extended examination here, so I have to treat them summarily, contenting myself with indicating their runic pieces. Four of Offa's moneyers use runes in their names. One,
Beagheard (who also calls himself *Beoghard, Bahhard*) was Kentish, active
in the period *c.*787–92. The other three, Botred, Wihtred and Eadnoth, were

13 C.E.Blunt, 'The Coinage of Offa', *Anglo-Saxon Coins*, ed. R.H.M.Dolley (London
    1961), 39–62.

Fig.37. Penny of Offa by the moneyer
Botred. (3:2)

East Anglians, striking from *c*.790 onwards. Wihtred continued as moneyer
for Offa's successors Coenwulf and Ceolwulf I in the first decades of the
ninth century, and continued to put runes on his coins. Though Botred issued
a few coins for Coenwulf, none are known with runes. Beagheard used only
'g' in a group of pieces with the legend +BEAgHEARD. Both Botred (fig.37)
and Wihtred made coins which have their names entirely in runes, and the
only Offa penny of Eadnoth also has his name completely in the script.[14] In
addition, Wihtred produced mixed inscriptions, often setting out his name in
curiously confused form: +w‖IH‖tr‖ED, wiHtR+ED, tw‖H‖ED‖IR, R‖HED
‖wt.

On broad pennies of East Anglian kings runes are rare and occasional, as
in RAEgENHEBE for *Rægenhere*, moneyer to Æthelweard (*c*.850). Comparatively frequent is the occurrence of 'm' in otherwise roman legends,
though there is always the possibility that the rune is not intended, its form
developing from an overcut roman M. This rune is quite common on pennies
of the ninth-century King Edmund, and particularly so on the memorial
coinage for him, as St Edmund, that the East Anglians put out in the closing
years of the same century. It occurs in the royal name, in moneyers' names
like DAIEmOND and SIIEmOND *(Dægmund* and *Sigemund)*, in mONE (the
abbreviation for *moneta*, 'coin', or *monetarius*, 'coiner, moneyer') and in the
maker's signature +TEDVVINVSmEFC (= *Tedwinus me fecit*). These are
among the latest examples. Thereafter the script vanishes from the coinage of
England.

The last forty years have seen great developments in Anglo-Saxon numismatic studies; nor is there reason to think those developments have reached
their end. It is interesting to observe how they have already affected our
knowledge of when and where the English used runes, specifically by stressing the importance of the south and the south-east at the expense of the north
and north Midlands. Using their own types of evidence numismatists have
removed the pieces bearing the names of Pada and Æthiliræd from Mercia,

---

[14] C.E.Blunt and G.van der Meer, 'A New Type for Offa', *British Numismatic Jnl* 38
(1969), 182–3.

have finally settled the coins of Beonna and Æthelberht/Lul in East Anglia, and have shown that the rune-bearing broad pennies even of Mercian kings issued from Kentish and East Anglian mints. To this there is a remarkable parallel in the way recent discoveries of rune-bearing portable objects other than coins have affected our conclusions. Examples discovered in late years come from eastern England and the East Midlands, as the Spong Hill, Wakerley, Undley, Harford Farm, Brandon, Keswick and Heacham finds; and from the south, those from Watchfield, Southampton, and the Chessell Down pail.

These constitute a dramatic increase in runic material from the south and east, and runologists, long held spellbound by the rich word-hoards of the later northern rune-stones, are increasingly turning their interest to the more southerly – and often earlier – inscriptions. Numismatists have helped us to see more clearly the role of runes in this phase of Anglo-Saxon culture, in particular in the seventh and eighth centuries. They have suggested something of the relationship of runic and roman scripts at a transitional period of English development. They have indicated the importance of the metal-workers in the spread of the runic script, and to that extent have encouraged us to link some of the earliest English runic activity with that of Continental Germania.

10

Rune-stones

There are thirty-seven Anglo-Saxon rune-stones known, a figure that takes in
the Leeds fragment which nobody has observed since 1838, and the Bingley
'font' whose runes are illegible. Nearly all the stones come from ecclesiastical contexts. Some of these are clearly defined. The Bewcastle monolith
holds its ancient site within the parish churchyard. The superb cross of Ruthwell, not far distant, stands within the church. It was there when Bainbrigg
saw it about the year 1600 and presumably had been since Anglo-Saxon
times, but seventeenth-century reformers threw it down, broke, scattered and
neglected it, and nineteenth-century enthusiasts reassembled and repaired it,
taking the bits from the churchyard where they had lain for years and putting
the restored cross up in the manse garden. It did not get back under cover for
ninety years or so. The three pieces of the Leek cross-shaft, now stuck
together again, stand to the south of the church, in the yard where they lay
until they were rescued in 1885. A number of stones were dug up in churchyards: Alnmouth (from near the old church of the town, long since fallen to
pieces), Lancaster, the two Maughold slabs and the Bakewell fragment. Later
builders reused some stones as raw material, for they came to light when
modern vandals or improvers pulled down or rebuilt old churches: Chester-
le-Street, Collingham, Crowle, Great Urswick, Kirkheaton, Leeds, Orpington, Overchurch and the three Thornhill examples. Perhaps we may find
more in the coming years as we turn mediaeval churches to secular uses or
tear them down for the value of their sites.

The two Monkwearmouth fragments come from the neighbourhood of the
existing (and the Anglo-Saxon) church. Most of the six Lindisfarne stones
are from the later mediaeval priory ruins, and presumably all are connected
in some way with the Anglo-Saxon house on the island. Navvies spotted the
Hartlepool name-stones when they came upon an ancient Christian grave-
field in their diggings, and the place where the Dover slab was discovered
may also have been a cemetery, that of the lost church of St Martin-le-Grand.
Bingley is linked to the town's old grammar school, whose yard adjoined the

church's. A runic fragment was found in the excavation of St Ninian's cave, an ancient oratory in the coastal cliffs of Wigtownshire, much frequented by pilgrims. Hackness, though first recorded in the outbuildings of the local hall, has inscriptions connecting it with the cloister of *Hacanos*, spoken of by Bede. Whithorn I had been built into a village wall, and Whithorn II used as a paving stone. Both were probably grave headstones and presumably come from the monastery/cathedral which flourished there in Anglo-Saxon times. Two examples only remain whose ecclesiastical origin is uncertain, and one of these has a pair of related inscriptions that are clearly Christian memorials. This is the Falstone memorial stone, found three feet below the ground at Hawkhope Hill, close by the village of Falstone. The other is a mysterious stone, now practically illegible, which labourers dug up by chance in a field somewhere near Sandwich and Richborough (see above, pp.27–8).

Thus the link between rune-stones and the church is strong and obvious. It remains to the present day in the disposition of some of them. As we have seen, Ruthwell, Bewcastle and Leek stand on or near their original sites. The Maughold slabs are set up in a shelter or cross-house, specially built to hold a group of incised slabs from the general locality, in Kirk Maughold church-yard. Several examples remain in the churches where or near where they were found: Bingley, Chester-le-Street, Collingham, Crowle, Great Urswick, Hackness, Hartlepool I, Orpington and Thornhill. Not all these are easy to get at. The Crowle stone, for instance, stands in the church nave, but the workmen who erected it there put the inscribed face close to a bench end that masks it, making study difficult and photography impossible. Moreover, it is hard to regulate conditions of lighting in a public building like a church, and consequently few of these pieces had, until recently, been as carefully studied and skilfully photographed as those that were transferred to museums. The latter comprise Alnmouth, Falstone and Hartlepool II (Museum of Antiquities, Newcastle-upon-Tyne), Bakewell (Sheffield City Museum), Dover (Dover Museum), Kirkheaton (Tolson Memorial Museum, Huddersfield, on long-term loan), Lancaster and Monkwearmouth I (British Museum), the Lindisfarne rune-stones (Lindisfarne Priory Museum), Monkwearmouth II (Sunderland Museum), Overchurch (Grosvenor Museum, Chester), St Ninian's cave and Whithorn I and II (Whithorn Priory Museum), and Sandwich/Richborough (Royal Museum, Canterbury).

In general the stones kept in museums are safer from vandalism and careless handling than those in churches. The latter are at the mercy of the visiting public and the ecclesiastical authorities who are not always well-advised in their treatment of these relics. They have often suffered curious vicissitudes in the course of their known history. For example, the Collingham stone is in two pieces now rejoined (fig.38). The lower one, which bears the runes,

Fig.38. The
  Collingham cross
  in its present state.

Fig.39. The
Collingham cross as
recorded in Stephens's
*Old-Northern Runic
Monuments*.

was found in 1841 beneath the ground and near the foundation of the church. At any early date it was complemented by the addition of bits of another cross, or perhaps even of two other crosses, and made into the curious composite structure that appears in early drawings and photographs (fig.39). For a time this stood in the vicar's garden and then in his greenhouse. By 1891 it was within the church, but was moved more than once before it reached its present site at the east end of the north aisle. We do not know when the correct top piece replaced the errant ones, but certainly by 1912 the two bits had been reunited.

When we are dealing with stones that have this sort of history, we must take into account the possibility that they have deteriorated since they first came to light, and that early drawings show their texts in better condition, more complete than they now are. An obvious case, noted in chapter 4, is the Ruthwell cross, where Bainbrigg's draft of *c*.1600 enables us to reconstruct the beginning of its *Dream of the Rood* text which was broken away in the reforming attack on this 'Idolatrous Monument'. Other drawings, made in the late seventeenth and eighteenth centuries, allow us to identify bits of letters that were damaged when the cross lay neglected in the church or churchyard, or when it stood exposed to wind and rain in the manse garden.

However, it is dangerous to use early depictions uncritically to reconstruct damaged or destroyed runes. The Collingham stone provides a stern warning, for we might hope to get help from nineteenth-century scholars who saw it before it went on its travels through the vicarage and round the church. As the cross now is, it has two lines of weathered and worn runes, one across the base of each of two adjoining faces. They read 'æ f *t* [. | .] s w i þ i', 'in memory of [.]swith'. The lines are curiously placed on the stone and could be later additions. They form a remarkably laconic inscription for a fairly elaborate memorial. The antiquary and rune-seeker D.H.Haigh was the first to report this stone, at a meeting of the Geological and Polytechnic Society of the West Riding of Yorkshire held at Leeds in 1857.[1] A drawing accompanies the printed text of his paper. He managed to see traces of runes on all four faces, two lines to the face, giving him a full inscription which he reconstructed:

+ŒDILBLÆD	ÆFTÆRGI	AUSWINIC	EGÆDDE
THISSETTÆ	NIFÆYMB	YNINGGIC	RSAULE

'Œdilblæd this set after her nephew after Auswini the king pray for the soul.'

---

[1] 'On the Fragments of Crosses discovered at Leeds in 1838', *Proc. Geological and Polytechnic Soc. W. R. Yorks.* 3 (1849–59), 512–13.

Part of this text is conjecture: for instance, Haigh admitted seeing on the fourth side 'an inscription almost defaced, of which the most distinct letter is an S at the beginning of the second line'. He completed his reconstruction by surmise and by recourse to other Anglo-Saxon memorial inscriptions. But even allowing for these additions there must have been, if Haigh is right, much more visible on the stone in 1857 than we can see now. But is Haigh right? By 1870 he complained that the runes had deteriorated. Nevertheless he could now read and restore the text +ŒONBLÆD THIS SETTÆ ÆFTÆR GISIBÆ YMB AUSWINI CYNING GICEGÆTH THÆR SAWLE which is different enough from the 1857 version to cast some doubt on both.[2]

George Stephens published Collingham in the first volume of *The Old-Northern Runic Monuments of Scandinavia and England* issued in 1866–7. Taking his information from photographs, rubbings and a drawing he gave not much more than now exists, admitting only traces of other runes. Stephens was not usually a cautious scholar in this sort of way, and the fact that he could see little of what Haigh saw is noteworthy. Haigh's runic work, in so far as it can be checked closely, is often erratic, showing an eagerness to find runes where none exist.[3] Moreover Haigh's readings of the Collingham inscription are curious Old English, with unexampled names like *Auswini* and *Œonblæd*, a strange use of the preposition *ymb* where we would expect *æftær* to be repeated, and of the verb *geciegan* (GICEGÆD), 'call upon, invoke', where *gebiddan* is usual. Runologically Haigh's drawing is suspect for it evidences 'ḡ' and 'k̄', neither found in other inscriptions from this part of the country, and shows the former as the first letter of GICEGÆD where it has no right to be since it ought to represent a back not a fronted *g*. All this should be enough to show how little we can trust Haigh's reading of the Collingham stone, and to suggest that even in the mid-nineteenth century its runic text was not much fuller than today. This does not mean that Collingham never held a more extensive text; nor that the weathered marks faintly visible on it may not once have been runes; nor indeed that in Victorian times the existing runes were not clearer than now. Perhaps I should take more seriously than I do the fact that both Haigh and Stephens read *-wini* not *-swiþi*, even though the 'þ' looks fairly clear to me and the form of Stephens's 'n' is not convincing. What, however, seems certain is that we are unlikely to get as much from nineteenth-century accounts of the Collingham runes as some of them want

---

2 'The Runic Monuments of Northumbria', *Proc. Geological and Polytechnic Soc. W. R. Yorks.* 5 (1869–70), 202.

3 R.I.Page, 'Runes and Non-runes', *Medieval Literature and Civilisation*, edd. D.A.Pearsall and R.A.Waldron (London 1969), 34–5.

to give. This is a special case of early drawings misleading the student, but it contains a general warning.

For the early history of a rune-stone practically the only evidence is the state of the stone itself. That many were re-used by later builders is both a help and a hindrance. These masons had no compunction in breaking, cutting or chiselling away part of a stone, since it would be largely meaningless to them by virtue of its obscure script and language. At Great Urswick they cut away the top, base and much of the right side to reduce it to the dimensions needed for a window lintel. At Crowle they chipped away part of the surface when they fitted it over the nave-tower door, perhaps to give keying to a coat of plaster. At Orpington they cut away about a third of its circular sundial before embedding the stone face inwards in the nave wall. In doing these things, though they destroyed part of the runic material, they also sealed the rune-stone in its new setting so that it remained unchanged from that time on. When the Crowle and Great Urswick stones were dug out of their walls in 1869 and 1911 they already showed signs of heavy weathering which must have preceded their re-use, and it is natural to guess that, in opposition to the Ruthwell but like the Bewcastle cross, they occupied much of their early existence in the open air, worn by the elements. When the Orpington stone was discovered in 1958 its surface was in good condition. It had spent little time out of doors, but could hardly do its job as a sundial under cover; so we might deduce that the dial was taken down not long after its erection. This would put it late in the Anglo-Saxon period (as, tentatively, the nature of its roman text also does), at a time when both language and architecture were about to change profoundly. Of the stones found in sealed contexts of the later Middle Ages, most show a good deal of weathering, as Collingham, Great Urswick, Kirkheaton and Thornhill I and III. Thornhill II, on the other hand, is little worn and can hardly have been long outside. It is a standing memorial stone, as are Thornhill I and III, so it looks as though some of these were set in churches, others in graveyards.

Seldom are rune-stones found in situ, so seldom is there archaeological evidence of their early history. The only clear case is Hartlepool where the two runic name-stones, as well as several similar specimens with memorial texts in roman script, occurred in graves. The discovery was accidental, not the result of controlled excavation, and the find-reports are consequently imprecise, conflicting and of uncertain authority.[4] In some graves the skulls rested on stones (though they were not all inscribed ones), and hence the Hartlepool slabs have sometimes been called 'pillow-stones'. In others the

---

4 For some of these accounts see G.Baldwin Brown, *The Arts in Early England* (1903–37), vol.5, 60–3.

inscribed stones seem to have been put near or over the head of the corpse, and this uncertainty of positioning has led recent scholars to prefer the neutral term 'name-stones'. The differing states of preservation of the two rune-stones are important evidence (figs. 11, 12). Hartlepool I shows little sign of weathering, and this could have been a pillow-stone for the corpse. The name may have been a pious memorial, or possibly an identification mark set with a corpse in case the grave had to be moved at some future date. Hartlepool II is heavily weathered. This may have lain over the body, originally at ground level but sinking in the course of years and gradually covered up. One or two of the non-runic Hartlepool slabs have prayer formulae, as ORA PRO UERMUND TORHTSUID, and this ought to imply that they were visible to the passer-by and so were above ground.

The shape and pattern of a stone sometimes indicates function. From Dover, for instance, comes a name-stone with the inscription '+*j* **i** s l h ea r d:'. This is a spelling of the masculine personal name *Gislheard*, using the rare 'j' for palatal *g* followed by stressed *i*, and the ambiguous rune '**i**' with its early value of a high front vowel (fig.40). The stone is a large roughly oval slab some 190 cm (75 inches) long. In relief is a cross on whose arms the name appears, cut upside-down with respect to the design. The stone is well weathered and probably came from a churchyard. It is fairly clear that this is a slab to cover a grave.

Fig.40. The Dover stone runes. (1:7)

Contrasting with it is Maughold I, also a slab bearing a cross with a masculine personal name, in this case 'b l a g c m o n' which is an unusual spelling of the common *Blacmon*, perhaps with a palatalised final consonant to its first element (fig.41). It is a piece of the local stone which forms natural slabs, so the face and back were left undressed and the sides cut only roughly. The base was left irregular, apparently so that it would stick easily into the ground. If so, this was presumably a grave headstone. Another stone meant to stand upright is the fragmentary Kirkheaton example, since it has a tenon cut for that purpose. Neither decoration nor inscription – a maker's signature – gives any indication of the purpose the stone served, so we must be grateful for this small clue.

Fig.41. The runes of the Maughold I slab.

Epigraphically the rune-stone inscriptions fall into a small number of categories. Most frequent are the memorial texts, though there are several different types. The simplest is the personal name alone: this is to be presumed in the nominative, as though expressing the idea '(this was) NN' or perhaps 'NN (rests here)', but in many cases it could equally well be accusative, as though in '(*æfter*) NN', '(in memory of) NN': cf. Collingham's 'æ f *t* [.] s w i þ i', though there the preposition seems to have taken the instrumental case. I have already listed Hartlepool I and II, Maughold I and Dover. There is also Monkwearmouth I, a stone with the name 't i d f i r þ' and some crude figure carving which art historians have recently ascribed to the first half of the

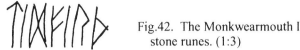

Fig.42. The Monkwearmouth I
stone runes. (1:3)

tenth century (fig.42).[5] From the late ninth is the Chester-le-Street standing stone, whose inscription mixes runes and roman capitals in the name EADm|VnD.[6] Some of the Lindisfarne stones may fit this group, though several are so fragmentary that it is hard to say. Lindisfarne I, however, is quite well preserved. Like its fellows it is a small round-headed slab with an incised decorative cross set within a border. In the two upper quadrants which

Fig.43. The Lindisfarne I
name-stone

the cross produces is a runic name 'o s ‖ g y þ', in the two lower ones the same in roman characters +OS‖GYÐ (fig.43). The two may refer to the same person, though not necessarily. They could be two different people, say mother and daughter, bearing the same name. The reason I suggest this is that other Lindisfarne fragments seem to record two different names, one in runes

5 R.Cramp, *County Durham and Northumberland*. CASS 1 (British Academy 1984), 123.
6 *Ibid.*, p.54.

Fig.44. The
Monkwearmouth II
name-stone.

above and the other in roman below the cross-arms. Lindisfarne V, for instance, appears to have two names with the second element *-wini*, apparently '[.] a m ‖ w i n i' and [.] AD ‖ WINI or [.] AÐ‖WINI: Lindisfarne II has BEANNA or BEANNAH with further roman letters making up an uninterpreted text, but above its cross-arms is '] o i n [.]', probably a name ending in *-oina*. Clinching is Monkwearmouth II, though only a small piece of it survives. In design it is closely similar to the Hartlepool and the Lindisfarne name-stone series. Like the Lindisfarne pieces it has runes above, roman below the cross-arms: 'e o [' and either AID [or ALD [, giving two distinct name elements (fig.44).

A stone bearing two names differentiated by the use of different scripts may record the two people most concerned with a memorial, the one commemorated and the one who put it up. Thus Lindisfarne I's two forms of

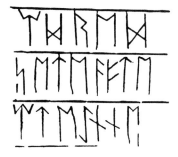

Fig.45. The Thornhill II stone
runes. (1:4)

Osgyþ, one preceded by a cross and one not, may abbreviate some formula such as 'Osgyth put this up in memory of Osgyth.' The full formula occurs in several rune-stones. Its simplest form is on two standing stones, perhaps ninth-century, from Thornhill. Thornhill II reads '+ ea d r e d | * s e t e æ f t e | ea t e ɨ n n e' (= +*Eadred* **sete æfte Eateɨnne*), '+Eadred set up (this memorial) after Eadthegn' (fig.45). The spelling 'ea t e ɨ n n e' is curious but there are parallels to the medial shift from *dþ* to *t* and to the inorganic doubling of 'n' so there is no reason to doubt the identification with *Eadþegn(e)* which H.M.Chadwick was the first to suggest. The use of 'ɨ' to represent the palatal *g*, almost vocalic, in the second element is notable and unexampled. Thornhill I has a much damaged text of a similar sort: '+ [.] þ e l b e | [.] *t* : s e *t* t < e > æ f t e | r e þ e l w i n i' (= + *Eþelberht sette æfter Eþelwini*), 'Ethelberht set up (this memorial) after Ethelwini.' Thereafter, and partly on the border, is an illegible addition.

On other stones this type of commemorative formula is expanded, with a request added for prayers for the soul of the dead. Complete examples are on the Great Urswick and Thornhill III stone. Great Urswick is a standing monument, with its carved foliage, beasts and human figures. The art historian dates it to the ninth century.[7] There are two inscriptions, the first being '+ t u n w i n i s e t æ | æ f t e r t o r o ɨ | t r e d æ b e k u | n æ f t e r h i s b | æ u r n æ g e b i d æ s þ e | r s ‖ a u | l æ' (= + *Tunwini setæ æfter Toroɨtredæ bekun æfter his bæurnæ gebidæs þer saulæ*), '+Tunwini set up a monument after Torhtred his son (taking *bæurnæ* as a form of *bearn*, though *beorn*, 'chief, prince' is also possible). Pray for his soul.' The word forms are archaic, in some senses perhaps distinctive of local dialect, but the sense is clear. Thornhill III, from the ninth century, has the similar '+ *j* i l s u i þ : a r æ r d e : æ f t [.] | b e r h t s u i þ e . b e k u n | o n b e r g i g e b i d͡d a þ | þ æ r : s a u l e' (= + *Gilsuiþ:arærde:æfte Berhtsuiþe · bekun on bergi gebiddaþ þær:saule*),

---

7   R.N.Bailey and R.Cramp, *Cumberland, Westmorland and Lancashire North-of-the-Sands*. CASS 2 (British Academy 1988), 150.

'Gilswith raised up in memory of Berhtswith a memorial on a mound. Pray for her soul.'

The very battered Falstone memorial has two inscriptions set side by side on the face of the stone. Both are fragments but enough is left to show that they were substantially the same, one in roman characters – insular majuscules to be precise – the other in runes. They read: +EO [.] | TA [.] *AEFTAER* | *HROETHBERHTÆ* | *BECUNAEFTAER* | *EOMAEGEBID-AEDDERSAULE* and '+ [.] | æ f t æ r r o e [.] | t æ [*b e c*] u n æ f t æ r e [.] | g *e* b [.] æ *d* þ e [.] s a u l e' (= + ... *æftærHroethberhtæ becun æftær eomæ gebiddæd þer saule*), '<NN set up> a monument after Hroethberht after his uncle. Pray for his soul.' The relationship between the two scripts at this date – perhaps the ninth century – is interesting for it seems that the carver, though acquainted with both, was more at home in the roman. For instance, in the name *Hroethberht* he followed the roman practice in using two characters 'o e' rather than the single rune 'œ' which would, by virtue of its name *oeþil*, more properly represent *o. . . .i*, *i*-mutated *o*.

The Overchurch stone is a flat slab, presumably designed for a grave. Its top has animal interlace and the inscription is in two lines on one of its sides. Workmen re-using the stone cut away one edge and with it the ends of both lines of text, so that a few letters of each are lost. The inscription remains comprehensible, reading, with a couple of errors corrected, 'f o l c {æ} a r æ r d o n b e c [|] *b* i d d a þ f o <r> e æ þ e l m u *n*['. (?= *Folc arærdon becun: gebiddaþ fore Æþelmun-*), 'The people (?host) raised a monument. Pray for Æthelmun<d>.'[8] Another variant on the commemorative formula was on the Crowle cross, whose text is so damaged and chipped away that very little remains. Art historians have commented on the late character of the crude ornament on this stone, and on the Danish influence it shows. Danish practice influenced the runes too, for they occupy a curving band cut in the stone in the Scandinavian fashion. Among the bits that remain we can distinguish the complex 'l i c b æ c *u* n' which it is natural to take as a compound noun, otherwise unrecorded, meaning 'corpse-monument', that is, 'memorial stone'.

A simple type of prayer formula occurs on the Lancaster cross, though it

8 A.Bammesberger is properly unhappy about the grammar of this statement, worried that a singular nominative, *folc*, should be thought to govern a plural verb *arærdon*. Accordingly he suggests that the subject is unexpressed, the indefinite 'they', and that *folcæ* is a dative singular. Thus he translates '(somebody) erected this monument for the people: (let them) pray for Æþelmund', which certainly wins a prize for ingenuity ('Three Old English Runic Inscriptions' in Bammesberger, *Old English Runes*, 130).

Fig.46. The runes of the Lancaster cross.

has its own problems. The piece is a free-standing cross of disputed date. Interlaces decorate its face, which also has a panel, within a raised border, carrying three lines of runes. They read 'g i b i d æ þ f o | r æ c y n i b a l | þ c u þ b e r e [.]' (= *Gibidæþ foræ Cynibalþ Cuþbere[.]*), 'Pray for Cynibalth, Cuthbere<ht>.' The ending is unfortunately lost in a damaged patch (fig.46). The presence of two names poses a problem of interpretation. Are we to read this as a request for prayers for two people, Cynibalth and Cuthberht? Or did the second name once have a patronymic ending as some have suggested: 'Pray for Cynibalth, Cuthberht's son'? Or is this an elemental version of the inscription that records deceased and commemorator: 'Pray for Cynibalth; Cuthberht (set up this stone)'?

Several of the more fragmentary or baffling texts could have been commemorative ones. The traditional reading of the Sandwich/Richborough stone is as a personal name, though David Parsons has pointed out how insecure this is.[9] The Maughold II fragment is similar to Maughold I, with incised cross and a group of runes that may be '] g m o n i' (if the last line is a half-length 'i') or perhaps just '] g m o n ·'. It is tempting to see this as part of the

[9] 'Sandwich: the Oldest Scandinavian Rune-stone in England?'

name *Blacgmon* which Maughold I also holds. A second element in the form -*moni* could be a dative/?instrumental following the preposition *æfter*, and Maughold II then compares with Collingham. Or it could be the genitive of a Latinised form of the name, the complete text being *(crux) Blacgmoni*. Leeds had the sequence '] cun' which may have been part of *becun* in an expanded commemorative inscription. Whithorn I has, cut along its edge, the group '[.] f e r þ s', obviously part of a personal name with the common second element -*ferþ*. Perhaps it is a genitive dependent on some noun like *becun* and giving the meaning '[.]ferth's monument', or it could be the beginning of a sentence [.]*ferþ s[ette]*, '[.]ferth set up', with the dead man's name elsewhere on the stone and now lost. Whithorn II is a slab with a low relief cross on its face. On the incised shaft of this cross are the remains of two full lines of runes, followed by a line that contained only two graphs. Most of the first line and part the opening of the second are worn away (for the slab had been re-used as a paving stone), and the bases of the two final runes are lost in a surface break, though they can be identified. Thus the only readable sequence is the very end of the text: '[.] h w i | t u', which could certainly be a name, or a byname, in an oblique case.

Finally in the series of commemorative monuments there is the great shattered cross of Bewcastle with its damaged, worn and worrying series of inscriptions. I have no space here to examine this cross and its runes in detail. I have considered elsewhere the epigraphical problems the monument raises, and here I simply sum up my discussion.[10] The cross-head is lost, but several draughtsmen copied its runes (though probably not independently) in the early seventeenth century (fig.1). They read 'r i c æ s d r y h t n æ s', 'of the powerful lord' or 'of the lord's power', which is no help without its context. The shaft, which survives more or less intact, is a single block of stone, intricately carved and extensively inscribed. Its west face, the principal one, has three figure panels representing St John the Evangelist with the *agnus dei*, Christ in majesty, and a figure with an eagle or hawk on a perch beside him, sometimes identified as St John the Evangelist.[11] An inhabited plant-scroll fills the east face, which thus has no space for runes. The north and south faces each have five panels of interlace, plant scroll, and chequers, one of them to the south enclosing a sundial. The inscriptions are set in the fillets or spaces above or between the decorative panels. All are severely worn, some virtually illegible. The main inscription, nine lines below the Christ panel, was I think tampered with in the nineteenth century so that much of it is irre-

---

10 'The Bewcastle Cross', *Nottingham Medieval Studies* 4 (1960), 36–57.
11 There is a detailed examination of the sculptured design in Bailey and Cramp, *Cumberland, Westmorland*, 61–72.

coverable. What remains seems to be a memorial inscription, for it contains the verb 's e t t o n' followed by a composite subject and governing an accusative 'þ i s s i g b [.] c [.]', *þis sigbecn*, 'this victory monument'. The penultimate line has the element 'g e b i d [.]', presumably a bit of a prayer formula. A fillet on the north face has the feminine personal name 'k y n i b u r * ḡ', but there is no indication why (fig.47). Two other recoverable inscriptions are not memorial. At the shaft head, where once there were several groups of runes, there now remains on the north face the fragment '[.] s s u͡ s', apparently a form of the name *Jesus*. Above the Christ panel of the west face is a similar text which serves to identify the carving it surmounts, '[+] g [e] s s u s | k r i s t t u s'.

Fig.47. 'k y n i b u r * ḡ' on the Bewcastle cross. (2:9)

Associated with Bewcastle in both style and date (set in the first half of the eighth century) is the runic cross at Ruthwell.[12] They differ in that Ruthwell preserves no text that can be called memorial, for what runes survive seem to serve the secondary Bewcastle purpose of identifying the carving that adorns the monument. They differ too in construction. Bewcastle was made up from a pair of stones, one of which formed the shaft still standing. Fixed to it by tongue and socket was the head, now lost. Ruthwell was also of two stones, an upper one being apparently both the cross head and the upper part of the shaft, a lower one comprising the greater part of the shaft and its base. When the reformers toppled the cross they shattered the upper stone into several bits. Four remain, built into the present cross and supplemented by new stone, and there is a fifth fragment, thought to be part of the cross beam, kept in a metal holder fixed to the railing of the pit wherein the cross stands. The lower stone was broken or cut midway across, and the two pieces are now rejoined, but with a good deal of the surface lost at the point of fracture. The cross base is sadly battered, and both carving and lettering are destroyed there.

The sculptures of the north and south faces of the cross form a group of figure panels identifying different aspects of Christ's life and ministry in its

---

[12] For details see the extended examination in *The Ruthwell Cross*, ed. B.Cassidy. Index of Christian Art Occasional Papers 1 (Princeton 1992).

Biblical record. In his reconstruction of the cross the early nineteenth-century minister of Ruthwell, Henry Duncan, fixed the topmost fragment, the upper limb of the head, the wrong way round, so in the following account I reverse its position. The south face has, beginning at its base: a severely damaged Crucifixion; the Annunciation; Christ healing the blind man; the sinful woman washing Christ's feet; two women embracing, usually identified as the Visitation; an archer shooting upwards; and a bird grasping foliage. The north face has, from base to top: a panel too battered for identification; the Flight into Egypt; the hermit saints Paulus and Antonius breaking bread in the desert; Christ in glory, his feet resting on two beasts; St John the Baptist holding the *agnus dei*, two male figures, identified as St Matthew and his angel; St John the Evangelist with his eagle. East and west sides have panels of foliage and inhabited vine scroll.

Broad borders surrounding the sculptured panels contain the numerous inscriptions. Several are in variants of the roman alphabet, Anglo-Saxon capitals and insular minuscules. They border some of the figure panels on the north and south faces and define their scenes, as for example the relatively complete legend [+]IHS X[*PS*] IVD[*E*]X:[*A*]EQV[*IT*]A[*TI*]S: BESTIAE: ET: DRACON[*ES*]: COGNOUERVNT: INDE:SERTO: SALVA[*TO*]REM: MVNDI:, 'Jesus Christ, judge of righteousness: in the desert beasts and dragons acknowledged the saviour of the world', which accounts for the Christ in glory.

The top stone of the cross had also runic texts on the north and south faces, but they are poorly preserved and only partly decipherable.[13] On the north face of the upper cross limb (as it is now set) is the sequence '] [.] æ f a u œ þ o [', standing amidst other, unidentifiable, runes. Attempts at interpreting this sequence have shown more ingenuity than judgment. Round two sides and along the top border of the ?Visitation panel runs the text, only partly legible, which seems to be 'm [.] r [.] a | m [.] e r | d o *m i n n* æ'. The first five runes apparently form the name *Maria* though from what remains *Marþa* is also possible and has sometimes been preferred. Since 'd o *m i n n* æ' is obviously Latin it looks as if this text, like the other Latin inscriptions of this side, was a title to the sculpture it accompanies. A group of runes remaining in isolation on the east face of the upper stone reads '] d æ g i s g æ f [.] [' – again a baffling sequence which has as yet only tentative explanation and for which there is no context of carving to give a clue to the meaning.

The runes of the top stone were cut sensibly so as to run in fairly long text

[13] A recent discussion is in B.Cassidy and D.Howlett, 'Some Eighteenth-Century Drawings of the Ruthwell Cross', *Antiquaries Jnl* 72 (1992), 102–17, particularly 116.

lengths along the borders they filled. Not so those of the lower stone, for where these occupy the vertical borders of east and west faces they are set, not along the length of the border, but in a succession of short horizontal lines of two, three or four letters each. Thus, that section of the text which fills the top and then the right-hand vertical border of the east face is divided up '[.] g e r e | d æ | h i | n æ | ḡ o | d a | l m | e ɨ | t t i | g þ | a *h* | e w | a l | d *e* | o n | ḡ a | l ḡ | u g | i s t | i ḡ a | *m o d* | i g f | [.] | [.] | m e n | [.]'. This looks absurd and is maddeningly hard to read. So odd does it appear that I incline to think it may not be part of the original design for the cross, and to wonder if these runes were added by a later carver who had less command over the space he had to fill. But this is a heretical view and not shared by art historians.

It was J.M.Kemble who first spotted that this group of inscriptions, all that remains on the top and side borders of the east and west faces of the lower stone, were a variant version of part of the *Dream of the Rood* poem otherwise known from the Vercelli Book.[14] The texts in free transcription and supplemented from early drawings of the cross and occasionally from Vercelli, are:

(a) '[+ .*nd*] geredæ hinæ ḡod almeɨttig þa *he* walde on ḡalḡu gistiḡa *mod*ig f[*ore* .] men ((*buḡ*)) [.]'

(b) '[.] ic riicnæ k̄yniηc h*e*afunæs h[*l*]afard *h*ælda ic *n*i dorstæ [*b*]ismær[*ad*]u uηk̄et *m*en ba æt[ḡ]ad[*re i*]c ((*wæs*)) [*m*]iþ blodæ bist[*e*]mi[*d*] *b*i[.]'

(c) '[+] kris[*t*] wæs on rodi hweþræ þer f*us*[*æ*] fearran kw[*o*]mu [*æ*]þþilæ til anum ic þæt al bi[*h*]((*eald*)) sa((*r.*)) ic w[*æ*]s mi[þ] s[*or*]ḡu[*m*] gi*dræ*[*f.*]d h[*n*]aḡ [.]'

(d) '[*m*]iþ s[*t*]re[*l*]um giwundad alegdun hiæ *hin*æ limwœrignæ gistoddu[*n*] *him* [.*li*]cæs ((*hea*))f((*du*))m ((*bih*))ea((*l*))[*d*]u ((*h*))i((*æ*)) [þ]e((*r*))[.]'

The speaker is the cross itself. Translated into modern English these verses become

(a) '+ Almighty God bared his body as he prepared to climb the gallows, valiant in men's sight . . . bow . . .'

(b) 'I . . . a mighty king, lord of heaven. I dared not bend down. Men mocked the pair of us together. I was stained with blood . . .'

---

14 'Additional Observations on the Runic Obelisk at Ruthwell . . .', *Archaeologia 30* (1844), 31–9.

(c) '+ Christ was on the cross. Yet to this solitary one there came men from afar, eager and noble. I beheld it all. I was bitterly distressed with griefs . . . bowed down . . .'

(d) 'Wounded with arrows. Down they set the man weary of limb. They stood at the corpse's head. There they beheld . . .'

These correspond, though perhaps not as closely as some think, to a group of verses 39–42, 44–5, 48–9, 56–9, 62–4 in the Vercelli *Dream of the Rood*. The upper stone sequence, '] d æ g i s g æ f [.]' has been completed '[*w œ p*] d æ g i s g æ f [*t*]' and likened to the phrase *weop eal gesceaft*, 'all creation wept', of the Vercelli poem, 55; but this theory remains unproven and probably is unprovable. The verses do not define any particular carving of the cross (even though the Crucifixion once appeared on the south face) but rather evoke the central act of sacrifice in the Christian myth which the cross as a whole represents.

This group of inscriptions is the most sustained piece of runic carving in Anglo-Saxon England, and so gives us the clearest opportunity for seeing English runes in action in formal expression. Transliterated the texts look surprisingly like early Old English ones that are not in runes, which is to say that using runes has made little difference to the language forms. In so far as these look unusual to many students of Old English it is in the main because they are early and Anglian; but nearly all the peculiarities can be paralleled in scribal material of early date and Anglian provenance. The use of doubled letters, as in 'a l m e i t t i g', 'r i i c n æ', '[œ] þ þ i l æ' and 'g i s t o d d u [*n*]' is curious and may be typical of rune-masters' practice. There is a skilled use of the various characters available for the palatal and velar stops: 'c' for front *c* in 'r i i c n æ', 'i c', '[*l i*] c æ s' (and, perhaps curiously, also for the final sound of '*k̄* y *n i ŋ* c'); 'k' for the back *c* before a consonant in 'k r i s [*t*]', 'k w [*o*] m u'; 'k̄' for the back *c* before a front or secondary palatal vowel in '*k̄* y *n i ŋ* c', 'u *ŋ* *k̄* e t'; 'g' for the front *g* in ' [+ . *n d*] g e r e d æ', '*m o d* i g', 'g i *d r œ* [*f* .] d', 'g i w u n d a d', 'a l e g d u n', 'l i m œ r i g n æ' and elsewhere; 'ḡ' for back *g* in 'ḡ o d', 'ḡ a l ḡ u', 'g i s t i ḡ a', 's [*o r*]ḡ u [*m*]', 'h [*n*] a ḡ'; 'i' for the spirant in 'a l m e i t t i g'.

The last type of inscription to be discussed is the craftsman's signature, which a few stones preserve. Complete is that on the Kirkheaton stone, 'e o h : w o r o | h t æ', 'Eoh made (this)' (fig.48). The name *Eoh* (also a common noun meaning 'horse, stallion') is not recorded elsewhere, but it is a likely Anglo-Saxon personal name comparable to other animal names such as *Fisc*, *Hauoc* and *Wulf*, and is equivalent in meaning to *Hengist* and *Hors(a)*. There are two fragmentary texts which we can certainly complete as signatures. Almnouth has the mixed MYREDaH·MEH·wO[, 'Myredah made me'. The

Fig.48. The Kirkheaton stone runes. (1:4)

Irish name *Muiredach* is not found elsewhere in Old English sources, but does occur in early Middle English, and this implies a later date for the Aln-mouth stone than the most recent art historical estimate (late ninth to early tenth century').[15] Beneath his main inscription and across the two facing figures that occupy much of the face of the stone, the Great Urswick carver proudly placed his announcement, 'l y l þ i ‖ s w [.] [', presumably 'Lyl made this'. The tiny fragment of a runic text remaining on the St Ninian's cave stone could also bear a form of the verb *wyrcan* so perhaps this too once held the artist's name.

Critics have long recognised the major Ruthwell cross texts as poetry and admitted them to the Anglo-Saxon verse corpus. What has often been ignored is that several of the memorial inscriptions too are in alliterative verse.[16] This is a loose form not always easy to distinguish from rhythmic prose, and some inscriptions fall on the borderline between the two. For instance, the Thornhill II text can be set out as an alliterative line:

> *Eadred sette   æfte Eadþegne.*

The stress pattern points the two personal names which, besides alliterating, possess the same first element, perhaps because the two men were relatives. There is a similar pattern in Thornhill I which we can normalise and com-plete:

> *Eþelberht sette   æfter Eþelwini.*

---

15 Cramp, *County Durham and Northumberland*, 162.
16 Belatedly, the inscriptions of Falstone, Thornhill III, Great Urswick, Overchurch and the Manchester ring were admitted to the poetic corpus in *Old English Verse Texts from Many Sources: a Comprehensive Collection*, edd. F.C.Robinson and E.G.Stanley. EEMF 23 (Copenhagen 1991).

In these two cases the resemblance to verse lines may be chance, dependent upon the personal name alliteration. Thornhill III has an extended memorial formula of two lines, where the extra wording shows that verse was intended even though the two names begin with different letters so that the first has no alliteration.

> *Gilswiþ aræde   æfte Berhtswiþe*
> *becun on bergi: gebiddaþ þær saule.*

Great Urswick i is similar:

> *Tunwini settæ   æfter Torohtredæ*
> *becun æfter his bæurnæ: gebiddæs þer saulæ*

while the Falstone texts apparently follow the same pattern.

Though these are formal texts, the carvers made no effort to show the verse form by refinements of punctuation or lay-out. Indeed the Anglo-Saxons' attitude to setting out and pointing inscriptions was lax compared with modern requirements of neatness and precision. Even in Anglo-Saxon times, however, different craftsmen had different standards and conventions. Most crude of memorial inscriptions is Great Urswick i. Here the carver cut a panel for the inscription to fit in, but failed to make it fit. He embarked upon his text without preliminary lay-out lines, so the runes are crude, ill-spaced and of unequal size. He started confidently with large letters, but by the time he came to the last line of the panel he was cutting smaller runes and cramping them together. Even then he did not get all his words in but had to complete the text below the panel. Here was a scene showing two facing figures with a cross standing between them. He cut his last six runes in the only space available, in three of the quadrants that the cross formed. Thus the final lay-out is:

> '+ t u n w i n i s e t æ
> æ f t e r t o r o ɨ
> t r e d æ b e k u
> n æ f t e r h i s b
> æ u r n æ g e b i d æ s þ e
>   r s ‖ a u
>   ‖ l æ'

There is no division into words, no punctuation, while only in line 1 does line-end and word-end coincide. The whole effect is casual, clumsy and coarse (fig.49).

Fig.49. The Great Urswick stone runes. (1:5)

Contrast with this Thornhill III. The inscription is cut on a panel divided into four lines by horizontal incisions. The lay-out is:

'+*j* i l s u i þ : a r æ r d e : æ f t [.]
b e r h t s u i þ e · b e k u n
o n b e r g i g e b i d̂ d a þ
þ æ r. s a u l e '

This is much better than Great Urswick i, but still not perfect. The last line is only half filled with lettering; the rest of it remains blank. But the rune-master has separated lines at word-ends, and in lines 1, 2 and 4 has split his text into discrete words by the use of points. Presumably he did not do the same in line 3 because he had no room; for the same reason he made it convenient to bind 'd͡ d'. He found his task too difficult. He had to lay out his material so that it occupied four lines without cutting up words, and he only half managed it. But he did make the attempt (fig.50).

The other two Thornhill stones, which also have inscription panels divided by horizontals into separate lines, use pointing rhetorically. Thornhill I is:

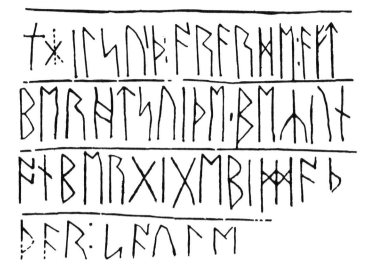

Fig.50. The Thornhill III stone runes. (2:5)

'+ [.] þ e l b e
[.] *t* : s e *t* t æ f t e
r e þ e l w i n i : [.] r'

followed by the illegible marginal addition. The carver has not taken note of
line endings nor has he pointed every word, but he uses the colon to stress the
two important elements of his text, the names of the man who commissioned
the monument and the dead man commemorated. The Thornhill II mason
does the same thing by the way he arranged words into lines:

'+ ea d r e d
* s e t e æ f t e
ea t e ɨ n n e'

each name filling its own line. Perhaps this arrangement accounts for the
inorganically doubled 'n'. The carver wanted his second name to fill the
space neatly. By the time he got to the first 'n' he realised he was too far to
the left. He could hardly double the final vowel rune so he duplicated the
penultimate, for purely decorative reasons.

   This comparison shows how differently individual rune-masters reacted to
the questions of neatness of lay-out and finish. Other examples confirm the
range of usages. From what remains it looks as though Crowle had no word
separation. Lancaster has none, nor did its carver bother to end lines at word-
ends:

'g i b i d æ þ f o
r æ c y n i b a l
þ c u þ b e r e [.] ['

Casual arrangement like this may continue the traditional practice that I noted in chapter 8 above: cutting runes is important, their appearance not. Falstone and Overchurch do not split their texts into separate words but as far as we can see their carvers tried to complete lines at the ends of words, though the Falstone one did not always succeed:

+EO[,]   '+ [.]
TA[.]*A*EFTAER   æ f t æ r r o e [.]
HROETHBERHT*Æ*   t æ [*b e c*] u n æ f t æ r e [.]
BECUNAEFTAER   g e b [.] æ *d* þ e [.] s a u l e '
EOMAEGEBIDAEDDERSAUL*E*

              'f o l c æ a r æ r d o n b e c [
              [.] *b* i d d a þ f o t e æ þ e l m u *n* ['

Alnmouth and Kirkheaton divide their material into separate words but end lines as space runs out, indifferent to the sense. The Alnmouth cross is an elaborate piece of sculpture, with a crucifix on its face and interlace and key pattern panels elsewhere. Its several texts are cut on fillets scattered over the surface of the stone, much of which is missing. So, there is one complete line of text which says SAV, presumably the beginning of the word *saul(e)*, 'soul'; the end was on a piece of the cross now lost. A personal name in the genitive divides between two lines EADV | LFES. The partly runic artist's signature is MYREDaH · MEH · wO, and the word *worhte* was, I suppose, completed elsewhere on the stone. Kirkheaton's signature divides:

          'e o h : w o r o
          h t æ '

roughness of arrangement matching crudeness of workmanship.

In many cases, then, the Anglo-Saxon mason did not plan his lay-out so as to give the runes a pleasing appearance. In others he obviously did, though nowhere near as strictly as the modern craftsman would. A passage as long as the Ruthwell *Dream of the Rood* would need a deal of preparation to ensure that, with its curious organisation into short horizontal lines cut one below the other in vertical borders, the wording fitted the space. Even there it is probable that the preliminary planning was general rather than detailed. Circumstances like these are bound to produce error, and some difficult readings on rune-stones may be the effect of carelessness rather than subtlety in representing language. Certainly, English rune-masters made mistakes, even in quite well-arranged inscriptions. As we have seen, Overchurch has two errors, while the Hartlepool II carver missed out a letter and added it above the line. The Ruthwell carver made two emendations, for he cut two full-length verticals for the last letter of '[*b*] i s m æ r [*a d*] u' and had to correct the 'œ' of 'l i m w œ r i g n æ' from a 'g'. Maughold I has a careful design of concentric circles containing a cross with arced arms. Its runes are neatly formed, yet between the 'c' and 'm' of 'b l a g c m o n' is a line which the carver cut but did not use or even widen out. Presumably it is a miscut, perhaps a first attempt at the beginning of 'm'. Thornhill I may have a letter missed out in 's e *t* t æ f t e r', though it is possible (but perhaps unlikely) that the rune-master intended 'æ' as both the final rune of 's e t t æ' and the initial of 'æ f t e r'. In the case of Thornhill II the carver's graver slipped when he was working on the last letter of 'ea d r e d' and deeply gashed the interlace panel above. This gives the additional, perhaps helpful, information that the carver cut his letters from the base upwards.

Such an incidence of mistakes makes the runologist more inclined to look on strange rune shapes or spellings as erroneous. For instance, Thornhill III has the clearly written name '*j* i l s u i þ', but the second 'i' is a small character squeezed precariously between the curve of 'u' and 'þ'. Though there is some evidence elsewhere for a half-length 'i' it is likely that the Thornhill III rune-master missed out his letter and inserted it later as best he could. Thornhill II has a case which is quite similar. Its second line starts with the verb 's e t e', but before 's' is a short vertical which, if it were 'i', would convert the word to the complex 'i s e t e' (= *gisette*, *gesette*, 'established'). Though it is far more likely to be an error, the beginning of a misplaced vertical of 's', yet I am so unsure of that interpretation as to transliterate the form '* s e t e'. We can only speculate as to what linguistic or runological conclusions should properly be drawn from strange spellings such as the Great Urswick 'b æ u r n æ' (with its unparalleled fracture diphthong), Maughold I 'b l a g c m o n' (with its curious 'g c') or the doubled letters which occur so often, as in Ruthwell's 'r i i c n æ', 'a l m e ᛁ t t i g' and 'g i s t o d d u [*n*]'.

However, we must not overstress the Anglo-Saxon rune-master's carelessness. We do not now see the rune-stones as they were meant to be seen. Illuminating in this respect is the word *becun*, 'beacon', which the monumental inscriptions use to denote these monuments. Semantically *becun* has three implications in Old English verse texts – and we must remember that many monumental inscriptions are in fact verse. The first implication is that of a token or symbol: the monument is a record or token of the departed, and if it is a cross it may also be remembered as a symbol of Christ who intercedes for the dead man's soul. The second is that of conspicuousness: a *becun* is something that can readily be seen, because of its position (*on bergi*, for instance) or its impressive and towering appearance. The third is that of brilliance: *becun* collocates very often with the adjective *beorht*, and refers to fiery or glittering objects. The last connotation may tell us something of how contemporaries saw the rune-stones. In the case of Scandinavian rune-stones we know that some were painted because a few survive with the original paint, while a quite common phrase 'inscribed runes' used the verb *fá*, 'paint'. As visitors to the National Museum, Copenhagen, will have seen with apprehension, Danish runologists have experimented with colouring replicas of Viking Age stones in bright hues. Probably English rune-stones were painted too. Little survives, but there is a slight suggestion of red colouring on Maughold I, blue and black on Great Urswick, and some have found traces of raddle on Collingham.[17] If the rune-stones were extensively painted, the runemaster's errors could be disguised by a painter who would obliterate wrong forms and replace them by right ones.

In this chapter I have spoken of rune-stones as though each was the work of a single craftsman; but it is possible and in some cases probable that several workers combined to make a monument. With a large product like the Ruthwell cross it is obviously unlikely that the workers at the quarry that supplied the stone blocks and roughly shaped them were the same as the highly skilled sculptor(s) who carved the elaborate decoration, nor need the latter have been the same as the rune-master(s) who cut the runic letters so absurdly in horizontal rows down the shaft. The question then arises whose concept the final work was, how carefully it was controlled, and whether the runes were part of the original design or were additions. If, as Rosemary Cramp has cautiously suggested, the carvers of Ruthwell came from Monkwearmouth/Jarrow, did the rune-masters too?[18] If so, what local dialect of Old English did they represent on the stone? In the case of the Hartlepool name-stones we note a common design in the monuments, but the inscriptions are not essential to that design. If commercial masons made these pieces, they may have prepared in advance numbers of incised slabs, adding names to them as they came into use, and the names may then belong to different traditions even though the slabs are closely similar. Elisabeth Okasha found tentative evidence for the practice on two of the non-runic stones from Hartlepool (her nos. IV and V) where the words *ora(te) pro* seem carved at a different time from the names they govern.

As this chapter has shown, the content of the Anglo-Saxon rune-stone

---

[17] Elisabeth Okasha has found traces of paint on some non-runic inscribed stones. S.B.F. Jansson illustrates the painting of Swedish rune-stones in *Runes in Sweden*, 153–61.

[18] *Early Northumbrian Sculpture*. Jarrow Lecture 1965, 10–11.

inscriptions is pretty dull. Nearly all are stylised in wording and sentence structure. There are few different types. What they say is fairly uninteresting. They add nothing to our knowledge of political or administrative history, and little enough to what we know of social history. (Here they differ from the Viking Age rune-stones of Scandinavia, which give valuable information on social ranking, land ownership and inheritance.) They make interesting suggestions about literacy in Anglo-Saxon England, but prove nothing. As records of the language, however, of what was recorded in certain places at certain times, they are invaluable, indeed unrivalled, though not unambiguous. To this aspect of the subject I return in chapter 15.

11

Runes Elsewhere

The rune-stones are not troublesome to sum up since they form a roughly homogeneous group, are all as far as we can tell Christian, and their inscription types are in the main few and platitudinous. Other runic objects are harder to survey. They spread over a longer time, from pagan to Christian. On an average they are earlier than the stones. Their legends, though often baffling, certainly cover a wider range of contexts. New examples appear with distressing frequency. It is hard to fit all known examples into a general summary; indeed some of them belong more properly in other chapters of this book.

As with the stones some objects have inscriptions so fragmentary, damaged or faint that we can hardly even guess at their meaning. Half a dozen examples chosen at random will suffice to illustrate the point. First, there is a plain bronze finger-ring dug up in the churchyard of Cramond, Edinburgh, the most northerly of our provenances. It is kept in the Museum of Scotland, Edinburgh. Round the outside of the hoop runs a sequence of runes, sadly affected by corrosion and modern polishing. What remains of the untidy rune-row is '[.] e w o r [.] e l [.] u', but there is no sign to show where the legend begins; which does not assist interpretation. The sequence 'w o r' would suggest a maker formula *NN worhte* or something of the kind, but the rest of the runes hardly support it. A personal name is possible, or a pair of names, but these are conjectures only.

A similar riddle is posed by a couple of gold strips, apparently part of the same object perhaps a finger-ring, found on the seashore near Selsey and now in the British Museum. The strips are about 5 x 18 mm (0.2 x 0.7 inches), broken off at each end and corrugated into zigzag shape. Each has runes scratched on one face, one with '] b r n r n [', which is meaningless to us and cannot have been articulate even to the Anglo-Saxons. The other has been variously taken as '] a n m æ [', '] a n m u [', '] a n m l [', '] o n m æ [' and so on. Whatever the correct reading of the text, it is too short to be of help. From a sixth-century woman's grave at Chessell Down, Isle of Wight, not so far from Selsey is a bronze pail, also in the British Museum. This is an import from the eastern Mediterranean, but it has, only recently noticed on its outer surface, mingled with a punched design representing a pair of hunting scenes, the remains of a mysterious runic sequence. What survives is '*b* w s [.] e c c c æ æ æ'. From the repetition at the end it appears this was not a plain language text, which is likely to lead runologists to believe it must be the remains of a magical or cryptic text.

Rather different is the case of a bronze sword-pommel in the Maidstone Museum. It was in 1863 that members of the Kent Archaeological Society found it in a sixth-century grave in the inhumation cemetery of Sarre, Thanet, but over a hundred years passed before the runes were spotted on it, when two scholars, S.C.Hawkes and V.I.Evison, came upon them independently and described them in articles published almost simultaneously.[1] The pommel was once gilded, but most of this surface has gone through wear, corrosion or vigorous cleaning. Since the runes were lightly scratched in the gilt on both sides of the piece, they now survive only as faint impressions in the bronze, and it is not surprising that they escaped notice until these two eagle-eyed archaeologists went to work on the object. As well as being faint the runes are hard to distinguish from other marks on the surface, and any attempt at identifying the graphs, at reading and interpreting them is bound to involve much speculation and probably more controversy.

The Coquet Island ring presents a rather different problem. This was a simple hoop of lead which, according to report, the island's lighthouse keeper found in his garden, a spot where he sometimes came upon human bones and which therefore may have been the grave-field of the Anglo-Saxon monastery recorded in the early *Lives of St Cuthbert.* Indeed, according to the local antiquary Edward Charlton the ring was actually on the finger of a skeleton, but I suspect this to be a romantic addition to the tale. The duke of Northumberland bought it for his museum at Alnwick Castle, and a number of excited antiquaries examined and drew it, bringing it to the attention of George Stephens of Copenhagen. In due course the duke allowed it to be sent to Stephens who had a careful drawing made. When it returned to the duke he put it in a wooden box, and there it quietly disintegrated into a greyish lumpy powder, lead carbonate, the common corrosion product of lead. It now remains, as a specimen of just that, in the British Museum Research Laboratory, and for its runes we depend on a group of nineteenth-century drawings

---

[1]   Hawkes and Page, 'Swords and Runes in South-east England', 1–3; V.I.Evison, 'The Dover Ring-sword and Other Sword-rings and Beads', *Archaeologia* 101 (1967), 89.

a

b

c

d

Fig.51. Four drawings of the Coquet Island ring: a from Stephens's *Old-Northern Runic Monuments* I (1866–7); b, c, d, successive drawings by Edward Charlton in Royal Library, Stockholm, dep.189: b March, c September, d November, all 1863.

(fig.51). These disagree save for the beginning of the text, '+ þ i s i s', and perhaps the rune 'r' towards its end.[2]

A more recently found example of these difficult texts comes from Heacham. A pair of tweezers, now in the Castle Museum, Norwich, has runes cut on both sides, apparently the same text on each. Unfortunately, the metal is severely corroded, and only parts of the letters are visible. Individual runes are identifiable – 'd', 'f', 'u' and others – but from what remains it is not clear which way round the text is to be read. Even a conflation of the two sides does not help.

Finally, from a pit at Southampton, and therefore unstratified – though the general context is ninth-century – are two adjoining fragments of a small bone plaque, its face decorated with a crudely formed interlace pattern. Following this, and damaged at the edge of the piece, is a group of runes, also crudely formed (fig.52). The first is certainly 'd'. The graphs that follow are indeterminate and have lost their bases. It is possible to make only tentative identifications. There may be 'p' bound with the 'd' (but what could that mean?). Thereafter perhaps 'l' and two more runes, the first apparently the bind 'ī n', the second the top of a vertical. At that the text breaks off.

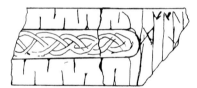

Fig.52. The fragmentary
Southampton bone plaque. (1:1)

Other English runic pieces have texts more or less complete, but though there may be few reading difficulties, problems of interpretation are often formidable. In chapter 1, I used as an illustration the various meanings that earlier scholars have attached to the seven letters of the Chessell Down scabbard mount. This inscription is not unique in its ambiguity. Indeed, we can confidently claim to know the meanings of fewer than half the runic legends preserved on portable objects other than coins. The rest either baffle us completely, or give the opportunity for several distinct interpretations of each. Usually there is no evidence to help us choose between them. An excellent example is a curious copper-alloy disc from the river Yare at Keswick. Its function is unknown. It is a sturdy object, 29 mm (1.1 inches) in diameter. There is a hole at its centre, plugged by a spherical-headed pin. The disc's top

2   Only one of the drawings was published, in Stephens, *Old-Northern Runic Monuments* vol.1, 480–1. The rest survive in the Stephens correspondence in the Royal Library, Stockholm.

Fig.53. The Keswick runic disc. (1:1)

surface has, circling round it, a sequence of eight runes (or possibly seven and a cross to indicate the text's beginning/end). They are deeply cut and clearly preserved, and read (taking the graphs counterclockwise as appears to be the intent) '+ (?or g, n) t l i m * (= ?s) u m (?or 'd')' (fig.53). John Hines wrote that this run of runes does not 'make clear lexical sense from any starting point', and I have to agree.[3] To sum up this unsatisfying opening of my chapter; how far it is worth while discussing possibilities with no means of reaching certainty is a question each student must answer for himself. My own response is that it is an occupation too many runologists have wasted their time, intelligence and erudition on.

This judgment puts in peril attempts at two sixth-century back-of-brooch inscriptions, from Wakerley and Heslerton. Both are quite clearly preserved though neither is unambiguous. Wakerley has the sequence 'b u h u' ('h' with a single cross-bar, so perhaps I should transliterate **buhu**), followed by a vertical that could be 'i' or may simply indicate the end of the text. Heslerton has four runes, either 'n e i m' or 'n e i e'. None of these makes obvious sense. However, they are simplicity itself compared with a new excavation find from the site of the Royal Opera House, Covent Garden, London. This is a hollow bone, 78 mm (3 inches) long, perhaps from a sheep or roe-deer. It is shaped for some sort of purpose and decorated with a series of incised and hatched bands. A smoothed area running along it is occupied by a sequence of runes, apparently retrograde. They contain the graph ⼂, which is a rare, manuscript, form of 'œ' interspersed with a number of verticals, which may be intended as 'i' forms or may be division symbols. The full text seems to be ← ' l œ l œ l þ l w l r d', though I cannot be sure of the distinction between 'þ' and 'w' here.[4]

Among the more promising texts, those whose meaning we know or stand a fair chance of determining, are some like those on rune-stones. There are,

---

3   'An Inscribed Disc from the River Yare near Norwich', *Nytt om Runer* 12 (1997), 13–15.
4   I have made the tentative suggestion that there may be a reference here to the personal name *Œþilward* but it is only a desperate guess: 'Runes at the Royal Opera House, London', *Nytt om Runer* 12 (1997), 12–13.

Fig.54. The Manchester ring legend. (3:2)

for instance, makers' signatures. Simplest is that on a ninth-century ring from the cabinet of the antiquary Sir Hans Sloane and now part of the foundation collection of the British Museum. Sloane's catalogue gave it only the general provenance, Lancashire, but this has been narrowed down to Manchester. The ring is a plain gold hoop, its legend, part runic part roman, set within beaded borders round the outer circumference. The craftsman cut away part of the surface and blackened it with niello, leaving the letters standing bright and clear in relief. They read, though the words are not separated, +æDRED MEC AH EAnRED MEC agROf, 'Ædred owns me, Eanred inscribed me' (fig.54).

A pious variant of the simple maker formula adorns the Mortain casket. This is one of the treasures of the church of Mortain, département Manche, Normandy, though nobody knows how it got there or when. It is a small house-shaped shrine or box, made of beech covered with thin plates of gilded copper. Its present form is that of a reliquary, for the roof has a window to allow the pilgrim to view the contents, but this is an alteration of the original construction and possibly as recent as the nineteenth century. The short sides of the box have buckles and loops through which could be passed a carrying-strap. It may have been a portable reliquary, but an alternative suggestion is that it was a travelling pyx for holding the consecrated host. On the front of the shrine the copper plates have repoussé decoration, representing, below, Christ flanked by the archangels Michael and Gabriel (identified by the legends SCSMIH and SCSGAB), and, above, a full-face figure of an angel with wings displayed. The runes are on the copper plate covering the back of the roof, cut or impressed in three uneven and untidy lines. They read:

'+goodhelpe:æadan
þiiosneciismeelgewar
ahtæ'

'God help Æada (who) made this *ciismeel*.' Some of the word forms suggest an Anglian provenance, while the stem vowel of *gewarahtæ* looks West Mercian. The last word of my translation, to be normalised *cismel*, presents the only interpretational difficulty since it does not occur anywhere else and its etymology is not self-evident. Explanations produced fall down on either formal or semantic grounds.[5] It has been compared with MLat *chrismal(e)*, 'box for the host', or *chrismarium*, 'reliquary', but the absence of -*r*- in the first element is against either of these. An alternative explanation derives it from MLat *cimelium*, 'treasure', but this requires an infix -*s*-. Formally convincing is Hermann Harder's suggestion of an OE **cistmæl* with the common loss of -*t*- in a three-consonant cluster. Here the meaning is a difficulty, for **cistmæl* should mean 'chest-cross' or conceivably 'choice cross', neither of which suits the Mortain shrine very well even though it has a small decorative cross on the roof, probably a later addition.

A slip of bone of unknown provenance may give a similar pious maker formula. It is commonly called the Derbyshire or Derby bone plate but I know of no evidence for the find-spot. The piece came to light in the collection of a Derby antiquary, and the British Museum accessions register for 1890 records it cautiously as 'perhaps found in Derbyshire'. It is a thin rectangular sliver of bone, 22 x 89 mm (0.9 x 3.5 inches), with the runes cut on one face within a double incised border. We do not know the object's function or whether we have the whole or part of it. It was riveted to something else, for two metal plugs remain piercing it. Janet Bately and V.I.Evison who examined the plate with care suggested that its seriffed runes link it to a scriptorium (though this is too daring a conclusion), and that it may be part of a ruler or an implement for turning pages, fixed to a strap or ribbon for convenience and security.[6] This is possible but no more. The runes read 'g o d g e c a þ a r æ h a d̂ d a þ i þ i s w r a t'. There are several translations formally possible, and no clear means of choosing between them. It depends in part on how you divide the text into its individual words – the original is no help here. Commonly it has been read *God gecaþ aræ Hadda þi þis wrat*. How does one take 'gecaþ'? As part of *geocian*, 'preserve', or of *ge-ecan*, 'increase'? Is 'aræ' a form of *ar*, 'honour, possessions, mercy', or of *ar*, 'minister': 'þi' a spelling of *þe*, 'who', or of *þy*, 'because'? Does 'wrat' refer to incising the plate or writing on some book it was attached to? Thus the range of meanings here includes: 'God will preserve the honour of Hadda who incised this', 'God preserves his minister Hadda who incised this', 'God saves by his mercy Hadda who wrote this', 'God increases the possessions of Hadda who wrote this', 'God will preserve the honour of Hadda because he wrote this.' Alfred Bammesberger has recently reexamined the interpretation of this piece and suggested an ingenious (perhaps too ingenious) new word

---

5   M.Cahen and M.Olsen, *L'inscription runique du coffret de Mortain* (Paris 1930), 44–8; F.Holthausen in *Anglia Beibl.* 42 (1931), 257–8; H.Harder, 'Zur Deutung von ags. *kiismeel*', *Archiv f. d. Stud. d. neueren Sprachen* 161 (1932), 87–8.
6   'The Derby Bone Piece', *Medieval Archaeology* 5 (1961), 301–5.

Fig.55. The Derby bone plate.

separation: *god geca þaræ Hadda þi þis wrat*, 'O God, help this (woman) Hadde who wrote this.'[7]

The Derby bone plate gives a first-rate demonstration of the care needed in examining an inscription (fig.55). So far I have implied that there is no difficulty in identifying its runes. In fact there are two ambiguous forms. Some scholars have read not 'g e c a þ' but 'g e c͡n a þ', which they take to be a part of OE *gecnawan*, 'know, acknowledge, declare'.[8] They are misled by a groove sloping across the stem of 'c' and resembling the cross-stave of 'n'. Under the stereo-microscope this shows itself clearly as an accidental gash not an incision, and the reading *gecaþ* is vindicated. Another, similar, case is more troublesome. The group 'h a d͡d a þ i' should perhaps be 'h a d͡d a n͡þ i'. Again, a line crosses the stem of 'þ' and this time the microscope reveals it as a cut, though shallower and less sharp than those of the runes. Both *Hadda* and *Haddan* are acceptable oblique name forms, the first being Northumbrian or North Mercian if it is not a simple mistake. I think it likely that the rune-master cut 'h a d͡d a þ i', and that a later hand amended it to 'h a d͡d a n͡þ i' in the belief that it contained a grammatical error.

The Whitby comb (in the Whitby Literary and Philosophical Society's Museum) retains part of a formula that also may have celebrated the man who made it (or since it is incomplete, its owner). This comb was made of at least three bits of bone, the teeth cut from one or more plates which rivets held to the two side-pieces split from cattle ribs. Both ends and most of the teeth are lost, and also part of the beginning and all the end of the runic inscription which ran along one of the side-pieces (fig.56). What is left is 'd͡[æ] u s m͡æ u s ‖ g o d a l u w a l u ‖ d͡o h͡e l i p æ c y ‖ ['. After the Latin beginning this continues in an Anglian dialect of Old English. Two words look strange because of the glide vowels that intrude between *l* and a following consonant: 'a l u w a l u d͡o' for West Saxon *eallwealda*, 'h͡e l i p æ' for West Saxon *helpe*. The sense is clear enough as far as it goes: 'My God: may

---

[7] 'Three Old English Runic Inscriptions' in Bammesberger, *Old English Runes*, 131–4.

[8] Quite recently K.Schneider, 'Six OE Runic Inscriptions', 46.

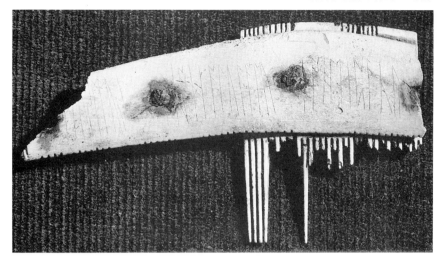

Fig.56. The Whitby comb.

God Almighty help Cy-', the last word presumably a personal name with the first element *Cyne-*. The comb comes from a rubbish dump near the ruins of Whitby Abbey and is traditionally associated with the Anglo-Saxon monastery of *Streoneshalh*, founded in 657 and destroyed in the second half of the ninth century. The language is consistent with this date range.

The Whitby comb stresses the obvious point that a personal name without any other details gives us little information. It could as well be the owner's, maker's, or that of someone else altogether. The Thames scramasax, in the British Museum, is a good case in point. It bears an inlaid *futhorc* and the personal name 'b ea g n o þ'. Dark Age blades carrying the name of the smith whose workshop forged them are common enough, and this may lead some to take Beagnoth as the craftsman. If the Thames runes were a real attempt to harness rune-magic for the sword's owner, Beagnoth may, I suppose, have been the rune-master's name adding its power to that of the *futhorc*. The scramasax is an impressive piece of equipment, one that an owner would be proud to see his name on, and distinguished enough to make a fine gift bearing the giver's name. We have no means of telling. There are several cases where we face this difficulty. An example is the ninth-century gold finger-ring from Llysfaen, in the Victoria and Albert Museum, London. This is a massive piece of jewellery, made up of eight members, four circles linked by lozenges. Each member has a leafed border, within it the field cut away and nielloed, leaving runes and ornamental devices standing clear. The lozenges have schematised beasts, the roundels hold the text, two symbols to each, with decorated forms as space fillers. The legend, roman save for the

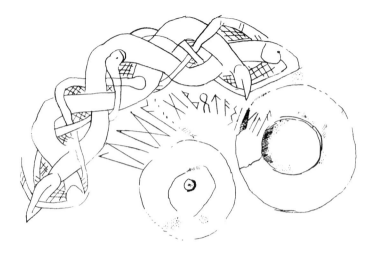

Fig.57. The repairer's inscription on the back
of the Harford Farm brooch. (3:2)

last letter, reads +A‖LH‖ST‖An, a well-recorded Old English masculine
name. The likelihood is that it is the owner's, but could also be a donor's, for
ring-giving was an Anglo-Saxon custom if the literary sources are to be
trusted.

Perhaps relevant here is the Harford Farm find.[9] This splendidly decorated
composite disc brooch, in the Castle Museum, Norwich, has been repaired,
not very skilfully, at some time in its use, perhaps in the seventh century. Its
back has elaborate incised decoration, part of it two panels of interlaced ser-
pents, following the line of the circumference. Within this, roughly following
the inner line of one of the interlaces, is the runic text: 'l u d a : g i b œ t æ s i
‖ g i l æ', the last four runes on the pin anchorage (fig.57), 's' looks an early
form, with five staves, ᚦ. There is no problem with the interpretation, 'Luda
mended (the) brooch', but it is worth observing that the name form, 'l u d a',
is in larger runes than the rest of the sentence, and divided from it by a row of
points in vertical line. This may be simply a device to give more prominence
to the personal name. Another possibility, which needs exploring, is that the
personal name, ?of the maker, was originally the only text on the back of the
brooch, but when it was repaired the rest of the sentence was added, uncom-
fortably fitted into the space available.

---

9   J.Hines, 'A New Runic Inscription from Norfolk', *Nytt om Runer* 6 (1991), 6–7.
     As well as the major text defined here there are traces of one or more runes on the
     pinhead of the brooch.

Where a name occurs on a less prestigious piece, it is perhaps more likely to record the owner of the property. An example could be the bit of a pair of silver tweezers from eighth-/ninth-century Brandon. These are neatly made, and one surface has framing lines and an inscription, incised and then darkened with niello. The runes are quite elegantly seriffed, and neatly arranged in the asymmetrical space available. They read: '+ a l d r e d', the common masculine personal name *Ealdred* in an Anglian form that lacks the breaking diphthong before *ld*. Fragmentary is the name on a copper-alloy object from Wardley that has been identified as part of a plate linking a set of pins, perhaps from the eighth century. What remains is '] *o* l b u r g', plausibly reconstructed as the feminine name *Ceolburg*. The letters are quite carefully formed, with rudimentary serifs. The final rune is less clearly cut than the others, which may imply a preliminary setting-out of the letter that was never recut. The inscription's lay-out was then planned with some care.

Fig.58. The Ash/Gilton pommel inscription. (5:2)

From the Mote of Mark excavations comes something much more casual – a small bone fragment inscribed with the letters 'a þ i l i' which looks to be a name form or element. Other, more problematic, cases where objects may record personal names and little or nothing else are the Ash/Gilton pommel, the Southampton bone and the Whitby disc. The Ash pommel presents several obscurities. There is no find-report for it. All we know is that it reached the cabinet of the Kentish antiquary, W.H.Rolfe, before 1845, and that the earliest people to report it say it came from the parish of Ash in Kent. Joseph Mayer of Liverpool acquired it and gave it to the local City Museum where it remains today. The runological difficulties of the piece lie primarily in identifying its letters. The sword-pommel, dated to the mid-sixth century, is pyramidal in shape and of silver gilt. Incised and nielloed patterns decorate its top, ends and faces, and one end has a rivet hole for the ring attachment. Contrasting with the elaboration of the decoration is the crudeness of the runes. These are scratched roughly but deeply on one face, their size varying with the pommel height. The other face is blank and in my opinion always has been, though some nineteenth-century writers professed to find runes there too. The inscribed face has a high proportion of unidentified symbols,

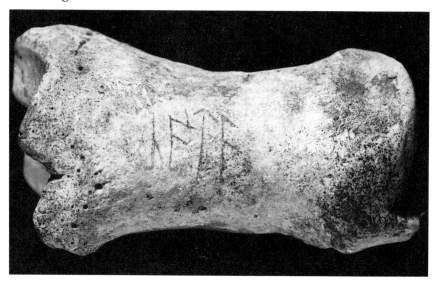

Fig.59. The Southampton (*Hamwih*) bone.

some of which may be only rune-like patterns added as space fillers, though they could also be early and local variant runes not otherwise preserved. The space available for the letters is small and irregularly shaped, hard to get letters in; and perhaps this accounts for some curious forms (fig.58). In 1938 Bruce Dickins wrote of the pommel that it 'bears the partly intelligible inscription ". . .sigim. . ."; this should perhaps be completed as "sigimund ah" (This belongs to Sigimund).'[10] Personally I do not think it useful to go beyond Dickins's admirably cautious comment on the text, but many scholars have dared to do so without carrying conviction. It is, however, worth noting R.W.V. Elliott's argument that the Ash pommel personal name was *Sigimer.*'[11]

The inscription on the Southampton bone shows another way of being difficult (fig.59). The runes here are unambiguous but we can only guess at their meaning. The bone came from an early rubbish pit linked to the settlement site of *Hamwih*. It had no cultural associations and only a general dating, between the mid seventh and the early eleventh century. It is cattle-bone, unworked save for the lettering, so there is no clue as to what purpose the inscription served. The runes read 'c a t æ'. Old English has the words *cat(t)*, 'cat', and *catte*, 'she-cat', and the bone may record either of these. My first

[10] 'The Sandwich Runic Inscription *Ræhæbul*', *Beiträge zur Runenkunde und nordischen Sprachwissenschaft*, ed. K.Schlottig (Leipzig 1938), 83.
[11] 'Two Neglected English Runic Inscriptions: Gilton and Overchurch', *Mélanges de Linguistique et de Philologie, Fernand Mossé* (Paris 1959), 141–2.

inclination was to take this as a personal name, parallel to other animal personal names like *Wulf*, *Culfre* and *Duva*, and allied to ON *kǫttr* which was used as a nickname. An alternative, ingenious, and probably correct interpretation is to take the inscription, not as Anglo-Saxon, but as Frisian.[12] To support this are the facts that *Hamwih* was a port with trading links to Frisia, and the form of 'a' is ᚹ, which some have thought a distinctive Frisian variant of the more common ᚠ. This would then give the word **katæ**, which can be compared with Old Frisian *kate*, 'knuckle-bone', defining the material it was carved upon.

Examples of such simplistic descriptions are not uncommon in the Scandinavian runic tradition. For instance, part of a stringed instrument from Trondheim has the word **ruhta**, 'lyre', on it: a box from the same town has [*tr*]**æzur**, 'jewel-case'. Perhaps nearest to this Southampton example is a mediaeval bone fragment from Lund, Skåne, which has cut on it the profound observation: **binisþitabinisþit[a]**, 'this is bone, this is bone'. A good if expanded English example of the self-evident is on a silver-gilt finger-ring, perhaps from the later eighth century, found at Wheatley Hill (Durham) and now in the British Museum. This legend was at first read 'r i n g i c h̑ a t t', 'I am called a ring', which makes good sense but bad grammar. Detailed examination revealed that decorative gem-settings riveted to the ring after the inscription was cut had obscured its first and last letters. For the first, serifs appropriate to 'h' could still be seen projecting beyond the setting, while radiography revealed beneath the second setting a short vertical with a central branch – the top of the vertical can perhaps be traced protruding above the setting. This could be the remains of 'æ'. So the text should probably be read '[*h*] r i n g i c h̑ a t t [.]' (= *hring ic hattæ*), which is more satisfying to the rigorous historical linguist (fig.60).

Fig.60. The Wheatley Hill ring. (1:1)

Perhaps a more subtle example of the same thing is the riddling inscription on an antler handle for some sort of tool, excavated at Brandon. This reads, 'w o h s w i l d u m d e [.] r a n', probably to be supplied and separated into individual words as *wohs wildum deoran*, '(I, it) grew on a wild beast'.

12 D.Hofmann, 'Eine friesische Runeninschrift in England', *Us Werk* 25 (1976), 73–6.

Fig.61. The Whitby disc.

However, this involves an irregular inflexion of the OE neut. *deor*, and an alternative has been suggested, *wohs wildum deor an*, the last two letters the preposition *an/on* in postposition, The meaning is unchanged.

The Whitby jet disc, perhaps a spindle whorl, came from the excavations at the site of the Anglo-Saxon monastery, and is now in the British Museum. It has three runes, cut neatly and set radially, all clearly to be seen (fig.61). Unfortunately two of them are ambiguous. The middle one is no doubt 'e'. The first could be 'l' or 'u', the third 'u' (but not if the first is 'u') or 'r'; possible readings are 'l e u', 'l e r', 'u e r'. A sequence 'u e r' is embarrassing unless the first rune represents the semi-vowel [w] which would be rather unusual. However, 'u e r' could be a northern form of West Saxon *wær*, 'token of friendship'. More likely is that *Wer* is a personal name. The simplex is not recorded save in place-names such as (*to*) *Wæresleage* (Waresley, Worcestershire), 'Wær's wood or clearing', but compounds with *Wær-* as first element are fairly common. 'l e u' too could be a personal name, possibly a form of *Leofu* or *Leof* or even *Hleow*. The difficulty about most of these suggestions is that they lead to masculine personal names unlikely to appear on a spindle whorl. Nevertheless I think the most likely interpretation of the Whitby disc legend is as an owner's mark or name. Runes on a spoon from York may serve the same purpose. This piece, ascribed to the late tenth or eleventh century, was found in 1884 during rebuilding work in the city. It is now in the Yorkshire Museum. The spoon is cut from a single piece of wood, some 22 cm (8.5 inches) long. Decorating the upper surface of the handle is a series of step patterns, alternatively hatched and plain. The letters, apparently 'c x', occupy one of the plain sections. Also probably to be taken as owners' marks are the single runes of the Sleaford brooch, in the British Museum, and the Willoughby-on-the-Wolds bowl, in the Museum of Archaeology, Nottingham University.

Two objects join the Ruthwell cross in using their runes to supply titles or explanations for the sculptures that adorn them. These are the oak coffin of St Cuthbert, made in Lindisfarne in 698, thereafter taken to Chester-le-Street and then Durham, dug from the despoiled shrine in 1827 and now kept in Durham Cathedral treasury; and the whale's bone Franks casket, first recorded in the hands of a family at Auzon, Haute-Loire, France, in the early nineteenth century, most of it now in the British Museum though one side is in the Museo Nazionale (Bargello), Florence.

For an Anglo-Saxon wooden object the coffin of St Cuthbert is well preserved. Yet a great deal of it is missing, and what survives was taken in small pieces from the saint's final resting place. Consequently any description of the object derives only from a reconstruction, fitting together as many as possible of the bits of oak the excavators found. The most recent conservation work, mainly carried out in 1978, was reported in a major monograph in 1985.[13] This latest rebuilding shows the coffin – or coffin-reliquary as it is sometimes called – some 168 cm long x 44 cm high x 39 cm wide (66 x 17.5 x 15.5 inches). Incised figure decoration, probably by more than one hand, covers its lid and four sides. On the lid the symbols of the four evangelists surround Christ. At the head end are two archangels, Michael and Gabriel; at the foot Mary holding the Christ child (fig.62). One of the long sides held the twelve apostles in two rows of six, the other the five remaining archangels, though both groups are sadly depleted. We can guess that each of the figures had the name incised near it, though not all survive. There are traces of a preliminary setting out and sketching of the figures, using a knife to score the wood. The figures were boldly formed, either by gouging or by double knife cuts. The names were made of single cuts with a knife, and are therefore very faint. At various times in the recent past these incisions were affected by the preservatives added to the wood, so that some scholars – Bruce Dickins, for instance – found aspects of them difficult to make out. This should give the early drawings of the coffin fragments, slight though they were, an added importance.[14] Most of the names were in roman script. It seems that all those of the apostles were, to judge from such complete forms as IOHANNIS, ANDREAS, THOMAS, PETRVS, MATHEǼS, together with fragments of the other names. So perhaps were the archangels' names and titles, though the occurrence of runic 'm' in the fragment of *Rumiael*,]VmIA[, suggests there were occasional runes mingled with them. Mary's name is almost illegible but seems to have been in roman, whereas the Christ title, *ihs xps*, certainly had the last three letters in runes and probably the first three too. LVCAS was

13 J.M.Cronyn and C.V.Horie, *St. Cuthbert's Coffin. The History, Technology and Conservation* (Durham 1985).
14 'The Inscriptions upon the Coffin', 305.

Fig.62. Christ and Mary on St Cuthbert's coffin.

the only evangelist to have roman characters for his name. The others, only in part readable, are in runes: '*m͡* a t *h* [.] s', '*m͡* a r c u s', '[.]*h* a *n n* [.] s'.

The Auzon or Franks casket is probably the best-known of English runic objects, and the most extensively studied. D.H.Haigh and George Stephens did the pioneering linguistic work on it in the mid-nineteenth century, and thereafter followed a host of their distinguished contemporaries including Sophus Bugge, Henry Sweet, C.W.M.Grein and R.P.Wulcker. But not until 1900 did A.S.Napier establish the main outlines of the texts and state the principal problems in a splendid and restrained monograph.[15] Thereafter there has been a plethora of notes and articles on the casket, but it is fair to say that the best of later research has added and modified, but done little to change the outlines that Napier drew, while the ingenuity of runologists has failed to solve the difficulties he enunciated. The twentieth-century bibliography of studies of the Auzon casket is a formidable one, though some of the work is trivial, wrong-headed or based on inadequate textual examination, and some is dogmatic, ignoring grammatical infelicities and pretending that uncertainties of translation do not exist. The effect of the complexity of the texts and the size of the bibliography is to make it impossible here to go beyond a summary account of the runic material and its treatment.

Each side of the Auzon casket is a plate of whale's bone, intricately carved. The plates were fixed to corner posts and were clamped by metal mounts, now missing. Grooves in the side plates held the plain bone base, much of which has been lost. There is the remains of a lid, but how it originally fitted is unknown; the back of the box has no uncarved panels where hinges should fit, yet the front has a hole for a lock or hasp which seems to posit a hinged construction.[16] A central strip of whale's bone running across the lid has carving like that of the sides, so there are altogether five sculptured panels, each with one or more runic legends, making up eleven discrete inscriptions on the casket. All letters stand in relief save for the runes 'm æ g i' (defining the representation of the Magi on the front) which are incised. All legends are in runes save for three words on the back in mixed capitals, uncials and half-uncials. The four major inscriptions border the four sides. Left and right faces have lines of runes surrounding the central carved field so as to form continuous texts broken only at the corners. The front is the same save for the panel holding the key-hole dividing its top line. The main legend of the back runs only along the two vertical sides and the top, where the design of the carving breaks it. On the front, left and right the carver had the problem of disposing his letters so that they ran virtually without interruption along four sides of a rectangle. On the left and right he cut them with bases consistently towards the panel centre, which meant he inverted the bottom line. On the front he tried a different solution, with the bottom line right way up but retrograde.

The front decorative panel is divided into two. Its left side shows a scene

15 'The Franks Casket', *An English Miscellany Presented to Dr Furnivall . . .* (Oxford 1901), 362–81.
16 Webster and Backhouse, *Making of England*, 101.

from the Weland (*Vǫlundr*) tale, known mainly from Old Norse sources.[17] The smith is at his anvil and speaking to a woman, while a second one stands behind her. Below lies the headless body of one of Nidhad's sons. Behind the whole group is a man with some birds, often identified as Egill, Weland's brother. To the right is an Adoration of the Magi – the 'm æ g i' of the inscription. The main text of the front describes not its carvings but the material the casket is made from. It reads:

> 'f i s c · f l o d u · ‖ a h o f o n f e r g ‖ e n b e r i g‖
> ←w a r þ g a : s r i c g r o r n þ æ r h e o n g r e u t g i s w o m‖
> →h r o n æ s b a n'

The general sense is clear but there are points of difficulty; the syntax of the first half and its link with the adjoining words *hronæs ban*, and the meanings of *gasric* and *grorn*. The first has aroused extensive discussion. Like many of my contemporaries I divide *hronæs ban* from the rest, regarding the words as a statement of the material used for the box: '(This is) whale's bone.' The rest of the text falls into two lines of alliterative verse:

> *fisc flodu ahof   on fergenberig*
> *warþ gasric grorn   þær he on greut giswom.*

In the first line the relationship between *fisc*, *flodu* and *ahof* is open to dispute. Is the word order subject-object-verb or object-subject-verb? Is it the fish that raised up the flood(s) or the flood that cast up the fish? Semantically either is possible, a stranded whale splashing up water on the *fergenberig*, 'mountainous cliff', or the sea casting the whale on the rocky shore (is this a possible meaning of *fergenberig*?). The verb *ahof* is singular. If (as I think) *fisc* is the subject, *flodu* can be either singular or plural; if *flodu* is the subject, it can only be singular. In any case it is either an irregular or a primitive form for, by the rules of sound-change, *-u* is lost early in this position. If *flodu* is singular, it is either early or irregular and unparalleled. If it is plural it may still be early, but it could also be a later form paralleled in a number of anomalous plurals in *-u*, of which examples are *wintru* and *applu* and a group of bisyllabic neuter plurals with that ending, particularly common in the Corpus Glossary.[18] These are not exact equivalents to *flodu*, but they go some way towards explaining it without requiring it to be early. My own suspicion

---

[17] References in A.Orchard, *Dictionary of Norse Myth and Legend* (London 1997), under *Völund*.

[18] I.Dahl, *Substantival Inflexion in Early Old English: Vocalic Stems*. Lund Studies in English 7 (Lund 1938), 69–70.

is that *flodu* is an irregular plural and that the Auzon carver may have added the final letter to fill a large space in his inscriptional panel, knowing of neuter plurals in *-u*. How you explain the ending of *flodu* will determine whether you put the casket early, say at the beginning of the seventh century, or not. The meanings of *grorn* and *gasric*, though important, are less significant in the general discussion of the Auzon casket. Though occurring nowhere else as an adjective *grorn* certainly means 'sad', for there is the noun *grorn*, 'grief', in the *Rhyming Poem*, related to such words as *grorne*, 'sadly', and *grornian*, 'mourn'. *Gasric*, also unrecorded elsewhere, is then the subject of this clause, and refers most naturally to the whale which 'became sad when it swam on to the shingle'. *Gasric is* a compound, its second element *-ric* common in Anglo-Saxon personal names, and perhaps, as has been suggested, in two compounds *hereric* and *heaðoric* in *Beowulf*.[19] It is cognate with Old Norse *-ríkr*, Gothic *reiks*, 'king'. The first element of *gasric* may be related to Gothic *gaisjan*, 'frighten', to OE *gar-*, ?'ocean' in the compound *garsecg*, or to Kemp Malone's postulated *gar*, 'storm'. A noun *gasric* would mean 'king of terror' (for the whale is a fear-inspiring beast in Old English literature) or 'king of the ocean' or 'king of the storm', all conceivable kennings for the whale. Thus the text, as I take it, means: 'The fish beat up the sea(s) on to the mountainous cliff. The king of ?terror became sad when he swam on to the shingle.'

The left side of the casket depicts the she-wolf feeding Romulus and Remus. A second wolf prowls above, and two figures with spears peer from either side. The text appears to present little difficulty but gives little linguistic information:

'r o m w a l u s a n d r e u m w *a l u s t w æ g e n* ‖ *g i b r o þ æ r*‖
a f œ *d d* æ h i æ w y l i *f* i n r o m æ c æ s t r i : ‖ *o þ l æ u n n e g* '

To be divided: *Romwalus and Reumwalus, twægen gibroþær, afæddæ hiæ wylif in Romæcæstri, oþlæ unneg*. The translation is usually given as 'Romulus and Remus, two brothers, a she-wolf nourished them in Rome, far from their native land'. The name forms are curious. *Romwalus* and *Reumwalus* are usually derived from Latin *Romulus* and *Remulus* (the latter an occasional variant of the commoner *Remus*), influenced by the Old English name element *-walh*. Some argue that popular etymology would produce a name **Romwalh* on the pattern of other dithematic names in *-walh*, and that the Latinised form of this, ending in *-us*, would in due course suffer loss of *h*

---

[19] K.Malone, 'A Note on *Beowulf* 2466', *Jnl of English and Germanic Philology* 50 (1951), 19–21.

between *l* and a vowel. The argument does not hold. The evidence of Latinised forms of -*walh* names shows that they do not produce -*walus* at any Anglo-Saxon date, for in Latin contexts the nominative remains endingless as -*walh* while an oblique case adds the ending without loss of *h*. Whatever the explanation of *Romwalus, Reumwalus*, they cannot be dated from Old English loss of *h*. *Romæcæster* is a name form not found outside the Auzon context, though *Romeburh, Romaburh* occur. As occasionally happens the element -*cæster* has been added to the genitive of a place-name. The ending in -*i* is notable, and is to be presumed a locative formed on the analogy of *a*- or *i*-declensions. It may indicate that the casket carver was unconventional in his grammatical usages, and that we should be cautious before citing the quality of vowel endings as evidence for dating or localising this object.

The back shows Titus's capture of Jerusalem. A stylised structure representing the temple occupies the centre. To the left above are armed attackers, and to the right above fugitives from the city. To the lower left and right are two scenes that seem to be defined by small discrete inscriptions in the very corners of the casket. The left one reads 'd o m', meaning 'court' or 'judgment', for a scene where a central seated figure presides over a group of individuals, one armed and one perhaps captive. The right one has 'g i s l' or 'hostage' for a rather indeterminate group of walking men, one of whom may be under escort. The main text of this side is only partly runic and only in part Old English. Its general sense is clear though details are baffling:

> 'h e r f e g t a þ ‖ t i t u s e n d g i u þ e a s u'
> ‖HICFUGIANTHIERUSALIM‖'a f i t a t o r e s'

The mixture of Old English and Latin is puzzling, while the Latin itself is inconsistent: 'a f i t a t o r e s' shows Anglo-Saxon pronunciation spelling of *habitatores* while the rest of the Latin is more or less Classical in form, though with the error FUGIANT for FUGIUNT. The existence of two spelling conventions in the Latin suggests something of the rune-master's method. He was not copying closely from an exemplar, for a written text would hardly have both usages. The accuracy and general precision of lay-out of his other texts implies that he had some sort of pattern before him, so for the Titus side too he was probably copying, but not doing it exactly. I suggest he had an original which was in Latin and in some form of roman script. He translated and transliterated as he went. Halfway through he forgot to do either, and copied direct. Noticing his error he finished his sentence necessarily in Latin but returned to runes, using a pronunciation spelling which he thought more appropriate to a vernacular script. This could also explain 'e n d' where we might expect the more common 'a n d' or 'o n d', for he may have begun to cut *et* (after the Latin name *Titus*) and realised his mistake in time. It may also explain 'g i u þ e a s u', a form that has caused much debate since its ending is etymologically impossible. The final vowel has been accounted an arbitrary appendage to a normal plural *Giuþeas*, 'Jews', but adding *-u* to an existing inflexional ending, even as a space filler, is most unlikely. Alternative explanations require the addition of some letters between the two bits of the inscription: *Giuþea su<mæ>, su<nu>, su<m>*, 'certain, sons, one of the Jews', and even *her fegtaþ Titus end Giuþeas u<t> hic fugiant Hierusalim afitatores*, 'here Titus and the Jews fight with the result that here its inhabitants flee from Jerusalem'. All these assume that the carver was careless, which in general he was not, and that he divided words between his text panels, which in general he tried not to do. My own tentative suggestion is that 'g i u þ e a s u' is a confused form of Latin *Giuþaeus*, a form for *Iudaeus*, 'Jew'. With the emendation to *fugiunt the* text now means, 'Here Titus and a Jew fight: here its inhabitants flee from Jerusalem'.

The carved panel of the top has a plain central disc to hold a mount for lifting the box lid. Disposed round it is a battle scene, vigorously conceived. A group of armed men attack a house that an archer defends. Behind him sits a figure, apparently a woman. Above the man's shoulder is the name 'æ g i *l* i'. He is customarily identified with Weland the smith's brother, Egill. The identification rests on three facts, that Weland appears on the front of the casket, that the late prose work *Þiðriks* saga tells of Egill's exploits as a bowman, that *Egill* and 'æ g i *l* i' are similar. Against it is the fact that no extant source tells a tale of Weland's brother fitting the carving. In consequence of the identification the Auzon name form has been derived from a Germanic original, and so has been related to such similar names as Continental Germanic *Agil*, *Egili*, Gothic *Agil*, and discussion has centred fruitlessly upon the length of the initial vowel. Yet I must stress that 'æ g i *l* i' need not be the same name as *Egill*. The latter is a strong noun, presumably *a*-stem: OE 'æ g i *l* i' must be either *ja*- or *i*-stem. If 'æ g i *l* i' is a direct descendant of a Germanic name it retains archaic unapocopated *-i* and so is very early indeed. But if, as I suggest, 'æ g i *l* i' does not = *Egill*, then it may be a name created within Old English itself, as such names as *Winele*, *Dudele*, *Hemele*, and then it need only antedate the shift of unstressed *i* to *e*. Place-name evidence implies that *Ægil(i)* was not particularly uncommon in Anglo-Saxon England (for example, Yelford (Oxfordshire), 'Ægel(e)'s ford'), so this carving may depict the adventures of an English hero.

I have left the casket's right side until last because of its difficulty. As I have already noted in chapter 6, its main inscription contains cryptic vowel runes, is very hard to interpret, and refers to a carving whose subject is both unknown and unusual. It divides into three scenes which are in no way formally linked to one another. To the left are two facing figures. One, seated upon a mound, is monstrous, with a beast's head, wings, but apparently human hands and feet. The other is a warrior with helmet, shield and spear. Central is a group of three, surrounded by short inscriptions, foliage and decorative devices. The most impressive of the three is a horse which stands with drooping head over a small human figure bowed down within a semi-elliptical cave or shelter. The third bears a staff and faces the horse, and between them is something that looks like a chalice. Above the horse's back is the word 'r i s c i' which ought to mean 'rush, reed'; beneath its belly is 'w u d u', 'wood'; over its head is 'b i t a' which may be the name of the horse (Biter) or of the man facing it. To the right are three hooded figures in consultation. What the scenes represent I do not know. Excited and imaginative scholars have put forward numbers of suggestions but none convinces. Indeed it is probable that the story illustrated has been lost in the course of years.

The main inscription, surrounding this mysterious group of carvings, has arbitrary or cryptic forms for most of its vowels: ⋏, ᚻ, ⋏, h, and also ⟓, ⟓, ⟓ and ⟓ which may be variant types of one symbol or different symbols. There are single examples of M and ᚷ (bound with 'f') and scholars differ over whether to give these their common values or to regard them too as cryptic. I think it best to transliterate them in the usual way, 'e' and 'a'. There has been general consensus of opinion as to how to take the first two forms: ⋏ as 'e', ᚻ as 'o'. The four zigzag symbols are commonly though not invariably read as 'i', and this too I accept. ⋏ and h have been read as 'æ' and 'a' respectively but doing so creates linguistic difficulties. Sir Christopher Ball has argued for a reversal of the two values, which certainly gives results no worse than the usual readings, and some might think them better.[20] I feel, as R.C.Boer did years ago, that the carver got confused over these two similar cryptic graphs, with the consequence that we cannot be sure which of the two values, *æ* or *a*, he intended for which symbol at any time.[21] It is a curious fact that the fewest emendations are needed if both are transliterated 'a'. However, to present the case impartially I retain these two symbols in my primary transcript:

'h e r h o s s i t ⋏ þ o n h ⋏ r m b e r g ⋏ ᚻ g l [.] ‖ d r i g i þ s w ⋏ ‖
h i r i e r t h e g i s g r h f s ⋏ r d e n s o r g ⋏ h ‖ n d s e f a t o r n ⋏'

Attempts at this have been too many, diverse and improbable for me to list them here, nor is there space to argue my own case. I content myself with

---

20 C.J.E.Ball, 'The Franks Casket: Right Side', *English Studies* 47 (1966), 1–8.
21 'Über die rechte Seite des angelsächsischen Runenkästchens', *Arkiv f. nord. Filologi* 27 (1911), 215–59.

putting forward an amended and divided text that seems to make sense, though it leaves much unexplained. It falls into three lines of alliterative verse:

> *Her Hos sitiþ   on harmberga*
> *agl[.] drigiþ   swa hirœ Ertae gisgraf*
> *sarden sorga   and sefa torna.*

'Here Hos sits on the sorrow-mound; she suffers distress as Ertae had imposed it upon her, a wretched den (?wood) of sorrows and of torments of mind', or, with different punctuation. 'Here Hos sits on the sorrow-mound; she suffers distress in that Ertae had decreed for her a wretched den (?wood) of sorrows and of torments of mind.'

Apart from the four sequences of magical runes – the legends of the three amulet rings and the Thames *futhorc* – there remain in the corpus only a heterogeneous group of objects with inscriptions to which I can give no certain meaning: the Caistor-by-Norwich astragalus (Castle Museum, Norwich), the Welbeck Hill bracteate, and the Loveden Hill urn, the Chessell Down scabbard mount, Dover brooch, Thames silver mount (all in the British Museum). And finally there are three baffling inscriptions which I leave to the end, for how we take them may affect our views on the date and nature of certain major runic developments.

The Caistor-by-Norwich piece is part of the contents of a cremation urn, apparently of the fifth century. Besides the burnt bones this held a toilet set, thirty-three plano-convex gaming pieces forming two sides, eleven black and twenty-two white, and over thirty-five astragali, variously affected by fire. The latter were probably used as pieces in some game. Only one astragalus is inscribed, and it is rather bigger than the others. The runes are neatly scratched across one broad face, and clearly read **raᛁhan** (fig.6). I transliterate it in bold because this is an early inscription and its runic affinities are uncertain. There is no direct clue as to what the text may mean. Elsewhere I have suggested two roots that could have been formative in such a word: **rei-*, 'scratch, cut', or **rei-*, 'dappled, coloured'.[22] Either of these could have produced a nomen agentis, 'scratcher, cutter' or 'colourer', which might mean 'rune-master' and so be appropriate for cutting in runes. Finally I suggest that the astragali could be pieces in a game played on a chequered board. One type of game is the hunt game, and the pieces in this often have animal names, like fox and geese, wolf and sheep. As a long shot, therefore, I

---

[22] 'The Old English Rune *eoh/ih*', 132–3.

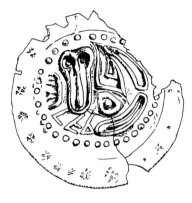

Fig.63. The Welbeck Hill bracteate.

link *raihan* to a Gmc **raiho* whence OE *raha*, *ra*, 'roe-deer'. It is then a curious coincidence that the Caistor astragalus, after masquerading for a long time as that of a sheep, was later declared by experts to belong to a roe. Indeed, this interpretation of the Caistor-by-Norwich text has become generally accepted.

From an inhumation cemetery at Welbeck Hill, Irby comes a silver bracteate which the German archaeologist Hayo Vierck assigned to the second half of the sixth century, thinking it local Anglian work. The design is so obscure that it is hard to tell what it represents or derives from (fig.63). The runes are clear, 'l æ w', set radially and retrograde. 'æ' is only a formal transliteration, for the character is ᚨ, the old *a*-rune; and the text could properly be presented as **law**. I link this legend to early bracteate inscriptions of Denmark, for these often have the sequence **la** or **al** in connexion with **u**, **w** or **þ** (the last an incompetent copyist could easily mistake for **w**). A bracteate from Darum (Jutland) has the retrograde **laþu** (a magical word) where **þ** has the form ▷, readily confused with Welbeck Hill's 'w'. Probably Welbeck Hill is a distant copy of some bracteate text such as this, and so descends from Scandinavian rather than West Germanic prototypes.

The major runic cremation urn from the great urn-field of Loveden Hill is also Anglo-Saxon work of the sixth century or later. The text was roughly cut in the unfired clay, below a row of cross-shaped stamps. Most but not all the runes are clear. There have been a number of attempts at the meaning, but none is satisfactory.[23] Double vertical lines divide the runes into three groups which seem to be:

' s i þ æ b l d ‖ þ i c w ‖ h l æ [.] '.

---

[23] Discussion in my 'Anglo-Saxon Runic Studies: the Way Ahead?' in Bammesberger, *Old English Runes*, 22–3.

I am not sure of the distinction between 'þ' and 'w' here (fig.29). I give the second letter as 'i' which is probably right. But there is the possibility of '1', for its lower twig is out of place and runs back perilously close to the initial 's', which of course may simply be a rune-cutter's error. It is possible that the sixth rune was intended as 'æ' but it is made up of double strokes and we cannot be sure. If my reading 'h' for the first letter of the last group is right, it is the single-barred form, though reversed. The final letter is a problem. I have suspected it to be a malformed 'f', but that has been challenged, and I am prepared to admit the challenge. The last two letter groups are quite baffling (unless the last is 'h l æ f' = *hlaf*, 'bread', which seems most unlikely). The first group could represent a personal name, something like *Siþæb(a)ld/ Siþæba(l)d*, but this is conjecture, no more.

I have several times referred to the many interpretations of the Chessell Down scabbard mount runes (fig.5). These again are clearly distinguishable but hard to interpret because we do not know the sort of message they record. The characters are 'æ c o : * œ r i', the only difficulty being the fourth rune. This is Ͱ which has sometimes been read 'w' by those who cannot accept the existence of an alternative 's' form Ͱ or who believe that that creation postdates the time of Chessell Down. The most common element of a Dark Age sword inscription is a personal name: 'æ c o' could be such a name, perhaps related to the recorded Old English masculine *Ac(c)a*. What 's œ r i' means I do not know.

The back of the Dover brooch has two inscriptions, both finely scratched between framing lines (fig.64). One looks more worn than the other, and seems more faintly and carelessly incised. It is retrograde, and apparently

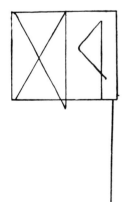
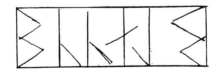

Fig.64. The Dover brooch runes. (11:2)

Fig.65. The Thames silver-gilt mount.

forms the letters 'i w d'. The second is clear enough in form, and begins and ends with 'b', one of them retrograde (or inverted) so that both face inwards. This makes it impossible to know which way round to take the runes, so I make nothing of them.

The silver-gilt mount from the Thames is a curious object (fig.65). It consists of a binding strip, 19 cm (7.5 inches) long, U-shaped in cross-section, ending in an animal's head in relief. The metal still holds some of the rivets that fixed it to whatever object, ?a knife sheath, it served. Its top is curved and decorated with oblique mouldings, and the back is plain. The runes are on the front, clearly cut, finely shaped and elegantly seriffed. Unfortunately they make no obvious sense: '] ‖ s b e͡r æ d h t i̇ b c a i ‖ e͡r h a͡ d æ b s'.

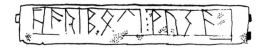

Fig.66. The Watchfield fitting. (1:1)

Three inscriptions remain, each with characteristics that require more study than they have received hitherto. The Watchfield fitting, now in the Oxfordshire Museum, Woodstock, is a copper-alloy strip that formed the side of a leather case containing a balance and weights, part of the grave goods that accompanied a young man (fig.66). The find-spot is surprising for Watchfield is in the Upper Thames valley, not a region noted for its runic inscriptions. Indeed, the grave assemblage as a whole does not look at home in the west there and may have travelled from Kent or even farther afield. Its date suggests the early sixth century. The inscription is quite clear in form: **haribo*i:wusa**. The **h**-rune is single-barred. The seventh rune, not identified above, is ⌃, otherwise unknown in England. It is likely to be a variant of ‹, an early form of **k**, 'c'. The inscription thus shows a couple of graphs that are not obviously characteristic of English texts. The first four runes would appear to be the word later recorded as *here*, 'army', which often forms the first element of a personal name, as it may do here. *Wusa* looks to me a possible hypocoristic personal name, derived from one beginning *Wulf-*. Thus

ᛚ ᛩ ᛗ ᛗᛂᚷ ᚻ ᛗᛁᚷ ᛒᛒ

Fig.67. The Undley bracteate (3:2)
with a schematic drawing of its runes.

there may be two names here, perhaps giver and recipient, a type of text that occurs occasionally elsewhere, though not in England unless you count the memorial stones.

The Undley bracteate poses a more specific question. It is of gold, a circle 23 mm (0.9 inches) in diameter, with a loop for suspension. Its design has two main elements: a right-facing helmeted bust with below it, rather sketchily rendered, a she-wolf suckling two children. There is a double spiral over the head and two minor features, a star and circle, behind it. Following the line of the circumference and occupying almost half of it runs a sequence of runes, retrograde, divided by points into three groups (fig.67). John Hines, who has examined this piece in detail, derived its design from fourth- or fifth-century Roman or Byzantine coins, and ascribed the bracteate to the second half of the fifth century. So much for the piece but the question arises: where was it made? The bracteate was a casual find made by a local farmer, so there is no archaeological context. Hines put its manufacture in southern Scandinavia, perhaps Schleswig-Holstein.[24] This presents an immediate problem, for the inscription contains one of the 'Anglo-Frisian' rune forms, ᚮ, **o**. Hitherto these have not been found epigraphically outside England and Frisia (save for non-significant examples in pilgrim's graffiti or on exported

---

[24] J.Hines and B.Odenstedt, 'The Undley Bracteate and its Runic Inscription', *Studien zur Sachsenforschung* 6 (1987), 73–94. But cf. C.Hills, 'The Gold Bracteate from Undley, Suffolk: Some Further Thoughts', *Studien zur Sachsenforschung* 7 (1991), 145–51.

Fig.68. The **skanomodu** solidus, with a detail of its runes.

objects). The text of the bracteate does not help: ←**gægogæ·mægæ·medu** – the transliteration is formal only and does not assert what phonemic value should be attached to the graphs ᚠ and ᛗ. The first group, three sets of bind-runes, is strikingly like that on a spearshaft from Kragehul, Fyn, which has **gagaga**. That is usually regarded as a charm formula, and I would take the Undley variant as the same. Whether the rest of Undley has meaning must be uncertain. **medu** could be OE *medu* 'mead', or perhaps a form of OE *mēd*, 'reward', or even OE *(ge)mēde*, 'consent, good-will'. The meaning of *mægæ* depends on what value you ascribe to the vowel runes here. By its early date and by its questioned origin the Undley bracteate has raised dispute among English runologists, and this seems likely to continue until parallel finds are made elsewhere in the runic world.

I have left to the end the gold solidus with the legend **skanomodu** because I suspect it should not be in this book at all though it has traditionally been treated as Anglo-Saxon. There is no find-spot, and the only known fact of its early history is that it was in George III's cabinet. Comparable runic *solidi* come from the Low Countries, and there is no numismatic objection to a Frisian provenance for this one. The **skanomodu** piece is usually described as a copy of an issue of the late fourth-/early fifth-century Emperor Honorius, with an obverse giving the imperial bust, and a reverse of the emperor, holding standard and Victoriola, trampling upon a captive. Its function is uncertain. On the whole it is unlikely it was intended as currency despite its appropriate weight, 4.35 grammes, for a solidus. Such a gold coin would be too heavy for most commercial uses in the late sixth/early seventh century. This specimen once had a loop to enable it to be worn as a pendant or brooch, so it is likely it was a copy of a Roman coin that had been converted into a jewel, as so many were in the Dark Ages.

The legends of the original have not survived on this copy. They have degenerated into meaningless letter-like groups save on the reverse where part is replaced by the runic **skanomodu** (fig.68), I transliterate it thus for convenience, for this is how it has traditionally been done, but it is important to note that the third rune is the Anglo-Frisian **a**, ᚠ, while the graph recorded twice as **o** is ᚷ, not ᛗ. The runes have usually been interpreted as a personal name, and I still think this explanation the most likely. The first element could derive from Gmc **skaun-* which gives OE *Scen-* in the rare name *Scenuulf* but is more common in Continental Germanic names, and the second element looks like the common *-mod*. There are two linguistic features that favour Frisia as the region of striking: the first element shows the Germanic diphthong *au* developed to a simple vowel represented by **a** (contrasting with the Old English diphthong *ea*), and the ending is the unstressed vowel *-u* found in other Frisian runic texts. Had the coin not appeared in an English king's collection, and been first published at a time when few Frisian runes were known, I do not think it would have been taken as Anglo-Saxon.

12

More Manuscript Runes

Denmark has a *Codex Runicus*, a manuscript written in the runic character, AM 28, 8^0 in the Arnamagnean Institute, Copenhagen. It is a historical and legal manuscript of the early fourteenth century, linked by its contents to Skåne, now a Swedish province but in the Middle Ages part of Denmark. It may well have been part of an attempt, which failed, to develop runes as a script to be written as well as carved. In general the English seem to have been too sensible to try to use runes for a purpose they were neither intended for nor suited to, particularly as they had a good range of roman scripts for writing. Consequently there is no Anglo-Saxon *Codex Runicus*. For all that, runes do occur in English manuscripts; I have already recounted some of the circumstances – as an important clue in *The Husband's Message*, as framework of the *Runic Poem*, as an esssential part of the antiquarian *runica manuscripta*, as occasional abbreviations for rune-names.

But there are other manuscript runes more important and frequent than these, for the Anglo-Saxons were pragmatic enough to adapt a pair of them to fill gaps which they found in their various roman-type alphabets. Roman had no symbol for the dental spirants [θ], [ð] that Old English contained, and early manuscripts use *d* or *th* for them. Clearly it was more efficient to take over 'þ', *þorn*, so that letter was borrowed into bookhand where it remained for centuries, side by side with the crossed *d* form *ð* which English also developed. Nor had roman a distinctive character for the semivowel [w]. Early manuscripts make do with *u* or *uu*, but some adaptive genius took *wynn*, the rune 'w', into his script and it came into common use. As a natural consequence, inscriptions cut in roman characters are likely to contain *þorn* or *wynn*. The Great Edstone (North Yorkshire) sundial has +LOÐAN ME ᚱROHTEA, '+Lothan made me . . .' (probably an unfinished text), and the Pershore censer-cover +GODRIC ME ᚱVORHT, 'Godric made me', while the extensively inscribed Brussels cross has examples of both these runes in a roman context.[1] Such examples as these are excluded from the lists of runic inscriptions, since their inspiration is patently non-runic.

Though these two graphs could readily be adapted to cursive use, many of the runic forms, 'h', 'p', 'm' and 'ŋ' for example, were ill-suited to it. Their general effect is epigraphical and monumental. This quality Anglo-Saxon scribes sometimes profited by when they wanted to make individual letters stand out from the surrounding text for some reason or another. A good example of this is in *Solomon and Saturn I*, a didactic poem surviving only in two Corpus Christi College, Cambridge, manuscripts, MS 422 where it is almost complete, and MS 41 which has only the beginning. One of the poem's characters Solomon, who represents Christian wisdom, describes the charismatic quality of the *pater noster*. He does it by taking each letter of the Latin text of the prayer in turn and recounting how it acts as a warrior striving against the great enemy of mankind. The first letter, P,

> Hafað guðmæcga   gierde lange,
> gyldene gade,   and a ðone grimman feond
> swiðmod sweopað;   and him on swaðe fylgeð
> ·A· ofermægene   and hine eac ofslihð.
> ·T· hine teswað   and hine on ða tungan sticað,
> wræsteð him ðæt woddor   and him ða wongan brieceð.

> This stouthearted warrior has a long staff, a golden goad, and keeps on beating the fell fiend. At his back comes A with his overwhelming strength, and knocks him down too. T wounds him, stabs him in the tongue, wrings his neck and breaks his jaws.[2]

And so on. MS 41 gives the poem – or rather its opening lines – in its early state, with the *pater noster* letters represented by individual roman capitals distinguished from the rest of the text by mid-line points. The scribe of the MS 422 version wanted to stress the individual letters of the prayer, and so added the runic equivalent before each roman character, dividing the runes off by points from the rest of the poem (fig.69). The effect is distinctive and striking.

Related but rather different is the use of runes in the Exeter Book riddles

1   Details of these inscriptions in E.Okasha, *Hand-List of Anglo-Saxon Non-Runic Inscriptions* (Cambridge 1971).
2   R.J.Menner, *The Poetical Dialogues of Solomon and Saturn* (New York 1941), 87. K.Sisam's criticism of Menner's handling of this poem's runes (*Medium Ævum* 13 (1944), 35) is relevant to my discussion.

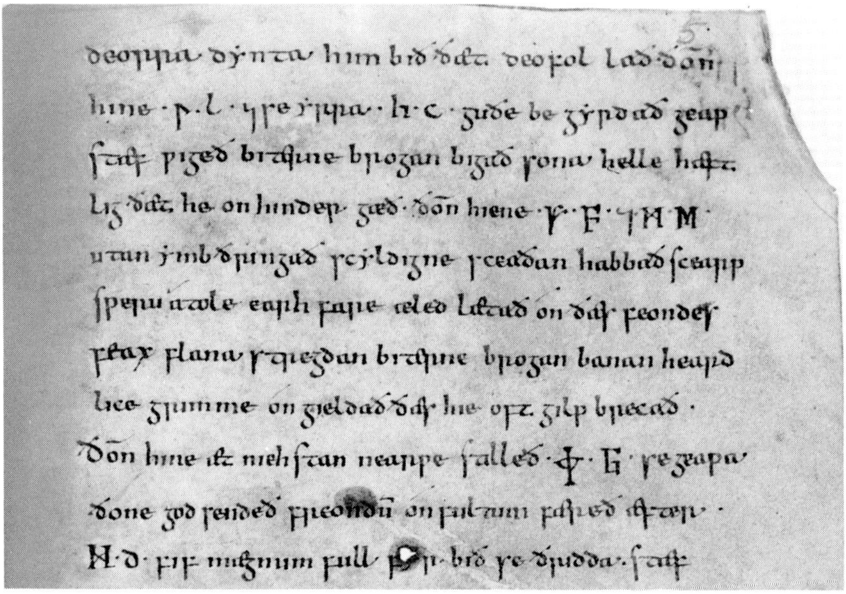

Fig.69. Part of the runic passage from *Solomon and Saturn I*
(Corpus Christi College, Cambridge, MS 422).

to give clues to the meanings of these cryptic verses.[3] *Riddle 19*, as set out on
fo.105r of the manuscript, is:

> Ic seah·ᚢᚱᛈᚾ.hyge wloncne heafod beorhtne swist
> ne ofer sælwong swiþe þrægan hæfde himon hrycge
> hilde þryþe·ᛏᛗᛗ.nægled ne rad·ᚠᚳᚧᛈ·widlast fe
> rede ryne strong onrade rofne·ᛣᛈᚠᛗᚾ·forwæs
> þy beorhtre swylcra siþfæt Saga hwæt ic hatte:7

Editors emend this and arrange it into verse lines, though not all in the
same way. If the rune-names are recited, they can form part of the verse form
for they may carry stress and alliteration. But taken like this they do not make
much sense.

> Ic seah   ·ᚢᚱᛈ
> ᚾ. hygewloncne,   heafodbeorhtne,
> swiftne ofer sælwong   swiþe þrægan.
> Hæfde him on hrycge   hildeþryþe
> ·ᛏᛗᛗ·   nægled ne rad.

---

[3]   The Exeter Book runes can be seen in the facsimile *The Exeter Book of Old
English Poetry* (Exeter 1933).

·ᚠᚷᛗᛈ· widlast ferede
rynestrong on rade   rofne·ᚻᛘ
ᚠᛗᛠᚾ· For wæs þy beorhtre
swylcra siþfæt.   Saga hwæt ic hatte:7

To make something of this passage, the runes have to be transliterated and the groups then taken retrograde: 'h o r s', 'horse', 'm o n', 'man', 'w e g a' *wega*, ?genitive plural 'ways' dependent upon *widlast*, 'h a o f o c', 'hawk'. 'I saw a horse, proud of spirit and bright of head, gallop quickly over the rich open field. Upon its back it bore a man mighty in battle: he did not ride in studded armour. Far over the paths, swift in his course, he carried a strong hawk. The journey was the brighter, the progress of such as these. Tell me what I am called.'

Riddle 24 (fo.106v) describes a creature that can imitate the cries of different birds and beasts. 'Sometimes I bark like a dog, sometimes bleat like a goat, sometimes honk like a goose, sometimes screech like a hawk. Sometimes I mimic the grey eagle, the battlebird's cry. Sometimes I call with the kite's voice, sometimes the song of the sea-mew, as I perch blithely.' There are six runes to give the answer.4

·ᚷ· mec nemnað,
swylce ·ᚠ· ond ·ᚱ·   ᛗ· fullesteð,
·ᚻ· ond ·ᛁ·

' 'g' names me, 'æ' and 'r' too; 'o' helps, 'h' and 'i'. These six letters clearly signify what I am called.' The answer is *higoræ*, 'magpie, jay'.

No other surviving riddle has the runic skill of these. *Riddle 64* (fo.125r) is more cryptic and less satisfying:

Ic seah ·ᚠ· ond ·ᛁ·   ofer wong faran
beran ·ᛒ·ᛗ·   bæm wæs on siþþe
hæbbendes hyht   ·ᚻ· ond ·ᚠ·
swylce þryþa dæl   ·ᚠ· ond ·ᛗ·
gefeah ·ᚠ· ond ·ᚠ·   fleah ofer ·ᛐ·
ᚻ· ond ·ᛇ·   sylfes þæs folces:

As it stands the verse is suitably riddling and indeed has never been convincingly explained, though that may be because the riddler was an unconvincing one.5 A common solution is to take each pair of runes as the beginning of a

---

4 In fact the scribe made a mistake with the first rune and wrote the roman letter *x* instead.
5 Indeed, F.H.Whitman, *Old English Riddles*. Canadian Federation Humanities

word that fits the context: 'w i' for *wicg*, 'steed', 'b e' for *beorn*, 'warrior', 'h a' for *hafoc*, 'hawk', but the rest not certainly identified. This gives a riddle whose content is very like that of *Riddle 19*, but needing more guesswork and giving vaguer clues: 'I saw a steed race over the field bearing a man. On their journey a hawk was its owner's delight . . . .'

All these riddles require the runes to be named otherwise the verse form fails. Presumably the audience knew the rune-names and could abstract them from the stanza as it was recited, and so were helped to solve it. Other runes in the Exeter riddles are nugatory. *Riddle 74/75* (fo.127r) – if it is substantial enough to deserve the name of riddle – reads *Ic swiftne geseah on swaþe feran*, 'I saw a swift creature travelling its way.' Thereafter are four runes, 'd n l h' usually amended to 'd n u h', *hund*, 'dog'.[6] A few other examples have runes written after them, probably by another hand and again to suggest the solution.

Two more contain runic clues, where the manuscript has no runes but only their names. *Riddle 42* (fo.112r) describes two creatures coupling. The clue is given *þurh runstafas . . . þam þe bec witan*, 'by means of runes . . . to those who know their books', and it is interesting to see the script so unambiguously linked to book-learning. The runes are enumerated:

> þær sceal nyd wesan
> twega oþer   ond se torhta æsc
> an an linan,   acas twegen
> hægelas swa some.

'There must be *nyd* and a second one of it, and the bright *æsc*, one in the line; two *ac*-runes and two *hægel*-runes as well.' Rearranged these make 'h a n a' and 'h æ n', 'cock and hen'.

Riddle 58 (fo.114v) is more enigmatic. It describes some engine for lifting water, single-footed with a heavy tail, small head, long tongue, no teeth. It neither eats nor drinks, yet it works in an earthen trench and raises water.

> þry sind in naman
> ryhte runstafas;   þara is rad foran.

'There are three correct runes in its name: *rad* precedes them (or *rad is* the

---

Monograph Series 3 (1982), 44 describes the riddle as 'quite crude', and claims that it is only the popularity of the 'horse and rider' theme that confirms the interpretation.

6   Needless to say, other solutions have been proposed. The most popular alternative seems to be to take 'd n l h' as *Hælend*, 'Saviour'.

first of them).'[7] What the Old English word for this machine is, we do not know.

Most famous, important and perhaps baffling of the cases where runes appear within literary texts are the runic signatures to the poems of Cynewulf. Indeed, it is only through these signatures that we know the name of this writer. They have been studied a good deal, more recently by literary critics trying to integrate the imagery suggested by the rune-names with the themes and structures of the individual poems.[8] This is not my present concern which is more with how the runes and their names fit into their immediate poetical contexts.

Four poems have passages which contain the runes that form either 'c y n e w u l f' or 'c y n w u l f'. These are *The Fates of the Apostles* and *Elene* in the Vercelli Book, and *Christ II* and *Juliana* in the Exeter Book.[9] The effect in all cases is a riddling one. The runes fit into the verse by alliteration and/or stress, and again their names would signal to the listener that a runic message was to come, and draw his attention to the personal name *Cyn(e)wulf* as the poet intended. *The Fates of the Apostles* goes further than a mere hint to the hearer: 'Here anyone who takes pleasure in poems recited, if he is sharp of intellect, may discover who wrote this verse.' Then follows the runic signature (ll.98–106 of the edited text: fo.54r), now in part obscured by a stain in the parchment and needing editorial treatment.

> ·ᚠ· þær on ende standeþ
> eorlas þæs on eorðan brucaþ: ne moton hie awa ætsomne
> woruldwunigende.   ·ᚹ· sceal gedreosan
> ·ᚢ· on eðle,   æfter tohweorfan
> læne lices frætewa,   efne swa ·ᛚ· toglideð
> Þonne ·ᚻ· ond ·ᚾ·   cræftes neotað
> nihtes nearowe,   on him ·ᛏ· ligeð,
> cyninges þeodom.   Nu ðu cunnon miht
> hwa on þam wordum wæs   werum oncyðig.

---

7   The last word of the riddle is *furum* in the manuscript. It is necessary to amend, and *foran*, 'in front of', and *fruma*, 'beginning, first' are suggested.

8   As, for instance, in D.W.Frese, 'The Art of Cynewulf's Runic Signatures', *Anglo-Saxon Poetry: Essays in Appreciation for John McGalliard*, edd. L.E.Nicholson and D.W.Frese (Notre Dame 1975), 312–34; E.R.Anderson, *Cynewulf: Structure, Style and Theme in his Poetry* (London/Toronto 1983).

9   A standard introduction to the runic signatures of these poems is K.Sisam, 'Cynewulf and his Poetry', first printed as a British Academy lecture but more readily available in his *Studies in the History of Old English Literature* (Oxford 1953). The Vercelli Book runes are available in the facsimile, *Il Codice Vercellese*, ed. M.Förster (Halle 1913), fos.54r and 133r.

Last stands *feoh*, money, which men of rank enjoy on earth –
dwellers in the world cannot have it for ever. *Wynn*, joy,
must perish; *ur*, our joy in the homeland. The brief trappings
of the body must decay, gliding away like *lagu*, water. While
cen, torch, and *yr*, ?bow, carry out their office in the close-
ness of the night, *nyd*, the king's service, lies upon them.
Now you may know who has been revealed to men in these
words.

Though this translation is grammatically and syntactically apt, it does not
mean much. Indeed, save that it is grammatical, it resembles many of the pro-
nouncements of modern sages, scholars, politicians and spin-doctors in
saying little while seeming to say a lot. In mitigation I could point out that it
is, after all, poetry. The sentence bringing together *cen*, *yr* and *nyd* has long
proved intractable. Elliott believes that its thought carries on the theme of the
passing of earthly joys, and that the *nihtes nearowe*, closely linked to *nyd*, is a
clear reference to the darkness of the tomb. In contrast, the torch and bow are
symbols of the continuing daily life of warriors in this world, even though
death may take the individual away.[10] I confess I find it hard to follow this
idea through the Old English verbiage. Brooks toys with the possible meanings of *yr*, and finally comes up with the tentative suggestion of 'ink-horn',
translating, 'while torch and ink-horn employ their function with labour in
the night, constraint, the service of the King, lies upon them.'[11] My translation follows earlier scholars in taking *ur* as 'our', and rejecting the *Runic
Poem* meaning 'aurochs' which it is difficult to get into a translation, or
indeed into an original poem, even in favourable circumstances. I have little
doubt that this is right, but I mention Elliott's alternative to show the ingenious twists runologists have recourse to in explaining Cynewulf's confusing
words. Elliott argues that the bond between rune, name and meaning was too
taut for a new sense, 'our', to intrude. Even he cannot get an aurochs into the
poem so he suggests that from early times the rune-name *ur* developed a secondary sense, 'manly strength', relying on Caesar's report that the Germani
hunted this beast as a trial of prowess.[12] He suggests for this partly illegible
passage the reading ·ᚢ· *on eðle æfter tohreoseð* and translates, 'and then in
the native land manly strength decays', which makes good sense if you accept
the initial premise. My own feeling is that if you can believe this you can
believe anything; but Elliott stoutly defends the interpretation in a recent

---

[10] R.W.V.Elliott, 'Cynewulf's Runes in *Juliana* and *Fates of the Apostles*', *English
Studies* 34 (1953), 196–7.
[11] K.R.Brooks, *Andreas and the Fates of the Apostles* (Oxford 1961), 125–6.
[12] See also Elliott, *Runes, an Introduction*, 50–1, reaffirmed 2.ed., 66–7.

study.[13] I suspect that the difficulties of translation reflect Cynewulf's difficulties in bringing a group of intransigent and sometimes unusual words into
his poem; we should rather admire that it is done at all than complain it is not
done well.

After his signature the poet explains why he included it in his verse.
Cynewulf was thinking of his inevitable death and the terrible judgment that
would follow, and so told his name, asking those who had enjoyed the poem
to pray for grace for him when he passed on his final journey to seek an
unknown land. The same context of the Last Judgment encloses the other
three signatures of Cynewulf and accounts for the desire, unusual in an
Anglo-Saxon vernacular poet, to be celebrated by name.

In *Elene* the signature (ll.1256–70: fo.133r) is the core of an apparently
autobiographical section appended to the tale of how St Helena found the
True Cross. When he had ended his story, Cynewulf admitted his former
ignorance of it, his carelessness about such a sacred thing, the weight of his
sins and his preoccupation with his daily labours. Then he turned from the
first to the third person (though commentators have usually assumed that he
continued to speak for himself), and after the signature wrote of the transitory world and the terrors of God's doom. There is no clear signal that the
runes are coming, as in *The Fates of the Apostles*, but a number of things may
have alerted the audience that something unusual was happening; the sudden
change of person, the introductory passage which is in the rare rhyming form,
the uncommon words *cen* and *yr* beginning the name.

> A wæs secg   [MS sæcc] oð ðæt
>   cnyssed cearwelmum,   ᚳ. drusende,
>   þeah he in medohealle   maðmas þege,
>   æplede gold.   ·ᚾ· gnornode,
>   ·ᛏ· gefera   nearusorge dreah,
>   enge rune   þaer him ·ᛗ· fore
>   milpaðas mæt,   modig þrægde,
>   wirum gewlenced.   ·ᚹ· is geswiðrad,
>   gomen æfter gearum,   geogoð is gecyrred,
>   ald onmedla.   ·ᚢ· wæs geara
>   geogoðhades glæm.   Nu synt geardagas
>   æfter fyrstmearce   forð gewitene,
>   lifwynne geliden   swa ·ᛚ· toglideð,
>   flodas gefysde.   ·ᚠ· æghwam bið
>   læne under lyfte.

---

13 'Coming Back to Cynewulf' in Bammesberger, *Old English Runes*, 246.

Until then the man was continually tossed by the waves of care. He was like a flickering torch (*cen*), even though he received precious gifts of embossed gold in the mead-hall. *Yr*, his comrade at need (*nyd*), mourned, felt clamming sorrow, secret oppression, where formerly the mettled steed (*eh*) galloped, measured the mile-long paths, splendid in its filigreed trappings. With the years pleasure, delight (*wynn*) has faded, youth with its former pomp is changed. Once the radiance of youth was ours (*ur*). Now the old days have passed away in the fullness of time, life's joys departed as water (*lagu*) ebbs away, the floods driven along. For every man under heaven wealth (*feoh*) is transitory.

The problems are much the same as those of *The Fates of the Apostles*: the uncertain line of thought, the sense of *yr* (can it credibly mean 'bow' here?), whether *ur* can mean 'our'. Only clearer in this context is the use of *cen*, for in *Elene* is it easy to defend a meaning 'torch' provided you can accept the sudden change of image from man as a ship buffeted by surging cares to man in his decline, the spark of life glowing fitfully like a dying torch.

Christ II is about the Ascension, but its thought ranges beyond that event to consider its significance for mankind, the reconciliation Christ's sacrifice brought between God and man, our need for divine grace to help us follow Christ's example, and the judgment our deeds will bring upon us (ll.797–807: fo.19v).

> Þonne ·ᚳ· cwacað,   gehyreð cyning mæðlan,
> rodera ryhtend,   sprecan reþe word
> þam þe him ær in worulde   wace hyrdon,
> þendan ·ᚾ· ond ·ᛏ·   yþast meahtan
> frofre findan.   Þær sceal forht monig
> on þam wongstede   werig bidan
> hwæt him æfter dædum   deman wille
> wraþra wita.   Biþ se ·ᚣ· scæcen
> eorþan frætwa.   ·ᚾ· wæs longe
> ·ᛚ· flodum bilocen,   lifwynna dæl,
> ·ᚠ· on foldan.

Then *cen* will tremble, will hear the king pronounce, the ruler of the heavens speak angry words to those who had been feeble in obeying him in this world, while *yr* and *nyd* could find solace most easily. In that place many a one, terrified, shall await wearily what harsh penalties he will adjudge him in consequence of his deeds. The joy (*wynn*) of

earthly treasures will have passed away. Our (*ur*) portion of
life's delights will long have been encompassed by the
water's floods (*lagu-* + *-flodum*), our wealth (*feoh*) in the
world.

Once this gets going it makes fair sense, though it involves a rather
dashing translation of the tenses of the last two sentences. I find the beginning quite baffling. I can hardly believe with Elliott that *cen* has the extended
sense of the fires of doomsday, nor does it seem very likely that the *yr* and
nyd passage refers to the worldly time when men 'relied overmuch on the
strength of their own arms, and on *nēd*, the need of the moment'.[14] (Elliott
translates the beginning, 'when the flame trembles he shall hear the King
speak, the Ruler of the skies utter stern words to those who formerly in the
world were remiss in their obedience to Him, at a time when their bow and
the necessity of the moment most easily availed to find help for them'.) I
applaud here Elliott's attempt, which is a really brave try at a hard passage of
verse, and it is certainly the most satisfying of the explanations I have seen,
but I find it hard to believe. Most commentators have cheated by arbitrarily
replacing some of the rune-names by words beginning with the same sound;
they put *cene*, 'bold', for *cen*, and *yfel*, 'evil', for *yr*, even though, as Sisam
has pointed out, such a reading of the runes would hide from the listener the
fact that a signature was beginning.[15] In fact, *Christ II* suffers from the same
troubles as *The Fates of the Apostles* and *Elene* in that some of the rune-
names, as we know or interpret them, will not fit the verse they are embedded
in. Of course, some of the traditional rune-names, as *ur*, represent things
seldom referred to in everyday speech; some, *cen* for instance, though signi-
fying common enough objects, are not recorded in Old English other than as
rune-names. This makes them difficult to get into everyday discourse.

In *Juliana*, as in *The Fates of the Apostles*, the poet followed his signature
(ll.703–9: fo.76r) by a plea for his readers' or reciters' prayers. The whole
forms an epilogue to the verse life of St Juliana. Cynewulf addresses the
reader or hearer, confessing that he will need the saint's help when his body
and soul part company, and his spirit travels to an unknown land to suffer the
consequences of his misdeeds.

---

[14] R.W.V.Elliott, 'Cynewulf's Runes in *Christ II* and *Elene*', *English Studies* 34
(1953), 54–6.
[15] *Studies in . . . Old English Literature*, 26.

Geomor hweorfeð
·ᛣ·ᚾ· ond ·ᛏ·   Cyning biþ reþe
sigora syllend,   þonne synnum fah,
·ᛗ·ᛈ· ond ᚾ·   acle bidað
hwæt him æfter dædum   deman wille
lifes to leane;   ·ᛚ·ᚠ· beofað,
seomað sorgcearig.

Sadly *cen, yr* and *nyd* will depart. The king, giver of victories, will be stern when *eh, wynn* and ur, stained with sins,
await in terror what he will adjudge them in consequence of
their actions, in requital of life. *Lagu, feoh* will tremble, will
lie in misery.

As Cynewulf points out, it will then be too late to repent, and he will need
all the help he can get, including St Juliana's. But also, 'I pray all mankind,
every man of good heart who recites this verse, to remember me earnestly by
name, and to beg the Lord of power, protector of the heavens, wielder of all
might, that he yield me help on that great day.'

The *Juliana* runes are not susceptible to the same interpretations, unconvincing though they may have turned out to be, as the other Cynewulf poems.
Here the runes are grouped together, and presumably the groups have significance. When the poem was spoken, the rune-names must have been pronounced, for they fit into the metre and alliteration, but the names hid a
meaning other than that of their names. The easiest explanation is Sisam's,
that each group of runes stands for the name *Cynewulf*: it is he who will
depart this life in misery, will wait in terror for the Lord's sentence, will
tremble wretchedly.[16] This is so simple that I would like it to be right, but it
has the weakness that it does not explain why the poet set out his name crypti-
cally in three groups of runes. They neither operate as letter sequences spelling out words, nor hold meaning when replaced by their rune-names.

A traditional way of reading the first two rune groups has been as the
words they spell, 'c y n' and 'e w u'. *Cyn*, 'kin, family, race', is expanded to
mean 'race of men, mankind', and *ewu*, a dialectal plural of *eowe*, 'ewe', is
made to carry the general sense, 'sheep', and the trick is done. So, Elliott, a
proponent of this view, translates, 'Sadly, the human race will depart. The
King, Giver of victories, will be stern when the sin-stained sheep await in
terror . . .', retorting wittily that the second runic cluster 'has puzzled modern
critics a good deal more than it would have puzzled an Anglo-Saxon'.[17] The

---

[16] *Ibid.*, 21–2.

final pair, 'l f', cannot be read in the same way, and here Elliott faces boldly
the reading *lagu-feoh*. He compares the *Christ II* quotation *laguflodum*
bilocen . . . feoh on foldan, and suggests that *lagu-feoh* is a compression of
this idea, 'all men's worldly treasures engulfed by the floods of Doomsday'.
So he translates the end of the signature passage, '(Earth's) flood-bound
wealth will quake; it will lie heavy with its burden of sorrow.'[18] Elliott's thesis
is open to objection. That 'l f' cannot be treated like 'c y n' and 'e w u' is
untidy, while the thought of flood-bound wealth lying heavy with its burden
of sorrow is one to daunt the bravest. As both Sisam and Rosemary Woolf
stressed, it is something of a liberty to translate *ewu* as 'sheep' rather than
'ewes', a word which fits the image of Judgment Day less happily.[19] Yet in his
interpretation Elliott works more closely with the *Juliana* text than does
Sisam, who cuts this Gordian knot with rather too ready a sword.

I have taken the poems in this order for ease of exposition: what order they
were written in we do not know. The riddle-like opening of *The Fates of the*
Apostles signature has been quoted as evidence that it is the first of them, yet
the poem's indifferent quality has been held to show the writer in the decline
of his powers. The unusual type of runic signature of *Juliana* implies that it
'must either have been the first or the last of his extant works', and Elliott
plumps for the first because 'the runic passage conforms closest to the type
of Anglo-Saxon runic riddle'.[20] When in the hands of judicious scholars the
evidence can lead to conclusions as far apart as these, it is wise to suspend
judgment.

So far I have dealt largely with runes in Old English literary texts, but
there are several other manuscript contexts for runes to appear in. Some are
marginalia, often trivial. For instance, the eleventh-century Corpus Christi
College, Cambridge, MS 41 was the property of a community acquainted
with runes. It is a large-letter copy of the Old English Bede, with a lot of marginal additions. One of the added texts is part of the verse *Solomon and*
Saturn, and though this version has no runes in its *pater noster* section it uses
'm' (= *man/mon*) as an abbreviation for the last syllable of *Solomon*. In the
lower margin of this manuscript's p.436 someone has written a trial *abc*, and
thereafter is the runic 'a b c d' and perhaps part of 'e'. In a different hand, in

---

[17] 'Coming Back to Cynewulf', 238.
[18] 'Cynewulf's Runes in *Juliana*', 200–2.
[19] *Studies in . . . Old English Literature*, 21; R.Woolf, *Juliana* (London 1955), 10.
[20] Woolf, *Juliana*, 7; Brooks, *Andreas*, xxxi; Elliott, 'Cynewulf's Runes in *Juliana*',
    203.

the outer margin of p.448 is the group 'x i i .7. x x x s w i þ o r'. The last six runes copy the neighbouring word *swiþor* in the main text at this point (the Old English Bede, book 5, chapter 19). The early part of the text is presumably a roman number, 12 + 30, and may refer to the hides of land (in fact 10 + 30) that, according to this passage, St Wilfrid received at Stamford and Ripon. An unnumbered opening page of the tenth-century Lauderdale or Tollemache *Orosius* (British Library MS Add.47967, perhaps from Winchester) has a curious group of runes in a late tenth-century hand: 'y r þ e r o ŋ t n æ o n ḡ o n ḡ': I have no idea what their significance is.[21] The final text page of the St Petersburg/Leningrad Gospels (St Petersburg Public Library MS F.v.I.8) has, scored in it with a knife, the group 'e þ e l st d r y þ', presumably a combination of *Eþelstan* and *Eþeldryþ*.

The distinctively epigraphical effect of runes on the page enables them to be used as reference marks, for they stand quite distinct from roman characters and cannot be confused with them. Examples are in the eleventh-century annotated text of Boethius's *De Consolatione Philosophiae*, Corpus Christi College, Cambridge, MS 214. The early pages had marginal notes most of which were lost when rats nibbled away the manuscript edges. Several different script forms linked the notes to the appropriate passages in Boethius – there are Greek and decorative roman capitals, and some forms that coincide with runes and presumably are them. Part of Corpus Christi College, Cambridge, MS 173 is a school book, Sedulius's *Carmen Paschale*. It has been roughly handled and has all sorts of later additions: marginal scribbles, doodles, sketches, comments and cribs. Written above the text are numbers of glosses, some in ink and some dry-point, translating the words, while here and there are symbols presumably telling the Anglo-Saxon reader what order to take the Latin words in. These include a few runes.

Derolez points to other types of manuscript rune, used in the signatures and comments of scribes, as ornamental letters, for marking the quires that made up a book, and so on.[22] No doubt a minute examination of the corpus of Anglo-Saxon manuscripts would reveal lots of further examples, and perhaps some quite new types. In the main, however, manuscript runes are fairly trivial. They are a secondary development. Scribes found runes useful as additional symbols, sometimes absorbing them into bookhand, sometimes keeping them distinct for practical purposes. In either case they have little

---

[21] See the facsimile *The Tollemache Orosius*, ed. A.Campbell. EEMF 3 (Copenhagen 1953), fo.*d*.

[22] *Runica Manuscripta*, 402–3.

connection with epigraphical runes, and, save in the matter of rune-names, it is an error (as I think, though not all agree with me) to believe that the two cast much light on one another.[23] However, I take up this point again in chapter 14.

---

[23] Challenged, for example, by Parsons, 'Anglo-Saxon Runes in Continental Manuscripts' in Düwel, *Runische Schriftkultur*, 195–220.

13

Anglo-Saxon and Viking

In chapter 3 I showed how the Anglo-Saxons adapted the Germanic rune-row to make it fit their developed form of the language. They gave some old runes new values. They modified some shapes, usually making them more complex. They created new characters so that the common English rune-row now had twenty-eight or more to the Germanic twenty-four. The North Germanic peoples of Scandinavia too found it desirable to alter the Germanic runes, but they did it more modestly if less efficiently by cutting down the number of characters to sixteen and simplifying some shapes. An effect of these changes was that by the time the Vikings poured into England their runes were noticeably different from the Anglo-Saxon graphs. Some forms in the two scripts coincided – **f, u, þ, r, i, l**, and in some versions of the Scandinavian rune-row **n, s, t**, and **b** – but others showed little resemblance.

In their homelands the Viking peoples used runes extensively. For much of the Viking Age it was the only script they knew. Comparative figures show how productive the Scandinavian rune-masters were, though we must be cautious about using statistics since new finds, made almost daily, keep on changing the picture. In a count made in 1965 Lucien Musset gave the following figures, for rune-stones alone, up to the year 1300: Sweden about 2,400 though they are unevenly spread about the country: Denmark and adjoining coastal areas that made up the mediaeval kingdom about 300: Norway about 50.[1] In 1983 the German runologist Klaus Düwel estimated there were (without dating limits) some 3,000 runic pieces in Sweden (1,200 of them in the region of Uppland), 1,100 in Norway, 700 in Denmark, 60 in Iceland.[2] New finds from urban archaeology will have added numbers of inscribed objects to the corpora, and to some extent changed the balance of inscription types recorded.

We would expect the Vikings to take to the countries they invaded, traded

---

[1] *Introduction à la runologie*, 241.
[2] *Runenkunde*, 2.ed. (Stuttgart 1983), 3.

with or colonised their practice of raising rune-stones and cutting runes on their various possessions, and so they did, though again not in even distribution. Iceland, which had a Viking Age settlement coming overwhelmingly from Scandinavia and its colonies, has apparently not revealed a single Viking Age rune, for its monuments are all, I think, of later date.[3] There are only half a dozen or so runic objects from the Faroe Islands though that too was a Norse-settled region. Normandy has no runes at all despite the Danish occupation there. From the eastern territories, from Russia and its neighbouring lands where people of Swedish origin were active, only a handful of runic texts was known until *glasnost* revealed to us more, though even then not many.

On the other hand the Celto-Norse community of the Isle of Man produced over thirty rune-stones by the latest count.[4] Katharine Holman's 1996 list of Scandinavian runic objects in Orkney and Shetland comprises twenty-five pieces (not including the immense corpus of late – post-Viking Age – runes scratched in the stone-work of the prehistoric mound at Maeshowe, Orkney)[5] and more have been found in the short time since she made that survey.[6] Ireland presents a dramatic example of how new finds may affect our understanding of the use of the script. Until the excavation of mediaeval sites in Dublin in the 1970s and 1980s, only three or four runic objects were known from Ireland despite the vigour of Viking activity there in the tenth and eleventh centuries. Dublin gave up a further fourteen runic (or in a couple of cases probably rune-like) specimens, on bone and wood surprisingly well preserved in the moist ground.[7] It is against this varied background of use of the script that we should view the Viking runes of Anglo-Saxon and later England.

One of the errors writers about the Vikings tend to fall into is the habit of treating the Viking peoples as though they were a single one, a homogeneous racial group with one culture common to all. In fact they were different if closely related races and their material and spiritual cultures showed local

---

3 A recent find from Viðey, Iceland, may be as early as the twelfth century: J.E.Knirk, 'Runepinnen fra Viðey, Island', *Nytt om Runer* 9 (1994), 20.

4 K.Holman, *Scandinavian Runic Inscriptions in the British Isles: their Historical Context.* Senter for Middelalderstudier Skrifter 4 (Trondheim 1996), 86–172.

5 Published as M.P.Barnes, *The Runic Inscriptions of Maeshowe, Orkney.* Runrön 8 (Uppsala 1994).

6 M.Barnes and R.I.Page, 'New Runic Inscriptions from Orkney', *Nytt om Runer* 12 (1997), 21–3.

7 M.P.Barnes *et al.*, *The Runic Inscriptions of Viking Age Dublin.* Medieval Dublin Excavations 1962–81, Ser.B. vol.5 (Dublin 1997). One more inscription has been found since that book came out.

variation. It is the same with the runes. There was not a single rune-row used by all literate Vikings. There were variants, sometimes regional, sometimes perhaps social and cultural. This is not the place for a detailed account of the development of Scandinavian runes in the early Middle Ages. All I am concerned with is to show that the script was occasionally employed to represent English and more often used in England to represent Scandinavian, and for this an outline of knowledge is adequate.

The Scandinavian peoples reduced their rune-row from twenty-four to sixteen letters by discarding runes, some of which were clearly otiose, some of which we would not think dispensable at all. The runes *eoh/íh, Ing* and *peorð* (to give them their English names) were of rare occurrence in the early Scandinavian inscriptions. *Eoh/íh*, representing some quality of medial front vowel in the region of *i* and *e*, was obviously not essential, while *Ing*, if it gave [ŋ], would seem to us a needless refinement since after all modern English manages without a special symbol for this sound. Why *peord* was dropped leaving **b** henceforth to represent both voiced [b] and voiceless [p] labial stops I have no idea, for this seems to us a distinction worth preserving.

As well as discarding these three rare runes the Scandinavian rune-masters got rid of five more common ones which again seem to us useful symbols, those for the two vowels **e** (*eh*) and **o** (*oeþil*), the two consonants **d** (*dæg*) and **g** (*gyfu*), and the semivowel **w** (*wynn*). The vowel rune **u** could easily replace the last of these. For the two voiced consonant stops [d], [g] the equivalent voiceless symbols **t** and **k** could be substituted, with the result that in the dentals and gutturals, as in the labials, the rune-masters did not distinguish between voiced and voiceless. The loss of the two vowel symbols **e** and **o** was never adequately compensated for, and the sixteen-letter *futhark* (or rather *futhąrk*, for that is what it became) was an imprecise instrument for representing vowel and diphthong sounds.

The younger *futhark* as it is called is represented on the ninth-century stone at Gørlev, Sjælland (Denmark) thus:[8]

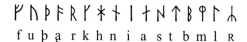

f u þ ą r k h n i a s t b m l ʀ

Compared with the Anglo-Saxon *futhorc* this shows two elementary formal variants, the English and the Norse forms deriving independently and differently from the Germanic runes. The typical northern **k** is ᚴ compared with

8 Jacobsen and Moltke, *Damnarks Runeindskrifter*, no.239.

the common English ᚲ. The final rune transcribed by the symbol **R**, ᛦ, is equivalent to the Anglo-Saxon ᛉ which the English came to use occasionally as 'x'. In the Norse *futhark* this graph has taken up a new position and stands last. Two other runes underwent severe modification in the younger *futhark*. Its rune-carvers avoided forms with two verticals, and so altered **h** and **m** to give them single verticals only. Two other runes developed new uses. Norse lost initial *j* early, and the rune-name **jāra* (Old English *ger*) became Old Norse *ár.* Accordingly the value of the **j**-rune (which had achieved the form ᛡ perhaps as a re-ordering of the elements of the curious Germanic graph ᛃ) became **a** in virtue of its name. The old **a**-rune ᚠ remained in use but with a nasalised value [ã], usually transliterated **a** in accordance with the development of its name **ansuR (> ąss).* and ultimately took the value **o** as in the rune-name *ós(s)* in the Norwegian and Icelandic *Runic Poems.*

These various changes occurred neither quickly nor surely. Nor, as for that, simultaneously. Over quite a long period there were variant forms for such runes as **h, m** and **a** (the old **j**), and the *futhark* given above is of the type that developed in Denmark for monumental purposes. These runes are therefore sometimes named the Danish runes, but as they were also used occasionally in Norway too and often in Sweden, they have also been known as the Common or Normal runes. All these names are rather outdated, and the letter forms of this type of *futhark* are now generally called 'long-branch' runes. They remained popular through the Viking Age, though usually with a simplification of **m** to ᛦ.

In Norway and Sweden, however, a yet simpler sixteen-letter *futhark* was used, its characters adapted to act perhaps as a sort of cursive script. In one version they are known as the Rök runes after the famous rune-stone in Östergötland where they occur. Slightly different and more common are the 'Swedo-Norwegian' runes. Today all these are usually grouped together as the 'short-twig' runes (Norwegian *kortkvistruner* or *stuttruner*); the reason will be clear from a comparison of their *futhark* with that of the long-branch runes. Derivable from inscriptions in short-twig runes is the *futhark.*

ᚠᚢᚦᚨᚱᚴ ᚼᚾᛁᚨᛋᛏ ᛒᛘᛚ ᛦ

f u þ ą r k   h n i a s t   b m l ᴿ

but it is wrong to consider this a typical *futhark*, for this version of the script has numbers of minor variants, as ᛎ for **ą**, ᛆ for **a**, ᛓ and ᛒ for **b**. Sometimes forms intrude from the long-branch into the short-twig *futhark*, as ᛒ for **h** and ᛦ for **m**. Inscriptions from the Isle of Man and the Norwegian province of

Jæren use the short-twig runes with the substitution of long-branch **m** (and some would add occasionally **h**, **a** and **n** too), and such a mixture of the scripts has often been called the Man-Jæren runes. For all this interpenetration, it is convenient for runologists to assert the distinction between long-branch and short-twig runes, and to label some forms, those for **n**, **a**, **s**, **t**, **b**, for instance, as 'diagnostic graphs', that is, forms that distinguish between the two types of *futhark*. But one should always keep in mind that this is a convenience rather than a statistical fact, and that in some cases an inscription may contain no examples of 'diagnostic graphs' and so may not be attributable to a specific *futhark* type.

In the later part of the Viking Age there were even further interminglings of the two main *futhark* types, and then, towards its very end, the Scandinavians created new rune varieties to overcome the obvious weaknesses the sixteen-letter *futhark* had. Thus **h** became restricted to the form ✳, and ↓ was used as a new e-rune. ↑ got the value /æ/ (transliterated **æ**) and sometimes /e/. ↲ served as a vowel rune usually transliterated as **o**. The distinction between voiced and voiceless stops was recreated by the formation of new, dotted, graphs, for instance ↱ for **g**, ↟ for **d**. Despite these developments, the sixteen-letter *futhark* remained in use side by side with the newly expanded one. What I have said in these last few paragraphs is an over-simplification of a complex set of facts, but it will do for the present.

Vikings brought their runes to England, and probably the script had a brief flowering here during the time of their establishment and settlement in the north and east. Subsequently the Norsemen lost their Scandinavian tongue, or at least were unable to keep it distinct from the English that resembled it, but that does not mean that cultural links – and so runic links – with Scandinavian territories overseas were cut. Indeed, though the evidence is slight, it seems that Norse runes continued to be brought into the north-west of this country, presumably across the Irish Sea, perhaps as late as the thirteenth century. The numbers that survive in England from all periods are small – Holman's list comprises sixteen examples, from which one (Settle) can now be removed as a modern copy[9] – and I cannot claim that the Scandinavian version of the script ever played much part in English civilisation. Yet there are Norse runes here, and this book should take some note of them.

But first, another distinction. The Scandinavian runes may represent different types of Scandinavian speaker in England. There was the casual visitor

---

[9]   As in Holman's Appendix 1 to *Scandinavian Runic Inscriptions*; M.P.Barnes, 'The Strange Case of the Settle Stone' in *A Frisian and Germanic Miscellany published in Honour of Nils Århammar . . .* edd. A.Petersen and H.F.Nielsen = NOWELE 28/29 (1996), 297–313.

Fig.70. The Penrith brooch *futhąrk*. (2:1)

who came to this country and, as casual visitors may do, scrawled some message on a building stone, or cut a text on a piece of wood or bone and threw it away. There was the settler, who retained some or much of his Scandinavian speech and recorded it in formal or informal terms – the Norse enclave in tenth-/eleventh-century Dublin would also be an example of this. There was the band of Scandinavians who took political control of a region of England and used their language to assert that supremacy – the Norsemen who commissioned the Manx rune-stones may be a parallel case. Or there was the entrepreneur who joined one of the Viking armies of, say, Cnut and came to England to make his fortune as a representative of a ruling power. In addition to all these there was presumably the traveller who brought with him from Scandinavia some piece of property that had runes already cut on it.

Of the Holman list of Scandinavian inscriptions in England two, from Rochester and Canterbury, are only small fragments of stone (both lost), with little to tell a present-day reader. Others are inscriptions that are manifestly and typically Scandinavian. An important instance is a short-twig *futhąrk* cut on the ring of a penannular silver brooch found at Penrith (Cumberland/Cumbria), now in the British Museum, apparently part of a scattered hoard. It is of a type ascribed to the later ninth or tenth century. Its *futhąrk* has only fifteen runes (fig.70).

Whether the last of these repeats the penultimate, as **m**, or is to be taken as a variant **R**, is unknown and indeed unknowable. There are two further, retrograde, runes on one of the brooch terminals, **fu**, presumably the opening of another *futhąrk*.

Another example is a bone comb-case found in uncertain circumstances at Lincoln (also in the British Museum), with the clear and forceful statement in long-branch runes: **kamb:koþan:kiari:þorfastr**, *kamb góðan giar<ð>i Þórfastr*, 'Þorfastr made a good comb.' The Danish runologist Erik Moltke accepted this as part of the Danish corpus – he put it perhaps in the later eleventh century, though admitting it could be younger.[10] If younger it is

---

[10] *Runes and their Origin*, 466, but cf. also his p.463. E.Ekwall pointed out that

quite likely it came to England already inscribed. Since there is no find-report the inscription's provenance must remain uncertain. A further bone piece from Lincoln has a fragmentary short-twig text divided into separate words from which **xhitirxstinx** may be extracted, but the context is too slight for us to interpret it with any certainty.[11]

Casual graffiti are the text groups on bits of bone, scapulae probably of roe-deer, found unstratified in excavations at St Albans (Hertfordshire). One has a pair of apparently related texts:] *þ*:**þu:uur:uur*** |**risti** and on another edge of the bone **runaʀ:tr**[. The group *risti rúnar* constitutes a well-evidenced formula, 'scratched runes', and implies a subject, which would presumably be the word represented by the combinations of **þ, u** and **r** – perhaps a personal name with the first element *Þor-/Þór-*. The second scapula has a text, part damaged at the end, probably **wufr***ik*, using as first letter the Old English rune *wynn* which has no equivalent in the younger *futhąrk*. The text is likely to be a personal name, Old English *Wulfric*, and then it implies an intermingling of Norse and English traditions. Aside from the English 'w', diagnostic runes of this group of texts are long-branch, and the whole is consistent with a Dano-English community of the Viking Age.

Another casual text, preserved in more august circumstances, is cut informally on a wall within the south transept of Carlisle cathedral, a building that was begun in the last years of the eleventh century. Dressing marks run across the stone and make reading of parts of its text difficult, but most is legible enough: **tolfinuʀaitþisarunraþisastain**, 'Dólfinn scratched these runes on this stone.' If this reading is correct, it is Norse but demotic Norse with odd word endings (*rúnr, þisa stain*), and word order (*þisa stain*) which may show English influence. *Dólfinn* is a fairly rare name in Scandinavia itself but quite widespread in England, and occurs in Cumberland in the centuries after the Norman Conquest. It is a fair guess that, whatever its language, the inscription is by a man with local connections. Though not all its letters are clearly distinguishable, the inscription seems to be in short-twig runes throughout except for the initial **t** which is long-branch, perhaps to give the rune-carver's name greater distinction. On a neighbouring stone in the wall is a further graffito: three runes, **aif** (?**aik**), of no obvious meaning.

Two rune-stones represent a more formal side of the Scandinavian runic input. The first (in the Museum of London) is from St Paul's churchyard,

'there is nothing to prove that [this comb-case] was made in England' ('How Long did the Scandinavian Language Survive in England', *A Grammatical Miscellany Offered to Otto Jespersen on his Seventieth Birthday* (Copenhagen 1930), 25).

[11] John McKinnell makes an attempt in 'A Runic Fragment from Lincoln', *Nytt om Runer* 10 (1995), 10–11.

Fig.71. The Bridekirk font runes.

London, where was found a sculptured stone whose design is plainly Scandinavian and may even be Swedish. It is part of a burial monument and bears the text: **k*i*na:let:lekia:st| in:þensi:auk:tuki:** in two opposing lines of longbranch runes: *Ginna lét leggia stein þensi auk Tóki*, 'Ginna and Toki had this stone laid.' The dead person's name was presumably recorded on a matching stone at the other end of the grave. From the mediaeval tower of a church at Winchester (now in the City Museum) comes a re-used rune-stone fragment, with two lines of text set between framing lines, and opposing one another in a Danish manner. Diagnostic letters **a, s** indicate long-branch runes. Too little survives for any reconstruction of the text, though the single word **auk**, 'and', is clear.[12]

Rune-stones like these are only marginally part of the history of English epigraphy. They are probably of Scandinavian workmanship (just as the Lincoln comb-case and the Penrith brooch could have been made and inscribed in Scandinavia). In contrast stands one object using Scandinavian runes where the language is unambiguously English. This is the great font in the parish church of Bridekirk (Cumberland/Cumbria). It is cut from a single block of stone, now mounted on a modern base. The block is roughly a cube, and is shaped into a bowl whose four faces are almost rectangular, and a pedestal with faces that taper towards their base. Elaborate carving covers all surfaces of the bowl and pedestal, with conventional foliage, plant scroll, beast and monster motifs and human figures. The inscription is on the east face of the pedestal. At either edge of this face stand two capitaled pillars, and between them curls a ribbon on which the text is displayed (fig.71). The

---

12 Published in detail in B.Kjølbye-Biddle and R.I.Page, 'A Scandinavian Rune-Stone from Winchester', *Antiquaries Jnl* 55 (1975), 389–94.

ribbon divides the face into two roughly equal parts which are occupied by plant scroll. At the left of the lower one stands the figure of a craftsman with hammer and chisel, still at work on the carving.

The font is well preserved, presumably because it has always been under cover. The surface has a skim of plaster or cement over it, and seems to have had when William Nicolson of Carlisle saw it in 1685, so it is likely to be of mediaeval origin. The skim obscures some of the letter shapes, and there is the further obstacle that it has been painted and the characters marked in, again making details hard to distinguish. Despite all this most of the characters are identifiable, and nearly all the legend can be read. It is in Scandinavian runes of a mixed type (with short-twig **a, s, n** but ✳ **h,** ⸙ **m,** ⸠ **o,** ↑ **t,** ⸝ **b,** ⸦ **e**) supplemented by the bookhand characters *eth, yogh* and *wynn* and the abbreviation symbol for *and*. The language is English, but nearer Middle than Old, which fits well with the art historians' twelfth-century date for the piece. The inscription forms a rhyming couplet, again appropriate to Middle English. Its subject matter throws light on the craftsman's figure beneath: **+rikarþ:he:me:iwr[o]kte:ꝼ:to:þis:me:rÐ:3er:**:me:brokte.** A short sequence towards the end of this has two letter forms odd enough to baffle the runologist, but the general sense is clear: 'Rikard he made me and . . . brought me to this splendour.' The sequence **3er:**** may be a second personal name, recording the man who commissioned the font (and so brought this piece of workmanship to a splendid end or a glorious place) or a second craftsman who embellished it further, perhaps with paint. The text looks entirely English: the Scandinavian element is in the graphs. **rikarþ** could, I suppose, be Old Norse *Ríkarðr*, but is more likely to be the Continental Germanic name *Ricard* which is recorded in England from the middle of the eleventh century. The rest of the couplet, as far as it can be understood, is good early Middle English. It follows that in this part of the north-west in the twelfth century, Viking runes were so far naturalised as to be used by people who spoke and presumably read and wrote English.

Nearby, at Dearham (Cumberland/Cumbria), and also at a short distance away, from Conishead Priory (Lancashire north of the sands/Cumbria), are two intriguing short texts. The Dearham example is a grave-slab, quite elaborate in design and with the name ADAM in decorative Romanesque capitals. Surrounding the whole is a plain border, and at one end of this – that opposite the personal name – someone has cut a rough line of runes, now broken at the beginning. The clearly readable bit of the legend is **hniarm** which has no obvious meaning and does not direct our attention to either the English or the Norse language. A nineteenth-century antiquary reported two further runic fragments found during the restoration of Dearham church, but they have not been seen since.

In the ruins of Conishead Priory was discovered a stone that was part of a thirteenth-century altar.[13] Cut in its surface are graphs that seem to be mason's marks, and on an inner face, where it would be hidden when the altar was set up, is the runic **dotbrt**, apparently a personal name with the second element *-bert*, its vowel omitted as sometimes happens in Norse usage (fig.72). The name is not recorded in either Scandinavian or English, so again it gives no indication of language. What is important about Conishead is the use of the distinctive **d**, ⇑, a dotted form of **t** which was not created until towards the end of the Viking Age – it occurs in the period 1050–1150 in Denmark, but is not found in Norway until the late twelfth century. Conishead is evidence that runic connections between England and Scandinavia continued until a fairly late date.

Fig.72. The Conishead Priory runes. Taken from a photograph.
Scale approx. 1:2

On the opposite side of the country, at Skelton-in-Cleveland (Cleveland/Yorkshire), is a fragment of a sundial: part of the dial itself and short bits of two texts, four lines of roman capitals below, and to their right two lines of runes set at right angles to the roman text. Both runic and roman inscriptions are divided into individual words by points set at centre height of the line. Not a lot can be made of either, but both could be Norse. Of the runes the sequence ****ebel·ok·** is all that can be identified, with diagnostic forms ⇃**o**, ⌐ **b** and ⊦ **e**.

There remains a single but most important monument, the twelfth-century tympanum now preserved in the church of Pennington (Lancashire north of the sands/Cumbria). This is a massive chunk of stone some 120 cm (47 inches) across, cut into a semicircle to fit the arch head it once adorned. An angel with wings displayed and below it a row of dog-tooth ornament occupy the central field, and these enable art historians to date the piece. Round the circumference runs a triple border, the central element of which holds the

---

[13] Michael Barnes and I have not been able to trace this stone. We know it only from the photograph published in P.V.Kelly, 'Excavations at Conishead Priory', *Transactions of the Cumberland and Westmorland Arch. and Ant. Soc.* NS 30 (1930), 149–68, pl.III.

runes. The tympanum has had a troubled history. Mediaeval masons took it for building stone, and it may be they who chiselled away part of the surface. When the old church of Pennington was pulled down in the early nineteenth century the tympanum was discovered in its fabric, taken away and set into the wall of a nearby outhouse where the weather attacked it. It stayed there for about a century and then returned to the church, where the authorities fixed it to an inner wall of the nave, but in poor lighting which makes inspection difficult. Only the first part of the text is at all legible, and some of this is disputed. For instance, Eilert Ekwall read ' . . . kial (*or* mial) seti þesa kirk. Hubert masun uan m.', while Bruce Dickins has 'KML:SETE:ThES:KIRK: HUBIRT:MASUN:UAN: M . . . .'[14] I can find only:]**kml:le*ta*:þena:kirk: *ub*rt:masu*n* :***:* +**, and I suspect the form of the first letter and certainly deny that a verb *seti* or *sete is* visible. Dickins translated the inscription, 'Gamal built this church. Hubert the mason carved . . . ', and this may be the very general sense, though we differ on points of detail. The form **masu*n*** may be the occupational title 'mason' as Dickins takes it, or a patronymic *Másson* as Ekwall prefers.

Identifying the language is trickier, for it has both Old English and Old Norse characteristics, and is not close to either in their 'classical' forms. The root *kirk*, 'church', has the Old Norse stem but not its ending, and if, as I believe, the demonstrative modifying it was *þena* this shows confusion of grammatical gender since ON *kirkia* is a feminine noun and *þena* a masculine accusative singular. If **kml** does stand for *Gamal* (with the vowels omitted as sometimes happens) that is certainly a Scandinavian name while *Másson* is a Scandinavian type patronymic. On the other hand the word order *þena kirk*, demonstrative + noun, is English. The Pennington inscription shows Norse influence but is not pure Norse. Neither is it pure English. It shows the two languages in intimate contact in north-west England in the twelfth century.

How little the Vikings affected English runic epigraphy this short survey of the Scandinavian material in this country will have shown. Norse inscriptions are rare in themselves, and only in the case of Bridekirk is there clear evidence of Scandinavian runes penetrating English epigraphical practice. This does not mean that the English knew little of Norse runes. Some of the *runica manuscripta* show acquaintance with the Scandinavian version of the script. For example, the runic page of the early twelfth-century manuscript St John's College, Oxford, 17, fo.5v has two Norse *fuþarks* with rune-names

---

[14] B.Dickins, 'The Pennington Tympanum with Runic Inscription' in A.Fell, *A Furness Manor: Pennington and its Church*, 217–19; E.Ekwall, 'How Long did the Scandinavian Language Survive?', 23–4. Holman produces yet another minor variant, *Scandinavian Runic Inscriptions*, 73–7.

attached. One is of the Gørlev type but with the letter order confused and some names or values wrong (fig.16). The other, more accurate, is also a long-branch *futhark*, with the simplification of Ｙ for **m**. The mid twelfth-century British Library MS Stowe 57, fo.3v has, among other alphabets, a Norse *futhark* with both short-twig and long-branch variants as well as cryptic rune forms. The fifteenth-century St John's College, Cambridge, MS E.4 (Thomas Betson's commonplace book), fo.4v has a complete Norse runic alphabet. For centuries, then, such *futharks* and alphabets occur in the English manuscript tradition, but they were antiquaries' toys and have little extended cultural importance.

In this chapter I have written specifically about Norse runes in England, but of course that makes use of a distinction that is artificial or anachronistic. Scandinavians did not restrict their activity in the British Isles to the regions that now form England. They came to Scotland too, in particular to the islands and their neighbouring coastlands, and left some of their runic monuments there. Some Norsemen came via Ireland or Man. My deliberately restricted English perspective here distorts the picture.

14

Runic and Roman

From time to time in this book I have mentioned the relationship between runes and roman in Anglo-Saxon England. Here I bring the material together in a more formal manner, discussing the interplay between the two scripts and posing a series of questions about literacy, though literacy from a pragmatic rather than a theoretical viewpoint. Did runic and roman scripts rival, supplement or complement each other? What was the link between runes in manuscripts and runes in inscriptions? Were there people literate in both alphabets throughout much of the period? Were there regions where one or other script predominated? Did the one writing system simply supersede the other? We are unlikely to be able to answer such queries in elementary terms, for the greater part of the evidence has just not survived. Moreover, an answer to some of these questions may be dependent upon date and/or place. An incautious runologist might be tempted to reply to general questions like these from extant, individual, examples; or rather, will be tempted and may fall. All a brief discussion can or should do is air some of the problems and warn against over-easy solutions.

In 1932 Bruce Dickins described runes as 'vastly superior as an instrument for recording the sounds of Old English . . . to the latin alphabet'.[1] If he is correct – for his statement was perhaps an overstatement – It should be cause for wonder that runic was not consistently the preferred script for representing Old English. The reason why it was not is obvious enough, and is a matter of politics rather than phonology. Manuscript writing was imported to England from Celtic lands and from the Continent, both regions where roman script, in one form or another, reigned. Roman has kept the prestige imparted to it by the Christian church from the date of its reintroduction to England at the end of the sixth century down to the present day. Yet Dickins's assessment has this in its favour, that Anglo-Saxons judged the imported alphabet not

---

[1] 'A System of Transliteration for Old English Runic Inscriptions', 15.

fully adequate for their purposes, so they supplemented it by incorporating the two runes *þorn* and *wynn*, adapting the ductus of their epigraphical forms to suit a written type. These two penetrated the roman alphabetic pattern and were used in representing the vernacular to the end of the Old English period and beyond.

Of the Germanic peoples who invaded England in the fifth century, some may have gained a knowledge of roman script on the Continent. Others presumably observed examples of its earlier use in this country, on monuments and formal records that Roman occupiers left behind them – some still to be seen today. Yet others certainly acquired Imperial Roman coins with their appropriate legends, though they may not have understood what the characters stood for. And others again may have observed a continued use of roman in surviving Celtic areas of the land.[2] There is, I think, no evidence of Anglo-Saxon practical use of roman from the earliest period. In the fifth and most of the sixth centuries the only recorded script for Anglo-Saxons seems to have been runic. But we must keep in mind the frail state of the evidence.

I suspect the earliest surviving example of roman used in an Anglo-Saxon environment to be the gold medalet issued by Bishop Leudhard, who accompanied the Frankish princess Bertha to England (*c.*580) on her betrothal to King Æthelberht of Kent. One specimen only survives, but there were presumably others. It has the legend LEV·DAR·DVS·EPS, retrograde and more or less roman.[3] Though this piece was current on the English mainland it can hardly be considered English, for the immediate context and presumably workmanship is Frankish and the circulation must have been minimal. At this early time Anglo-Saxon England apparently had no coinage of its own, though it knew Merovingian and late Imperial Roman issues, both found in fair numbers in Anglo-Saxon burials and hoards. Through them some English became acquainted with roman graph forms, if not their values. When indigenous coins were first issued, *c.*600 or a little earlier, they copied such exemplars, even attempting their legends with greater or lesser success. Indeed, it is in the early coins of Anglo-Saxon England that the relative importances of the two scripts, roman and runic, seem most clearly defined.

I have already discussed English runic coins in some detail in chapter 9. Here in part I summarise, in part add further material. There are, for instance,

---

2   C.Thomas discusses the continuity of Latin in the British Isles in *Christianity in Roman Britain to AD 500* (London 1981). E.Okasha has included relevant inscribed stones in *Corpus of Early Christian Stones of South-west Britain. Studies in the Early History of Britain* (Leicester 1993).

3   C.H.V.Sutherland, *Anglo-Saxon Gold Coinage*, no.l; M.Werner, 'The Liudhard Medalet', *Anglo-Saxon England* 20 (1991), 27–41.

Fig.73. New runic coin type from Billockby. (2:1)

some quite early English gold coins with roman superscriptions that are more relevant to English circumstances than that of the Leudhard medalet – forms of personal names or name elements, occasionally a title, *monetarius*, 'moneyer', in one form or another, sometimes the name of a town, presumably the mint that issued the coin – Canterbury (DOROVERNIS CIVITAS), London (LONDVNIV). And there is one royal name and style, AVDVARLÐ REGES tentatively identified, despite some peculiarities of form, as that of Eadbald of Kent (616–40). Here, then, are administrators within an English society using roman script more or less accurately, to represent Romanised name forms and titles in south and south-east England.

However, there are also, among these early gold issues, examples of runic texts that replace roman. Noteworthy are the three with the legend now commonly read **desaiona**. These are based on an Imperial Roman model, but with the runes replacing the original reverse legend. The runes have not yet been interpreted, and that may be because they were in fact meaningless, added at random because a coin ought to have a legend and because runic shapes were more familiar to the users than were roman. This theory may be supported by a very recent find, a *tremissis* also derived from Roman Imperial coins, perhaps those of Constantine I. Hitherto six specimens of the type had been known, but none with runes. On the new discovery, from Billockby (Norfolk), part of the legend is replaced by a (retrograde) runic group, **ltoed‖** or perhaps **ltoedh**, which again has no obvious meaning and contains a vowel sequence **oe** which looks implausible (fig.73). The runes are preceded by fragments of letters, probably roman and derived from the original obverse legend, and are followed by what could be **g** (?or marginally **n**) or may be a cross ending the text. Again, a legend was needed and was supplied, but we do not know if it was read.

The importance of coin evidence in this discussion is that it often provides considerable numbers of individual examples, and they can usually be dated and localised with some precision, As we have seen, English issues from *c*.660 onwards, the silver pennies, continued the practice of putting runic legends on indigenous coins derived from Roman types. Pada's had blundered versions of original obverse roman legends, but runes to give the moneyer's name on the reverse. Epa's have his name in runes on the obverse, sometimes set beside fragments of the roman text. Pennies of other moneyers, of Wigræd, Tilberht and Æthiliræd, display only runes. In all these cases officials preferred to use runes rather than roman, whatever may have been on their models. Is there significance for runic literacy here?

The mid-eighth-century East Anglian coins of Beonna and Alberht/Æþelberht provide a useful set of examples, extensive and datable within a short time range. The individual moneyers had varying practices. Efe supplied his name in roman save for an occasional use of 'f', and royal name and style are either fully roman, or part roman, part runic. Werferth had the royal name and style part roman, part runic; his own name in runes. Wilred used runes only. A type without moneyer's name shows royal name and style again in runes. The solitary known coin of the contemporary king Alberht demonstrates runes only. There is strong evidence here for some official use of runic script at one time in one part of England. Roman was not rejected though it suffered strong competition. But what does this tell us of literacy? The merchant who used the coinage was happy to accept runic, roman or both. We do not know if he could read the legends, or only required their presence. Nor do we know how much royal control there was to determine what script should be used, what script was most acceptable to all involved, king, moneyer, public; though Marion Archibald has presented formidable evidence of a planned development in the design of Beonna's coinage which implies some centralised organisation.[4] Well into the eighth century, then, in the south-east and east, there is material that suggests double (or alternative) literacy, with both scripts acceptable for some purposes. The coin evidence for East Anglia in the latter part of the eighth century confirms this point. Lul's Æthelberht coin and the East Anglian issues of Offa of Mercia show runes in use but not exclusively or perhaps even commonly, and the royal name and style on Offa's coinage, wherever minted, is firmly roman. In Northumbria there is a general use of roman, but with an occasional input of runes as late as the ninth century.

D.M.Metcalf has interpreted the numismatic evidence for runic and/or roman literacy pragmatically and in loosely statistical terms:

> If there are a dozen or twenty moneyers working concurrently in the city of York in the Anglian period . . . and just two or three of them sometimes wrote their names in runes, there is an implication that they did so by individual choice, and not by instruction from higher authori-

---

4 'The Coinage of Beonna in the Light of the Middle Harling Hoard', 22.

ties. It seems that these two or three were sufficiently bi-literate to attempt an orthography in either Roman letters or runes, according to their inclination. Similarly, among Offa's thirty or so moneyers, just a few used runes, and again there may be the implication that the choice was at the personal level.[5]

How does this fit in with other evidence of the rivalry of the two scripts? Taking south-east England and East Anglia in the period of the sixth to eighth centuries, the contrast between the numismatic evidence and that from other epigraphical sources is striking. There appear to be no surviving roman inscriptions there but several runic ones; which suggests how cautious we must be in assessing data that are likely to be inadequate. However, from the late seventh and eighth centuries survive written documents in skilled roman lettering from the south-east, royal charters in Latin such as that of the Kentish Hlothere in favour of Reculver (679), recorded in confident uncial characters (British Library MS Cotton Augustus ii.2; Sawyer 8); of Wihtred of Kent, dated 697, granting land to the church at Lyminge (British Library Stowe MS Ch.1; Sawyer 19); a charter, somewhat altered, of one Œthilred of Essex (*c.*690), giving an estate to Barking (British Library Cotton MS Augustus ii.29; Sawyer 1171). Of course, these come from a royal/aristocratic/Christian milieu where Continental influence was strong. It is unfortunate that no parallel material survives from East Anglia. What preceded these late seventh-century documents we do not know. Their form hardly suggests the work of novices. In earlier times rulers must have had some way of promulgating their wishes to their subjects, of recording their decisions, though it may not have been a literate one. We have no indication of what was the audience for the early charters, who could read or understand them, but we can safely assume it was small. Yet there is what moderns call a 'literacy event' here, and it is distinct from the 'literacy event' implied in the coins and inscriptions. The charters constitute some sort of public sign of an intention or action and give it permanent record.[6] The coin legends may be a similar public sign, validating the quality of the material, giving the customer confidence in the product.

Other early epigraphical texts from the south-east and East Anglia add little, for most of them are of uncertain meaning; yet what they add hardly

---

5 D.M.Metcalf, 'Runes and Literacy: Pondering the Evidence of Anglo-Saxon Coins of the Eighth and Ninth Centuries' in Düwel, *Runeninschriften*, 435.

6 S.Kelly deals with this type of evidence in 'Anglo-Saxon Lay Society and the Written Word', *The Uses of Literacy in Early Mediaeval Europe*, ed. R.McKitterick (Cambridge 1990), 39–45.

supports this assessment of literacy as a public act. The Chessell Down scab-bard mount runes (assuming they are acceptable geographically) were not intended to be generally seen and may not have been cut much before burial. The runes of the Loveden Hill urn look purposeful enough, even though as yet uncomprehended; but for what readership would one inscribe a cremation pot? The second Chessell Down text, casually scratched on an imported pail amidst an engraved decoration, does not seem to have been immediately comprehensible or markedly visible. The Harford Farm brooch inscription was cut on the back of the piece, again not for public viewing. Its inscription, perhaps the only one of this group that can be interpreted with certainty, is banal enough. Yet it shows a metalsmith (even if not a very skilled one) able to command the script for vernacular and everyday use. Sad that we have not more early examples of this inscription type.

Remaining within this general area but moving to a rather later period, we have two runic finds whose significance is relevant here. Brandon disclosed a bone tool handle with, again, a vernacular inscription, this time riddling. This site suggests a high status community which also was acquainted with roman script in a learned context; witness the early ninth-century gold plaque (perhaps from a book cover or a cross terminal) with an incised Latin text from there or nearby.[7] There is no reason to think the workman who used the inscribed tool was literate also in roman; but then, there is no reason to think he was not. From Blythburgh, of unknown date, is a bone writing tablet which has important implications. It is in the British Museum. Three runes, part of a longer text, are cut in the raised surface that surrounds the writing area, 'u i þ ['. On the writing area itself, that cut out to hold the wax, are several sequences of runes, very faint and part overlapping one another. David Parsons interprets these as traces of runic writing that had been scratched into its lost wax coverings, possibly (in view of some of the letter sequences) using the Latin language. He suggests this shows runes employed, even in a learned society, for informal messages and notices, though this goes a little beyond the evidence.[8] Are there here the remnants of a continued use of runic script for everyday transitory purposes, most of the evidence lost simply because it *was* transitory?

There seem to be no Anglo-Saxon roman inscriptions surviving from this region (or from these regions) substantially older than the Brandon plate. From later Anglo-Saxon times there are a few from both East Anglia and south-eastern/southern England, and these coincide roughly in date with a few runic texts in the south. Thus, there is some, but not striking, correlation

---

7 Webster and Backhouse, *Making of England*, no.66 (a).
8 Parsons, 'Anglo-Saxon Runes in Continental Manuscripts', 208–10.

in the uses of the two writing systems at any rate from Middle Saxon times onwards. Epigraphical evidence for literacy in either script is weak, but this could be a chance of survival.

It is interesting then to compare the geographical distributions of the known runic and roman inscriptions. Numbers of sites preserve memorial, or at least formal, stones using each or both of the scripts: Alnmouth, Chester-le-Street, Falstone, Hackness, Hartlepool, Lancaster, Lindisfarne, Monkwearmouth, Ruthwell, Thornhill. In contrast, there are a few sites that evidence only runes on stones; but considerably more with only roman, as Aldborough, Billingham, Bishopstone, Breamore, Canterbury, Carlisle, Coldingham, Deerhurst, Dewsbury, Great Edstone, Haddenham, Hexham, Ipswich, Jarrow, Kirkdale, Lincoln, London, Manchester, Ripon, Stratfield Mortimer, Thornton-le-Moors, Wensley, Whitby, Whitchurch, Winchester, Yarm.[9] Of course, these lists must be regarded only as general guides, partly because of the small numbers of examples in each case, partly because dating of some stone fragments is very uncertain; partly also because, in the case of some sites, there may be evidence of Anglo-Saxon runic usage on material other than stones – London, Manchester, Whitby and perhaps York. Moreover there may be a couple of sites quite close together geographically, where the pair between them demonstrate the two scripts, though each may have only one – Carlisle is near Bewcastle, Dewsbury near Kirkheaton. Thus it would be foolhardy to use much of this evidence to suggest districts of exclusive use of the one or the other script. Yet there are a few striking points; points probably significant for any discussion of the relative importance of the two scripts. For instance, Winchester has quite a number of roman inscriptions, but not a single runic one (save its Scandinavian stone, which is irrelevant here). York has extensive later Anglo-Saxon roman texts, many of them formal, but only a couple of uncertain runic examples in minor use. Though the West Country and the south-west are not particularly rich in any sort of Anglo-Saxon inscription, yet these regions evidence some later roman texts but not a single epigraphical rune – Worcester is the nearest example. This at least suggests a limited literacy in runes at certain times and places of Anglo-Saxon England.

Parsons's suggestion that the later runes were essentially an informal script can perhaps be followed up by examining the non-stone inscriptions of Christian Anglo-Saxon England. How informal are they? In fact, not always. One could hardly regard the ambitiously inlaid runes of the Thames scramasax or the carefully cut ones of the Thames mount as informal; or those of

---

[9]   Details of these inscriptions are in Okasha, *Hand-List of Anglo-Saxon Non-Runic Inscriptions* and its supplements.

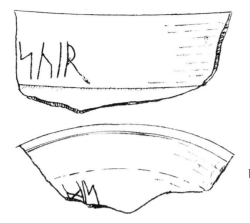

Fig.74. Runes on a sherd
from Worcester.

the quite elaborate Manchester gold ring; or those of the Auzon and Mortain caskets; or of the coffin of St Cuthbert; or even of the Thames silver mount. Others, however, could be; as the apparently personal request for God's help on the Whitby comb; or the elementary annotation, whatever its significance, on the Southampton/ *Hamwih* bone; or the name (?name element) on the Mote of Mark bone. Most casual of all is perhaps the scribble from Worcester, a few runes cut in two lines on a fragment of Roman pottery found in the infill of a pit and so, unfortunately, unstratified (fig.74).

Again, there are inscriptions that present runic and roman characters side by side, or indeed mix them in the same inscription. The Falstone memorial stone has essentially the same text twice, once in each script. In the main St Cuthbert's coffin uses roman for the names of figures represented on it, but perhaps surprisingly some of the most important are in runes. The Mortain casket seems to distinguish: roman script identifies the Latin names and titles of saints Michael and Gabriel, but the vernacular maker's signature is in runes. The Auzon casket also presents a mixture of scripts. For the vernacular texts on front, left and (apparently) right sides, and to identify the Magi runes are used. On the back, runes give the Latin text save for one sentence that begins in roman and concludes in runes. Here there is the bizarre circumstance that the roman bit is more or less classical in form but its final, runic, word 'a f i t a t o r e s' gives a pronunciation spelling (see above, p.176). Was a deliberate distinction of use signalled here? The lower stone of the Ruthwell cross has its vernacular poetical text in runes, its Latin descriptive texts in roman; but the upper stone seems to have had at least one Latin text in runes.

Further variants of the roman-runic mix are those inscriptions where an occasional rune invades an otherwise roman text, as in the Manchester and Llysfaen rings and the Alnmouth stone. Here a different distinction may be implied, one that affects the shaping of small-scale letters. A straight line

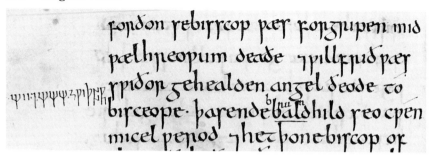

Fig.75. Runic marginalia in Corpus Christi College, Cambridge, MS 41.

may be easier to cut than a curve. A die-cutter, as for a coin, may not have suitable tools to carve elaborate shapes and so may prefer easy ones. As Metcalf has pointed out, X is simpler than G, and hence such a mongrel form as DAEgBERCT in a moneyer's name.

In some centres that had productive scriptoria, there are (as yet) no examples of epigraphical runes even in unofficial use. Winchester is an obvious case but there are others – Abingdon, Malmesbury, Christ Church, Canterbury, Bury St Edmunds, for example. There is a further complexity. In the south-west of England there is some small evidence of manuscript runes where there is none from epigraphy. Corpus Christi College, Cambridge, MS 41 which was in the Exeter library by the eleventh century, has a few runic marginalia (fig.75). The Exeter Book employs runes in riddling fashion here and there. Intriguing is the case of Worcester whence many Anglo-Saxon manuscripts survive. Some years ago I drew attention to a short passage in runes embedded in an otherwise roman text from that house, Copenhagen, Royal Library MS GkS 1595 4⁰.[10] This sequence of seventeen runic/rune-like graphs could be interpreted as part of a Latin instruction *in altar et inuoluit*, but only because the text is known from parallel sources. Otherwise, errors in forming ten of the runes make it hard to follow. There was here some sort of tradition of runes in manuscripts but it was not a strong or precise one. Why runes were used in this one passage in the middle of an otherwise orthodox roman text I do not know. This makes it all the more interesting that graffiti runes have since appeared, though again in small numbers, at Worcester.

There are also examples where manuscript runes were used to some degree as an alternative script, of runic marginalia and perhaps pen trials beside orthodox roman-script texts. I have discussed a few of these in chapter 12, and presumably there are more awaiting discovery or publication. What

---

[10] R.I.Page, 'Runes in Two Anglo-Saxon Manuscripts', *Nytt om Runer* 8 (1993), 15–19.

their implications for runic literacy are I do not know. Do they imply a two-script community, which chose to use runes only occasionally or for trivial or day-to-day purposes? Or are these the work of a few specialists, antiquaries who happened to know runes? What sort of 'literacy event' do they represent?

When the runic forms *þorn* and *wynn* were adopted into bookhand, their distinctive epigraphical forms were disguised. They were made to conform to the general appearance of written roman characters. Quite different is the scriptorium use of runic as a characteristic set of letter forms which stand apart in some way from common roman practice. Examples occur in riddling use, where the runes which reveal the answer project their distinctive forms on the written page. Yet this did not always work well. Take, for instance, the case of Exeter Book Riddle 24 (above, p.189). The six runes that reveal the solution *higoræ* were intended to be 'g', 'æ', 'r', 'o', 'h', 'i'. When the Exeter scribe came to the first of these, X, he failed to spot it was a rune, representing it by the roman character nearest in appearance, minuscule *x*. Only when he reached ᛈ whose form could not possibly be roman did he realise he should be forming runes. Yet he might have expected that script, for Riddle 19, a couple of pages earlier, had used it to reveal its answer. This implies knowledge of runes, but no expectation of finding them in a written text. For all that, the creators of some of these riddles must have assumed a reader's or a hearer's recognition, for their verse lines often require the rune-names to be spoken – they complete a verse line's alliteration.

I have alluded above (p.77) to the manuscript use of a rune form in place of its rune-name, but this too needs further consideration. As far as our evidence goes, only a few runes served this purpose. Of course, a number of the names were not commonly needed in Old English discourse. It seems that few wanted to write about *ur*, the wild ox. Whatever *peorð* meant, the term is known only from an enigmatic definition in the *Runic Poem*. The word *cen* survives only as a rune-name (though its meaning, 'torch', is commonplace enough). There was no occasion for 'u', 'p', 'c' to be used to represent the nouns that constitute their names. On the other hand, ᛞ for *dæg*, ᛗ for *man* are quite common and ᛟ for *œþel* is occasional. Why certain others never appear is a mystery. The Lindisfarne Gospels gloss is a text which uses ᛞ and ᛗ not infrequently (though even then in a minority of cases). Yet the Gospels also speak of *feoh* (*feh*), *gyfu* (*geafa*) and *ger* quite often and *nyda* (*ned*) occasionally, but never give them by their runes. The related Rushworth Gospels gloss does not have a like use of runes, though in his signature one of its scribes, Farman, puts the rune 'm' for the final syllable of his name. The first *Beowulf* scribe used 'œ' to represent *eþel* on three occasions, but wrote the word or element out in full on several others. Rune-graph used for rune-name is a subject that calls for more precise and perceptive examination; this preliminary look suggests it is quite rare and restricted, perhaps a learned conceit of a few scribes.[11]

A quite different use of runes in the scriptorium reflects their appearance rather than their signification. Some sumptuous manuscripts from Anglo-Saxon times have the opening words of major texts magnificently presented in display scripts. Here readability is not an important consideration, splendour is. For variety, scribes often imported into their display lettering graphs from non-roman sources. Greek is one such; but runes also invade these decorative pages. An excellent example is the Gospels of St Chad, an eighth-century codex from the West Country or Wales, in Lichfield Cathedral Library. Display letters adorn the openings of Matthew, Mark and Luke. In the Mark opening, *Initium euangelii lhu Xpi filii di sicut scrip | tum est*, the Christ title *Xpi*, has a variant form of the rune 'p', while the *p* of *scriptum* is also runic, this time the graph for 'm'. Luke begins *Quoniam quidem multi conati sunt ordin | are narrationem rerum* with the final letter of *quoniam* the rune 'm' and the first letter of *multi* either a doubled 'm' or a variant 'p'.[12] How far this decorative artist was aware of the signification of his graphs is a question, but at least he had some knowledge of runic graph forms. I do not think such runes quite present a 'literacy event', for these examples present no evidence that workers in this scriptorium would use runic script for discourse, to articulate the vernacular. Some similar pages in contemporary manuscripts employ occasional Greek characters in their display scripts, but this can hardly mean they would commonly write Old English or even Latin in Greek characters. All we can really say of such examples is that they demonstrate scriptorium awareness of runic graphs.

There are two further examples of the interaction between runic and roman. The scribe borrowed *þorn* and *wynn* in presenting Old English because he had no convenient roman equivalents. When a rune-master came to represent Latin, he was faced with a reverse problem. Latin had the symbol <x> which in general was not needed in spelling Old English words – *hs* did just as well for [ks]. In representing a formal Latin word containing *x* (as in the royal title *rex* on some coins), the rune-carver could make an adjustment. Beonna's moneyer Werferth seems to have tried out a spelling 'r e ɨ s'; but the unnamed moneyer who issued that king's interlace reverse pennies attempted

11 There is a useful opening discussion in R.D.Eaton, 'Anglo-Saxon Secrets: *Rūn* and the Runes of the Lindisfarne Gospels', *Amsterdamer Beiträge zur älteren Germanistik* 24 (1986), 11–27.
12 Illustrated in J.J.G.Alexander, *Insular Manuscripts 6th to the 9th Century* (London 1978), pls. 50, 78.

Fig.76. The Orpington sundial.

'r e x'. For this he needed a new final graph. He could not borrow roman X, for that would conflict with runic 'g'. Instead he took over the otiose graph ᛉ and used it for <x>, producing the.group ᚱᛖᛉ. A variation is on St Cuthbert's coffin. When it came to reproducing the Christ symbol XPI (originally three Greek characters XIII), the carver cut ᛉᛈᛁ.

The Orpington sundial illustrates a different overlap. The dial, formed from a block some 60 cm across, was originally circular, with two roman texts running in opposite directions round its circumference, each presumably occupying half (fig.76). When mediaeval builders reused it they cut away part, removing about one third of the circumference. two bits of texts remain: (a) clockwise,]ECÐÐANÐESECANCANHV+ (b) counterclockwise,]ELTELLAN7HEALDAN+. Presumably they refer to the sundial's function, *ðan ðe secan can hu*, 'for the one who can seek out how', and *tellan and healdan*, 'to count and to keep'. The dial itself seems to have been divided into sixteen equal sectors by incised rays, each second one crossed at its end for ease of counting. A third roman inscription filled eight of these sectors, only the beginning and end surviving: OR [. . .] VM, presumably a form of MLat *orologium*, 'sundial'. In three more of the sectors are runes or rune-like graphs, one to a sector, ᚠ, ᚩ and ᛗ, ?'æ', 'œ' and 'o'. These have no

Fig.77. Runic graffito at
Monte Sant' Angelo,
Italy. Taken from a
photograph.

obvious meaning, and it is likely they are markers to identify distinct sectors of the dial, those for the early and mid-morning which indicated important canonical hours. There is some similarity here to the manuscript use of runes as reference marks.

A final example of the runic/roman relationship is in some ways the most interesting, though its implications remain obscure. This is seen in graffiti cut by travellers, perhaps pilgrims. So far they have been spotted only in Italy, probably on the way to the Holy Land; but it is likely they will be found elsewhere – on the road to Santiago (Spain), for instance – if antiquaries keep their eyes open for them. A most important collection is in the pilgrimage church of St Michael, Monte Sant' Angelo, Gargano, on the Italian east coast. There is a great collection of personal names in various tongues cut into the façade of the gallery beneath the present church. Among them are Anglo-Saxon masculine names, some in roman, some in runes. Not surprisingly, they display varying skills in cutting. Some look more formal than others, with seriffed graphs. Clearly readable are 'w i g f u s', 'h e r r æ d' (fig.77), 'h e r e b e r e h c t' and 'l e o f w i n i'.[13] A second Italian site is the Cimitero di Commodilla, Rome, where several English names are carved, including one in runes, 'e a d b a l d'.[14] Runes may have been a common script for giving one's name in an informal setting – as so often in Scandinavian runic inscriptions. Or could there be a distinctive usage here, Englishmen writing their signatures in what they regarded as a characteristically English script? In discussing this subject we have to keep in mind the bias of evidence. There is a continuity of written texts (in the modern sense of the word 'written') from Anglo-Saxon times, through the years after the Norman Conquest to the fifteenth century, and then the tradition was taken over by the printers. There is no similar continuity to be traced in inscriptions. When we contemplate a mediaeval English text it is natural to assume it will be on parchment, and not on wood, bone, metal or stone. Traditionally, 'literacy' has meant 'book liter-

---

[13] Derolez and Schwab, 'Runic Inscriptions of Monte S.Angelo'; 'More Runes at Monte Sant' Angelo', *Nytt om Runer* 9 (1994), 18–19.

[14] R.Derolez, 'Anglo-Saxons in Rome', *Nytt om Runer* 2 (1987), 14–15.

acy'. If we are to review the question, we must put more stress on other forms of literacy. But we then face the problem of inadequacy of material, of the statistical poverty of our samples. To go further than I have done here requires a book rather than a chapter. Like Ibsen I have contented myself with asking questions leaving others to find the answers.

15

The Study of Runes

Anglo-Saxon runes did not survive the Norman Conquest. By the twelfth century, it seems, only antiquaries knew the script. Thereafter for some centuries nobody knew it. Scribes continued to write the graphs *wynn* and *thorn* for they had become part of bookhand, but I do not suppose any of the later scribes realised the two letters were runic. Symbols that coincide with runic graphs – ↑ and ᛁ for instance – occur among the marks by which mediaeval masons identified the stones they had carved, but whether this is chance or whether the masons' marks descend from runes there is no means of knowing. Words related to OE *run* appear in Middle English – a noun *run(e)* which often has connotations of writing, secrecy and counsel, and compounds like *runstauen* (OE *runstafas*) and *leodrunen* (OE *leodrunan*), for instance. But there is no reason to think there was much awareness of runes as a distinct alphabet in the period between the end of Anglo-Saxon times and the sixteenth century, when people again became aware of the script.

From about 1600 onwards there has always been someone in England who knew about runes, tenuous though the acquaintance may have been in some decades. Since the eighteenth century the knowledge has been quite widespread, even in some degree or other fashionable. Carvers used the script as an attractive archaism – in the 1720s the distinguished sculptor J.M.Rysbrack created a group of statues for the park at Knowle each representing a day of the week. Appropriate gods were given their names in runes, 't i w', 'w o d n', 'þ u n r', 'f r i g' for *Tiw, Woden, Thunor, Frig*. 'Runic' became a popular word round about 1800, and the script was occasionally printed. The nineteenth century was a great age for finding, reading, interpreting and copying runic inscriptions, and journals of the newly founded local archaeological societies abound in references to them. In the early twentieth century the editors of the authoritative *Cambridge History of English Literature* found it proper to include in volume 1 a chapter on 'Runes and Manuscripts', while the *Cambridge Bibliography of English Literature* had a section on runic epigraphy but none on the much more numerous non-runic inscriptions of

Anglo-Saxon England. Recent years have seen a marked increase in the number of runic forgeries or perhaps I should say, to avoid any suggestion of deceit, runic creations. This is in part due to the cult of unreason that now links the script to supernatural practice or prophecy; part the effect of the whimsical travesties of runes that appear in J.R.R.Tolkien's *Lord of the Rings* and its multitude of successors and imitators; part the copying of earlier types of jewellery and ornament that is characteristic of commercial ventures like the very successful *Past Times*; and part, I suppose, because of the startling number of new finds that metal detectors have come upon.

Despite all this, in Great Britain today the study of runes remains a minority interest. Conditions are far different from those in Scandinavia; in Sweden and Denmark where runic inscriptions are found with a frequency that almost outstrips publication; or in Norway where urban excavation has revealed multitudes of runic texts which throw new light on social and commercial history; or even in Iceland where the old script survived so late that it is hard to distinguish between the last traditional runes and the earliest antiquarian revivals; perhaps also in America where the discovery – and many sceptics would add the manufacture – of rune-stones confirming the Viking discovery and exploration of the land has become something of a national industry. Compared with the immense and long-enduring Scandinavian material the English runic corpus remains tiny, almost insignificant. Scandinavian rune-stones supply data for the history of law, inheritance and religious change, data for gender studies and other fashionable topics, in a way the English cannot. Compared with the splendid stories that Americans have pieced together from their dubious petroglyphs the content of English inscriptions is usually pedestrian where it can be ascertained, baffling where it cannot. Why then should even a minority ponder English runes?

They are, of course, part of English cultural history, and their study can be justified as a historical study. They reveal, intentionally or not, some aspects of life in Anglo-Saxon England, and they suggest questions to be put to the historian and the archaeologist, questions that are easier to frame than to answer. Why are there no epigraphical runes in Wessex? Is this runeless region of England in any way connected with runeless areas of the Continent, that, say, between Jutland and Frisian, Frankish or Alemannic territories? What is the wider significance of the few, very early, inscriptions in England whose runes may suggest North Germanic inspiration; of the geographical and temporal distributions of single-barred **h**, for instance? Again, why did the church in the north of England foster the script, while that of the south seems to have overwhelmed it? What deductions can be made from Anglo-Saxon runic monuments and graffiti found outside England? What can we conclude from runic marginalia found in some manuscripts? Such questions are invitations to the historian, archaeologist or codicologist to examine his own source material in the search for an answer.

Alternatively we can expound runic facts to the historian or archaeologist in the hope of exciting him to more general questions. Runic name-stones of similar design occur at Lindisfarne, Monkwearmouth and Hartlepool; in York there are comparable stones with roman letters only. Lindisfarne and Monkwearmouth (one example from the latter) use runes in similar ways, on stones that also carry roman texts though the two scripts are kept distinct. From Hartlepool there are name-stones with runes and name-stones with roman characters, but as yet no certain examples with both. There looks to be a progression from, most southerly, York using roman script only, to, most northerly, runic and roman on the same monument. The archaeologist is invited to consider what this might imply about cultural relationships between the great religious houses of the north-east coast.

Again, in the desolate region in the neighbourhood of the Solway Firth are two major and costly runic monuments, the Bewcastle and Ruthwell crosses, whose purposes we do not know. Nothing else in the area suggests a very wealthy or influential Anglo-Saxon community, or as for that a literate one. We would like to know how these two high crosses fit into the general cultural life of the area, and as a consequence whether we may think of them as local products or the work (?with the language) of people imported from afar. Does the newly-discovered provenance of the Linstock Castle runic ring, not far from Bewcastle, help here? Again, Leeds and its neighbouring townships, Collingham, Bingley, Kirkheaton and Thornhill, have a tight group of rune-stones all connected with churches. It would be interesting to know if there is anything in the ecclesiastical history of the region to account for the concentration.

Speculations and questions of this sort are fascinating and could be fruitful if scholars could be got to address them. But it is perhaps in the linguistic field that the great importance of the Anglo-Saxon runic inscriptions lies. Not only do they include the earliest specimens we have of the English tongue; they also give the first indications of English literacy. In manuscript there is nothing so early by two or three centuries as the Caistor-by-Norwich or Loveden Hill texts. The linguistic value of these legends is certainly impaired by the fact that we have only the faintest idea of what they mean, yet they are not by that token linguistically valueless. This makes it all the more surprising that modern historical linguists appear ignorant of or nonchalant about this primary evidence. The Scandinavian affinities of these and of the Spong Hill and Welbeck Hill inscriptions remind us that a rigid division into North and West Germanic language groups is outdated and unrealistic, and that we must reckon on the likelihood of some northern influence upon the forms of Old English.

The early texts can suggest something of the chronology of the prehistoric sound changes. Caistor-by-Norwich apparently preserves early *h* between vowels where it was later to be lost, and it may also show Gmc *ai* remaining, not yet monophthongised to *a* – but of course this assumes that Caistor is an English, not a Norse inscription. The sixth-century **skanomodu** solidus – though again its legend may not be Old English – seems to show that *i*-mutation was not so advanced as to prevent the rune *oeþil* representing *o* unaffected by the sound change. There is then room for dispute as to whether such a conclusion clashes with what may be drawn from the roughly contemporary Chessell Down scabbard mount, since that appears to distinguish between *o* susceptible and *o* not susceptible to *i*-mutation.

Even now we can derive a small amount of linguistic material from early and baffling runic texts, and we can hope for more in the future, if some intuitive genius can be persuaded to work upon them so as to produce explanations that will satisfy both the facts of the case and the proper scepticism of the critics. For the time being, however, it is the later inscriptions, where we know the meaning with some precision, that are of most importance to the study of the history of English, and again one can only express surprise that historical linguists have tended to ignore them. After all, some of these texts are from areas whence we know no other Old English texts, and they may contain hints about the dialectal variants to be expected there – hints that may be taken into account by place-name scholars working on those regions. There is a little material from East Anglia, much of it incomprehensible save for the coin names. North Lincolnshire has the tiny Crowle fragment of wording. The north-west coastal area has the great texts of Ruthwell and the lesser ones of Mote of Mark, Whithorn, Bewcastle, Lancaster, Great Urswick, while further south, from the Wirral, is Overchurch. Late runic inscriptions from the north-west reveal the strength and pertinacity of Scandinavian subdialects there.

Inscriptions from the later period supply some additions to Anglo-Saxon vocabulary: *fergenberig, gasric, grorn* on the Auzon casket; *cismel* on the Mortain casket; *licbæcun* from the Crowle cross; the preposition *æfte* on Thornhill II. They give a specific contextual meaning for *becun* ('monument') which occurs so often that it must have been a current one, though it appears rarely outside these and certain non-runic inscriptions. They supply personal names not elsewhere recorded in independent usage, or variants upon known personal names: *Pada Epa/Æpa, Æþiliræd, Wigræd, Beonna/Benna Ægili, Aþili* and so on.

They add to our knowledge of Old English syntax in demonstrating new or unusual case usages. There seems to be a locative in *on bergi, in Romæcæstri, on rodi.* An instrumental may follow the preposition *æfter* in Collingham's 'æ f t [.] s w i þ i'. A dative after the verb *gebiddan* is several times recorded in such requests as *gebiddaþ þær saule* though there is also the more common construction in *gibidæþ foræ Cynibalþ.*

Probably it is in their implications about the pronunciation of Old English at various dates and places that the main interest in runic inscriptions lies. To the elementary student of Old English – which usually means late West Saxon – the runic spellings will often look strange and barbarous, the inflexional endings curious. He may deplore the fact that the rune-masters show scant respect for some of the sound-changes he has learned so assiduously. Thus the runic inscriptions are important in drawing attention to the vast mass of the language that once existed, but is not recorded because it stands outside the main manuscript traditions of Anglo-Saxon England.

Sometimes the inscriptions show the language as it was before the shift of the unstressed vowels. The endings *-æ* and *-e* have not fallen together in the indefinitive vowel which manuscripts represent as *-e*. Unstressed *u* has not been lowered so that it could be represented by *a*. Great Urswick retains such spellings as 's e t æ' (WS *sette*), 's a u l æ' (WS *saule/sawle*), and these endings contrast with that of its 't u n w i n i', (WS *-wine*). There is a methodological trap here, for we cannot assume without further thought that the rune-masters' contrast between 'æ' and 'i' in representing lightly stressed vowels is the same as that which manuscript writers intend when they distinguish between *-æ* and *-i*. Probably it is, for the rune-masters' distinction fits etymological propriety and phonological development in the same way as does that of the scribes, but I stress the point because we should keep in mind, when dealing with runic texts, that we may face a rather different system of representing sounds from what we are used to. We should never equate runic and manuscript spellings unthinkingly. Great Urswick is a stone which preserves the older unstressed vowels consistently, save in the rather special case of 'æ f t e r'. The Auzon casket is similar in that it too retains older forms and records the contrast between early unstressed *i* and *æ*. While in general recording the older types of ending the Ruthwell cross occasionally shows the newer forms, as 'w a l d *e*' and probably 'f [*o r e*]' and 'æ t [ḡ] a d [*r e*]'. In this it compares with a few transitional scribal texts which show the new indefinitive vowel endings gradually replacing the older and distinctive ones.

Our inscriptions abound in local dialectal features that can be paralleled in the few manuscript sources available. The Auzon casket, for instance, has several Anglian and possibly Northumbrian spellings: smoothing of the fracture diphthong in 'f e g t a þ' and '*u n n e g*'; retraction of PrOE *æ* to *a* in the neighbourhood of a labial (instead of fracture before *r* + consonant) in 'w a r þ'; absence of front diphthongisation and a distinctive quality of the stem vowel in 'c æ s t r i'; loss of inflexional -*n* in 's e f a'. The Mortain casket has the stem vowel *a* in 'g e w a r a h t æ' which looks a West Mercian characteristic.

The way we can relate these distinctive forms to features of local dialect that are recorded in manuscripts gives us some confidence in the validity of curious spellings for which we have no parallels. Great Urswick's 'b æ u r n æ' has a very odd representation of the fracture diphthong usually given as *eo* (if the word is *beorn*) or *ea* (if it is *bearn*). Crowle's 'l i c b æ c u n' may show that locally the smoothing of the diphthong derived from Gmc *au* produced an open vowel rather than the more closed one usually suggested (cf. Thornhill III 'b e k u n'). Again, manuscript texts from several dialect regions record a glide vowel developing between liquid and consonant. Such glides are particularly common in inscriptions – Mortain's 'g e w a r a h t æ', Kirkheaton's 'w o r o h t æ', Lancaster's 'c u þ b e r e [.]', Whitby comb's 'a l u w a l u d o' and 'h e l i p æ', Great Urswick's 't o r o i t r e d æ', Monte Sant'Angelo's 'h e r e b e r e h c t' – and this may be evidence that in the folk tongue Old English had even more glides of this sort than the manuscript evidence implies.

This brief account is intended, not to exhaust the linguistic material of the English runes, but to show the beginner something of its richness. I have given texts here in transliterated form, but it is important to keep in mind that a transliteration embodies an interpretation. Strictly, I should have presented all examples in their runic characters, but that would have been difficult in practice and would have made them less accessible to readers. Each case needs more careful examination and discussion than I give it in this book, and the known corpus of Anglo-Saxon runic inscriptions has other features that merit consideration. This corpus increases annually. We can confidently expect to find new runes in coming years, which will both present fresh examples and illuminate those already known. It is some years since René Derolez revealed the great importance of English manuscript runes. Elisabeth Okasha's *Hand-list of Anglo-Saxon Non-runic Inscriptions* with its supplements has given scholars the chance to compare the runic and non-runic epigraphy of the Anglo-Saxons. The Catholic University of Eichstätt, Germany, has announced its plan for a databank of Old English and Old Frisian runic materials. The Oslo-based annual *Nytt om Runer* keeps the enthusiast informed about the latest discoveries and publications. Thus the great bulk of relevant English material is rapidly becoming available to students.

These developments are perhaps both a symptom of and a cause for the increase of younger scholars entering the field, prepared to spend time examining these primitive English texts in preference to writing yet more articles on *The Wanderer, The Seafarer* and *The Battle of Maldon*; or tentatively tracing yet another source for an eleventh-century homily. Who knows what may be found by investigators trained in the modern, supersubtle, methods of linguistics, scholars who have command of computerised access to materials, scientists who can seize the opportunity of microscopic examination of rune-cutting techniques? They are bound – are they not? – to derive more from the English runic inscriptions than the old-fashioned philologists like myself who have worked upon them so far – if of course they have the perceptivity to spot the weaknesses as well as the strengths of their new approaches. For inevitably these promising developments have weaknesses. They may encourage the student to look at inscriptions in runes in isolation from those in other writing systems. Yet some houses were clearly bi-alphabetical. They may tempt the student to examine inscriptions out of context, to take them as collections of word forms rather than efforts to represent language in a variety of materials and circumstances, some of them unfavourable to the attempt. Throughout this book I have stressed the need to observe more than a set of texts, the importance of seeing inscriptions as parts of artefacts, conditioned by space, material, tools, by the time taken and the care employed. In other words, to ensure that runologists do not confine themselves to the study or library, but go outside to meet archaeologists, numismatists, art historians, craftsmen, indeed all others whose work might affect our appreciation of the work of early rune-masters.

Bibliography

The standard bibliography of English runic inscriptions up to 1961 is H.Marquardt, *Bibliographie der Runeninschriften nach Fundorten* 1, Abhandl. d. Akademie d. Wissenschaften in Göttingen, phil.-hist. Klasse, 3. Folge 48 (1961). This is perhaps too elaborate for the beginner who needs guidance through the huge list of items, of varying merit, entered there. A much more modest bibliography, directed towards the English runes, appears in vol. 1 of the *Cambridge Bibliography of English Literature*, 2.ed. (Cambridge 1974), 220–6. There is a continuous bibliography of runic publications (most of them non-English but including also the work on Anglo-Saxon runes) in the Norwegian annual *Nytt om Runer* (1986–), which also includes brief notes on new finds. The following bibliography, a short and select one, lists for the beginner the main books and papers needed to start work on English runes. If there are too many of my own publications in it, this is because, like most runologists, I suspect that only my own opinions and observations are valid.

General Works on Runes and Appropriate Collections of Runic Inscriptions

G.Stephens, *The Old-Northern Runic Monuments of Scandinavia and England*, 4 vols. (London, Copenhagen and Lund 1866–1901).
———— *Handbook of the Old-Northern Runic Monuments of Scandinavia and England* (London and Copenhagen 1884). Reprinted in reduced size (Felinfach 1993).
W.Viëtor, *Die northumbrische Runensteine* (Marburg 1895).
H.Arntz and H.Zeiss, *Die einheimischen Runendenkmäler des Festlandes* (Leipzig 1939).
R.I.Page, 'The Inscriptions' in D.M.Wilson, *Anglo-Saxon Ornamental Metalwork 700–1100 in the British Museum* (London 1964), 67–90.
L.Musset, *Introduction à la runologie* (Paris 1965).
W.Krause and H.Jankuhn, *Die Runeninschriften im älteren Futhark*, 2 vols. (Göttingen 1966).
E.Okasha, *Hand-List of Anglo-Saxon Non-Runic Inscriptions* (Cambridge 1971) with supplements in *Anglo-Saxon England* 11 (1983), 83–118 and 21 (1992), 37–85.
K.Düwel, *Runenkunde*, 2.ed. (Stuttgart 1983).

———— ed. *Runische Schriftkultur in kontinental-skandinavischer und -angelsächsischer Wechselbeziehung.* Ergänzungsbände zum Reallexikon der germanischen Altertumskunde 10 (Berlin and New York 1994).

———— ed. *Runeninschriften als Quellen interdisziplinärer Forschung.* Ergänzungsbände zum Reallexikon der germanischen Altertumskunde 15 (Berlin and New York 1998).

E.Moltke, *Runes and their Origin. Denmark and Elsewhere*, trans. P.G.Foote (Copenhagen 1985).

R.I.Page, 'New Runic Finds in England', *Runor och runinskrifter.* Kungl.Vitterhets Historie och Antikvitets Akademien, Konferenser 15 (Stockholm 1987), 185–97.

R.W.V.Elliott, *Runes, an Introduction*, 2.ed. (Manchester 1989).

J.Hines, 'The Runic Inscriptions of Early Anglo-Saxon England', in *Britain 400–600: Language and History*, edd. A.Bammesberger and A.Wollmann. Anglistische Forschungen 205 (Heidelberg 1990), 437–55.

Old English Runes and their Continental Background, ed. A.Bammesberger. Anglistische Forschungen 217 (Heidelberg 1991).

R.I.Page, *Runes and Runic Inscriptions. Collected Essays on Anglo-Saxon and Viking Runes* (Woodbridge 1995): includes many of the individual essays referred to in this book, often with postscripts expanding or modifying my original presentations.

Frisian Runes and Neighbouring Traditions, edd. T.Looijenga and A.Quak. Amsterdamer Beiträge zur älteren Germanistik 45 (1996).

Works on Various Aspects of English Runes

J.M.Kemble, 'On Anglo-Saxon Runes', *Archaeologia* 28 (1840), 327–72.

B.Dickins, 'A System of Transliteration for Old English Runic Inscriptions', *Leeds Studies in English* 1 (1932), 15–19.

K.Sisam, 'Cynewulf and his Poetry', *Proc. British Acad.* 18 (1932), 303–31. Reprinted in his *Studies in the History of Old English Literature* (Oxford 1953).

J.Blomfield, 'Runes and the Gothic Alphabet', *Saga-Book of the Viking Soc.* 12 (1937–45), 177–94, 209–31.

R.J.Menner, *The Poetical Dialogues of Solomon and Saturn* (New York 1941).

J.A.W.Bennett, 'The Beginnings of Runic Studies in England', *Saga-Book of the Viking Soc.* 13 (1946–53), 269–83.

R.W.V.Elliott, 'Cynewulf's Runes in *Christ II* and *Elene*', *English Studies* 34 (1953), 49–57.

———— 'Cynewulf's Runes in *Juliana* and *Fates of the Apostles*', *English Studies* 34 (1953), 193–204.

———— 'The Runes in *The Husband's Message*', *Jnl of Engl. and Germanic Phil.* 54 (1955), 1–8.

———— 'Runes, Yews, and Magic', *Speculum* 32 (1957), 250–61.

———— 'Coming Back to Cynewulf' in Bammesberger, *Old English Runes*, 231–47.

R.Derolez, *Runica Manuscripta: the English Tradition*. Rijksuniversiteit te Gent, Werken Uitgegeven door de Faculteit van de Wijsbegeerte en Letteren 118 (Brugge 1954), addendum in *English Studies supplement* 45 (1964), 116–20.

———— 'Runic Literacy among the Anglo-Saxons' in Bammesberger, *Britain 400–600*, 397–436.

R.I.Page, 'On the Transliteration of English Runes', *Medieval Archaeology* 28 (1984), 22–45.

———— 'Anglo-Saxon Runic Studies: the Way Ahead?' in Bammesberger, *Old English Runes*, 15–39.

———— 'Runic Writing, Roman Script and the Scriptorium', *Runor och ABC*, ed. S.Nyström (Stockholm 1997), 119–40.

M.Halsall, *The Old English* Rune Poem. McMaster Old English Studies and Texts 2 (Toronto 1981).

Scandinavian Runes in England

M.Olsen, 'Runic Inscriptions in Great Britain, Ireland and the Isle of Man', *Viking Antiquities in Great Britain and Ireland* 6, ed. H.Shetelig (Oslo 1954), 153–233.

A.Liestøl, 'Runer frå Bryggen', *Viking 27* (1963), 5–53.

———— 'Correspondence in Runes', *Mediaeval Scandinavia* 1 (1968), 17–27.

———— 'The Literate Vikings', *Proc. Sixth Viking Conference* (Uppsala 1971), 69–78.

R.I.Page, 'How Long did the Scandinavian Language Survive in England? The Epigraphical Evidence', *England before the Conquest*, ed. P.Clemoes and K.Hughes (Cambridge 1971), 165–81.

———— 'The Manx Rune-stones', *The Viking Age in the Isle of Man*, edd. C.Fell *et al.* (London 1983), 133–46.

S.B.F.Jansson, *Runes in Sweden* (Stockholm 1987).

K.Holman, *Scandinavian Runic Inscriptions in the British Isles: their Historical Context*. Senter for middelalderstudier, Skrifter 4 (Trondheim 1996).

Individual English Runic Inscriptions

Readers will note the controversy there is likely to be over the interpretation of runic inscriptions. All I give here is a short list showing where inscriptions have been adequately – though not necessarily definitively – published. Naturally I do not always agree with the interpretations offered. My lists omit a few examples where the validity or identity of the graphs is in doubt. In some cases the text of this book will give further details.

1. *Runic coins*

Many runic coins will be found illustrated in the Anglo-Saxon volumes of the British Academy's *Sylloge of Coins of the British Isles* (1958–), while the Anglo-Saxon volumes of *A Catalogue of English Coins in the British Museum*, though outdated in many ways, remain useful. More up-to-date are the relevant sections of P.Grierson and M.Blackburn, *Medieval European Coinage with a Catalogue of the Coins in the Fitzwilliam Museum, Cambridge*, vol.1 (Cambridge 1986). A valuable study aimed specifically at the English material is M.Blackburn, 'A Survey of Anglo-Frisian and Frisian Coins with Runic Inscriptions' in Bammesberger *Old English Runes*, 137–89. A rather different range of material is discussed in D.M.Metcalf, *Thrymsas and Sceattas in the Ashmolean Museum Oxford*, 3 vols. (= Royal Numismatic Society Special Publications 27 A–C (London/Oxford 1993–4). Modern treatments of individual issues are:

C.H.V.Sutherland, *Anglo-Saxon Gold Coinage in the Light of the Crondall Hoard* (Oxford 1948).

C.S.S.Lyon, 'A Reappraisal of the Sceatta and Styca Coinage of Northumbria', *British Numismatic Jnl* 28 (1957), 227–43.

S.E.Rigold, 'The Two Primary Series of Sceattas', *British Numismatic Jnl* 30 (1960–1), 6–53, with addenda and corrigenda, 35 (1966), 1–6.

———— 'The Principal Series of English Sceattas', *British Numismatic Jnl* 47 (1977), 21–30.

C.E.Blunt, 'The Coinage of Offa', *Anglo-Saxon Coins*, ed. R.H.M.Dolley (London 1961), 39–62.

———— C.S.S.Lyon and B.H.I.H.Stewart, 'The Coinage of Southern England, 796–840', *British Numismatic Jnl* 32 (1964), 1–74.

———— and G.van der Meer, 'A New Type for Offa', *British Numismatic Jnl* 38 (1969), 182–3.

R.I.Page, 'Ralph Thoresby's Runic Coins', *British Numismatic Jnl* 34 (1965), 28–31.

H.E.Pagan, 'Northumbrian Numismatic Chronology in the Ninth Century', *British Numismatic Jnl* 38 (1969), 1–15.

M.M.Archibald, 'The Coinage of Beonna in the Light of the Middle Harling Hoard', *British Numismatic Jnl* 55 (1985), 10–54.

———— and V.Fenwick, 'A Sceat of Ethelbert I of East Anglia and Recent Finds of Coins of Beonna', *British Numismatic Jnl* 65 (1995), 1–19.

2. *Rune-stones*

Most of these will be published in the British Academy's *Corpus of Anglo-Saxon Stone Sculpture* (Oxford 1984– = CASS).

Alnmouth: *CASS* i, 161–2.
Bakewell: Stephens, *Old-Northern Runic Monuments* 1, 373–4.
Bewcastle: R.I.Page, 'The Bewcastle Cross', *Nottingham Med. Stud.* 4 (1960), 36–57; *CASS* 2, 61–72.
Bridekirk font: M.D.Forbes and B.Dickins, 'The Inscriptions of the Ruthwell and Bewcastle Crosses and the Bridekirk Font', *Burlington Mag.* 25 (1914), 24–9.
Chester-le-Street: *CASS* 1, 53–4.
Collingham: G.Baldwin Brown, *The Arts in Early England* (1903–37), 6 part 2, 153–7.
Crowle: Stephens, *Old-Northern Runic Monuments* 3, 185–8.
Dover: *CASS* 4, 143.
Falstone: Okasha, *Hand-list of Anglo-Saxon Inscriptions*, 71–2; *CASS* 1, 172–3.
Great Urswick: W.G.Collingwood, 'A Rune-inscribed Anglian Cross-shaft at Urswick Church', *Trans. Cumberland and Westmorland Antiq. and Archaeol. Soc.* NS 11 (1911), 462–8; *CASS* 2, 148–50.
Hackness: Derolez, *Runica Manuscripta*, 140–2; *CASS* 3, 135–41.
Hartlepool: F.S.Scott, 'The Hildithryth Stones and the Other Hartlepool Name-stones', *Archaeologia Aeliana* 4 ser. 34 (1956), 196–212; *CASS* 1, 98–9.
Kirkheaton: Stephens, *Old-Northern Runic Monuments* 4, 51–2.
Lancaster: Stephens, *Old-Northern Runic Monuments* 1, 375–7.
Leeds: D.H.Haigh, 'On the Fragments of Crosses Discovered at Leeds in 1838', *Proc. Geological and Polytechnic Soc. W.R. Yorks.* 3 (1849–59), 512–13.
Leek: R.W.V.Elliott, 'A Runic Fragment at Leek', *Medieval Archaeology* 8 (1964), 213–14.
Lindisfarne: C.R.Peers, 'The Inscribed and Sculptured Stones of Lindisfarne', *Archaeologia* 74 (1923–4), 255–70; *CASS* 1, 202–4.
Maughold: P.M.C.Kermode, *Manx Crosses* (London 1907), 110–11, 217–18.
Monkwearmouth: *CASS* 1, 123–4.
Orpington: R.I.Page in *Archaeologia Cantiana* 82 (1967), 289–91; Okasha, *Hand-List of Inscriptions*, 105; *CASS* 4, 147–9.
Overchurch: R.W.V.Elliott, 'Two Neglected English Runic Inscriptions', *Mélanges de Linguistique et de Philologie, Fernand Mossé* (Paris 1959), 144–7.
Ruthwell: *The Ruthwell Cross*, ed. B.Cassidy (Princeton 1992).
St Ninian's Cave: C.A.R.Radford and G.Donaldson, *Whithorn and Kirkmadrine Wigtownshire* (Edinburgh 1957), 44–5.

Sandwich/Richborough: D.Parsons, 'Sandwich: the Oldest Scandinavian Rune-stone in England?', *Developments around the Baltic and the North Sea in the Viking Age*, ed. B.Ambrosiani and H.Clarke (Stockholm 1994), 310–20; *CASS* 4, 168–70.

Thornhill: Elliott, *Runes, an Introduction*, 2.ed., 113–15.

Whithorn: Radford and Donaldson, *Whithorn and Kirkmadrine*. 40–1.

3. *Other Epigraphical Runes*

Ash/Gilton pommel: S.C.Hawkes and R.I.Page, 'Swords and Runes in South-east England', *Antiquaries Jnl* 47 (1967), 3–4; V.I.Evison, 'The Dover Ring-sword and other Sword-rings and Beads'. *Archaeologia* 101 (1967), 97–102.

Auzon (Franks) casket: A.S.Napier, 'The Franks Casket', *An English Miscellany presented to Dr Furnivall . . .* (Oxford 1901), 362–81; Elliott, *Runes, an Introduction*, 2.ed., 123–39.

Blythburgh writing tablet: D.Parsons, 'Anglo-Saxon Runes in Continental Manuscripts', *Runische Schriftkultur in kontinental-skandinavischer und -angelsächsischer Wechselbeziehung*, ed. K.Düwel (Berlin 1994), 209–11.

Bramham Moor/Harewood/Sherburn-in-Elmet amulet ring, and the related Kingmoor and Linstock Castle rings: D.M.Wilson, 'A Group of Anglo-Saxon Amulet Rings', *The Anglo-Saxons*, ed. P.Clemoes (Cambridge 1959), 159–70; Page in *Anglo-Saxon Ornamental Metalwork*, 73–5; R.I.Page, 'A Rune Provenanced?', *Anglo-Saxon England* 27 (1998), 291–4.

Brandon handle, pin and tweezers: D.Parsons, 'New Runic Finds from Brandon, Suffolk', *Nytt om Runer* 6 (1991), 8–11.

Brunswick casket: U.Schwab, *Die Sternrune im Wessobrunner Gebet* (Amsterdam 1973), 73–5; R.Marth and R.I.Page, 'Gandersheim, Kästchen von', *Reallexikon der germanischen Altertumskunde* 10 (1997), 422–6.

Caistor-by-Norwich astragalus: R.I.Page, 'The Runic Inscription from N59' in J.N.L.Myres and B.Green, *The Anglo-Saxon Cemeteries of Caistor-by-Norwich and Markshall, Norfolk* (London 1973), 114–17.

Chessell Down scabbard plate: Hawkes and Page, 'Swords and Runes in South-east England', 4–6, 11–18.

Chessell Down pail: C.J.Arnold, *The Anglo-Saxon Cemeteries of the Isle of Wight* (London 1982), 26–8, 46–7; Page, 'New Runic Finds', 193–4.

Coquet Island ring: Stephens, *Old-Northern Runic Monuments* 1, 480–1.

Cramond ring: Stephens, *Old-Northern Runic Monuments* 3, 215–16.

Derby(shire) bone plate: J.M.Bately and V.I.Evison, 'The Derby Bone Piece', *Medieval Archaeology* 5 (1961), 301–5.

Dover brooch: V.I.Evison, 'The Dover Rune Brooch', *Antiquaries Jnl* 44 (1964), 242–5.

Harford Farm brooch: J.Hines, 'A New Runic Find from Norfolk', *Nytt om Runer* 6 (1991), 6–7.

Heacham tweezers: Page, 'New Runic Finds', 193.

Heslerton brooch: Page, 'New Runic Finds', 193; D.Powlesland, 'The Heslerton Anglo Saxon Settlement' (North Yorkshire County Planning Department 1987), unpaginated.

Keswick disc: J.Hines, 'An Inscribed Disc from the River Yare near Norwich', *Nytt om Runer* 12 (1997), 13–15.

Lindisfarne (St Cuthbert's) coffin: J.M.Cronyn and C.V.Horie, *St. Cuthbert's Coffin: the History, Technology and Conservation* (Durham 1985); R.I.Page, 'Roman and Runic on St Cuthbert's Coffin' in *St Cuthbert, His Cult and His Community*, edd. G.Bonner *et al.* (Woodbridge 1989), 257–65.

Llysfaen ring: Okasha, *Hand-List of Inscriptions*, 98–9.

London (Royal Opera House) bone: R.I.Page, 'Runes at the Royal Opera House, London', *Nytt om Runer* 12 (1997), 12–13.

London (Thames Exchange) ring: K.Gosling, 'Runic Finds from London', *Nytt om Runer* 4 (1989), 12–13.

Loveden Hill runic urn: B.Odenstedt, 'The Loveden Hill Runic Inscription', *Ortnamnssällskapets i Uppsala Årsskrift* (1980), 24–37; Elliott, *Runes, an Introduction*, 2.ed., 50–2.

Manchester ring: Page in *Anglo-Saxon Ornamental Metalwork*, 75–7; B.N.J.Edwards, 'An Anglo-Saxon Ring Provenance Narrowed', *Antiquaries Jnl* 63 (1983), 132–4.

Monte Sant' Angelo graffiti: R.Derolez and U.Schwab, 'The Runic Inscriptions of Monte S. Angelo (Gargano)', *Academiae Analecta* 45, 1 (1983), 95–130; M.G.Arcamone, 'Una nuova iscrizione runica da Monte Sant' Angelo', *Vetera Christianorum* 29 (1992), 405–10; U.Schwab and R.Derolez, 'More Runes at Monte Sant' Angelo', *Nytt om Runer* 9 (1994), 18–19.

Mortain casket: M.Cahen and M.Olsen, *L'inscription runique du coffret de Mortain* (Paris 1930).

Mote of Mark bone: L.Laing, 'The Mote of Mark and the Origins of Celtic Interlace', *Antiquity* 49 (1975) at p.101 and pl.X.

Rome graffito: R.Derolez, 'Anglo-Saxons in Rome', *Nytt om Runer* 2 (1987), 14–15.

Sarre pommel: Hawkes and Page, 'Swords and Runes in South-east England', 6–7.

Selsey fragments: R.I.Page, 'Anglo-Saxon Runic Studies: the Way Ahead?' in Bammesberger, *Old English Runes*, 37.

skanomodu solidus: R.I.Page, 'The Runic Solidus of Schweindorf, Ostfriesland, and Related Runic Solidi', *Medieval Archaeology* 12 (1968), 12–25.

Southampton/*Hamwih* bone: R.I.Page in *Proc. Hampshire Field Club* 26

(1969), 86–8; but cf. D.Hofmann, 'Eine friesische Runeninschrift in England', *Us Wurk 25* (1976), 73–6.

Southampton plaque: Page, 'New Runic Finds', 193.

Spong Hill urns: C.M.Hills, 'A Runic Pot from Spong Hill, North Elmham, Norfolk', *Antiquaries Jnl* 54 (1974), 87–91; P.Pieper, 'Spiegelrunen' in *Runor och Runinskrifter.* Kungl. Vitterhets Historie och Antikvitets Akademien, Konferenser 15 (Stockholm 1987), 67–72.

Thames fitting: Page in *Anglo-Saxon Ornamental Metalwork* 77–9.

Thames scramasax: Page in *Anglo-Saxon Ornamental Metalwork* 69–73.

Undley bracteate: B.Odenstedt, 'The Inscription on the Undley Bracteate and the Beginnings of English Runic Writing', *Umeå Papers in English* 5 (1983); J.Hines and B.Odenstedt, 'The Undley Bracteate and its Runic Inscription', *Studien zur Sachsenforschung* 6 (1987), 73–94; but cf. R.I.Page, 'Anglo-Saxon Runic Studies: the Way Ahead?' in Bammesberger, *Old English Runes*, 24–6.

Wakerley brooch: Page, 'New Runic Finds', 193.

Wardley plate: K.Gosling, 'An Anglo-Saxon Runic Inscription from Leicestershire, England', *Nytt om Runer* 3 (1988), 14.

Watchfield fitting: C.Scull, 'A Sixth-century Grave Containing a Balance and Weights from Watchfield, Oxfordshire, England', *Germania* 64 (1986), 105–38; idem, 'Excavation and Survey at Watchfield, Oxfordshire, 1983–92'. *Archaeological Jnl* 149 (1992), 249.

Welbeck Hill bracteate: H.Vierck in K.Hauck, *Goldbrakteaten aus Sievern* (München 1970), 337–9.

Wheatley Hill ring: R.I.Page, 'An Anglo-Saxon Runic Ring', *Nytt om Runer* 12 (1997), 11–12.

Whitby comb: R.I.Page in *Whitby Lit. and Phil. Soc. Annual Report 1966*, 11–15.

Whitby disc: Sir Charles Peers and C.A.R.Radford, 'The Saxon Monastery of Whitby', *Archaeologia* 89 (1943), 74.

Willoughby-on-the-Wolds bowl: M.J.Dean and A.G.Kinsley, *Broughton Lodge. Excavations on the Romano-British Settlement and Anglo-Saxon Cemetery at Broughton Lodge, Willoughby-on-the-Wolds, Nottinghamshire 1964–8.* Nottingham Archaeological Monographs 4 (1993), 27 and fig.34.

Worcester sherd: R.I.Page, 'Epigraphical Runes in Worcester', *Nytt om Runer* 9 (1994), 17.

York spoon: D.M.Waterman, 'Late Saxon, Viking, and Early Medieval Finds from York', *Archaeologia* 97 (1959), 85–6.

Indexes

An italicised number refers to a page with an appropriate text-figure. The symbol † before a reference to an inscription suggests that there is some doubt about the validity of its runes.

INDEX OF INSCRIPTIONS

GENERAL INDEX